The Juvenile Justice and Residential Care Treatment Planner, with DSM-5 Updates

Practice*Planners*® Series

Treatment Planners
The Complete Adult Psychotherapy Treatment Planner, Fifth Edition
The Child Psychotherapy Treatment Planner, Fifth Edition
The Adolescent Psychotherapy Treatment Planner, Fifth Edition
The Addiction Treatment Planner, Fifth Edition
The Continuum of Care Treatment Planner
The Couples Psychotherapy Treatment Planner, with DSM-5 Updates, Second Edition
The Employee Assistance Treatment Planner
The Pastoral Counseling Treatment Planner
The Older Adult Psychotherapy Treatment Planner, with DSM-5 Updates, Second Edition
The Behavioral Medicine Treatment Planner
The Group Therapy Treatment Planner, with DSM-5 Updates, Second Edition
The Gay and Lesbian Psychotherapy Treatment Planner
The Family Therapy Treatment Planner, with DSM-5 Updates, Second Edition
The Severe and Persistent Mental Illness Treatment Planner, with DSM-5 Updates, Second Edition
The Intellectual and Developmental Disability Treatment Planner, with DSM 5 Updates
The Social Work and Human Services Treatment Planner, with DSM-5 Updates
The Crisis Counseling and Traumatic Events Treatment Planner, with DSM-5 Updates, Second Edition
The Personality Disorders Treatment Planner
The Rehabilitation Psychology Treatment Planner
The Special Education Treatment Planner
The Juvenile Justice and Residential Care Treatment Planner, with DSM-5 Updates
The School Counseling and School Social Work Treatment Planner, with DSM-5 Updates, Second Edition
The Sexual Abuse Victim and Sexual Offender Treatment Planner, with DSM-5 Updates
The Probation and Parole Treatment Planner, with DSM-5 Updates
The Psychopharmacology Treatment Planner
The Speech-Language Pathology Treatment Planner
The Suicide and Homicide Risk Assessment and Prevention Treatment Planner, with DSM-5 Updates
The College Student Counseling Treatment Planner
The Parenting Skills Treatment Planner, with DSM-5 Updates
The Early Childhood Intervention Treatment Planner
The Co-occurring Disorders Treatment Planner, with DSM-5 Updates
The Complete Women's Psychotherapy Treatment Planner
The Veterans and Active Duty Military Psychotherapy Treatment Planner, with DSM-5 Updates

Progress Notes Planners
The Child Psychotherapy Progress Notes Planner, Fifth Edition
The Adolescent Psychotherapy Progress Notes Planner, Fifth Edition
The Adult Psychotherapy Progress Notes Planner, Fifth Edition
The Addiction Progress Notes Planner, Fifth Edition
The Severe and Persistent Mental Illness Progress Notes Planner, Second Edition
The Couples Psychotherapy Progress Notes Planner, Second Edition
The Family Therapy Progress Notes Planner, Second Edition
The Veterans and Active Duty Military Psychotherapy Progress Notes Planner

Homework Planners
Couples Therapy Homework Planner, Second Edition
Family Therapy Homework Planner, Second Edition
Grief Counseling Homework Planner
Group Therapy Homework Planner
Divorce Counseling Homework Planner
School Counseling and School Social Work Homework Planner, Second Edition
Child Therapy Activity and Homework Planner
Addiction Treatment Homework Planner, Fifth Edition
Adolescent Psychotherapy Homework Planner, Fifth Edition
Adult Psychotherapy Homework Planner, Fifth Edition
Child Psychotherapy Homework Planner, Fifth Edition
Parenting Skills Homework Planner
Veterans and Active Duty Military Psychotherapy Homework Planner

Client Education Handout Planners
Adult Client Education Handout Planner
Child and Adolescent Client Education Handout Planner
Couples and Family Client Education Handout Planner

Complete Planners
The Complete Depression Treatment and Homework Planner
The Complete Anxiety Treatment and Homework Planner

Practice*Planners*®

Arthur E. Jongsma, Jr., Series Editor

The Juvenile Justice and Residential Care Treatment Planner, with DSM-5 Updates

William P. McInnis

Wanda D. Dennis

Michell A. Myers

Kathleen O'Connell Sullivan

Arthur E. Jongsma, Jr.

WILEY

Published by John Wiley & Sons, Inc., New York.
Published simultaneously in Canada.

Library of Congress Cataloging-in-Publication Data:

The juvenile justice and residential care treatment planner/William P. McInnis . . . [et al.].
     p. cm. — (Practice planners series)
  Includes bibliographical references.
  ISBN 9781119073284
  ePUB 9781119075097
  ePDF 9781119075080
  1. Juvenile delinquents—Mental health—Handbooks, manuals, etc. 2. Juvenile delinquents—Mental health services—Handbooks, manuals, etc. 3. Mental illness—Treatment—Planning—Handbooks, manuals, etc. I. McInnis, William P. II. Practice planners

RJ506.J88 J885 2001
362.2′086′923—dc21   2001046655

Printed in the United States of America.

V10018441_050820

To my wife Lynn for her constant love and support.

—*William P. McInnis, Psy.D.*

To my niece Amanda and nephews David, Darius, Zelma, and Adri.

—*Wanda D. Dennis, Ph.D.*

To my sister who made it normal for me to dream.

—*Michell A. Myers, Ph.D.*

To my newborn son Patrick Connell for waiting until my writing was complete to make his grand entrance.

—*Kathleen O'Connell Sullivan, Psy.D.*

To my colleague, Bill McInnis, for his loyalty, support, and insightful professionalism.

—*Arthur E. Jongsma, Jr., Ph.D.*

CONTENTS

PracticePlanners® Series Preface   xi
Acknowledgments   xiii
Introduction   1

Academic Underachievement/Learning Disabilities   14
Assaultive/Aggressive   30
Attention-Deficit/Hyperactivity Disorder (ADHD)   47
Cruelty to Animals   63
Deceitful/Manipulative   74
Depression   85
Drug Selling   99
Enuresis   112
Family Instability/Violence   124
Family/Societal Reintegration   133
Fire Setting   146
Foster Care Placement   161
Gang Involvement   173
Grief/Abandonment Issues   186
Isolated/Distrustful/Angry   197
Low Self-Esteem   214
Peer Conflict   229
Physical Abuse Victim   242
Probation Noncompliance   258
Runaway/Street Living   270
Sexual Abuse Victim   281
Sexual Misconduct   294
Sexual Promiscuity   305
Stealing/Breaking and Entering   321

Substance Abuse   338
Suicidal Ideation/Self-Harm   353
Truancy   365
Vandalism/Trespassing   379

Appendix A—Bibliotherapy Suggestions   391
Appendix B— Recovery Model Objectives and Interventions   402
Appendix C— Bibliography   409
Appendix D—Resources for Therapeutic Games,
    Workbooks, Toolkits, Videotapes, and Audiotapes   413

PRACTICE*PLANNERS*® SERIES PREFACE

Accountability is an important dimension of the practice of psychotherapy. Treatment programs, public agencies, clinics, and practitioners must justify and document their treatment plans to outside review entities in order to be reimbursed for services. The books in the Practice*Planners*® series are designed to help practitioners fulfill these documentation requirements efficiently and professionally.

The Practice*Planners*® series includes a wide array of treatment planning books including not only the original *Complete Adult Psychotherapy Treatment Planner*, *Child Psychotherapy Treatment Planner*, and *Adolescent Psychotherapy Treatment Planner*, all now in their fifth editions, but also *Treatment Planners* targeted to specialty areas of practice, including:

- Addictions
- Co-occurring disorders
- Behavioral medicine
- College students
- Couples therapy
- Crisis counseling
- Early childhood education
- Employee assistance
- Family therapy
- Gays and lesbians
- Group therapy
- Juvenile justice and residential care
- Mental retardation and developmental disability
- Neuropsychology
- Older adults
- Parenting skills
- Pastoral counseling
- Personality disorders

- Probation and parole
- Psychopharmacology
- Rehabilitation psychology
- School counseling and school social work
- Severe and persistent mental illness
- Sexual abuse victims and offenders
- Social work and human services
- Special education
- Speech-language pathology
- Suicide and homicide risk assessment
- Veterans and active military duty
- Women's issues

In addition, there are three branches of companion books that can be used in conjunction with the *Treatment Planners*, or on their own:

- *Progress Notes Planners* provide a menu of progress statements that elaborate on the client's symptom presentation and the provider's therapeutic intervention. Each *Progress Notes Planner* statement is directly integrated with the behavioral definitions and therapeutic interventions from its companion *Treatment Planner*.
- *Homework Planners* include homework assignments designed around each presenting problem (such as anxiety, depression, substance use, anger control problems, eating disorders, or panic disorder) that is the focus of a chapter in its corresponding *Treatment Planner*.
- *Client Education Handout Planners* provide brochures and handouts to help educate and inform clients on presenting problems and mental health issues, as well as life skills techniques. The handouts are included on CD-ROMs for easy printing from your computer and are ideal for use in waiting rooms, at presentations, as newsletters, or as information for clients struggling with mental illness issues. The topics covered by these handouts correspond to the presenting problems in the *Treatment Planners*.

The series also includes adjunctive books, such as *The Psychotherapy Documentation Primer* and *The Clinical Documentation Sourcebook*, contain forms and resources to aid the clinician in mental health practice management.

The goal of our series is to provide practitioners with the resources they need in order to provide high-quality care in the era of accountability. To put it simply: We seek to help you spend more time on patients, and less time on paperwork.

ARTHUR E. JONGSMA, JR.
Grand Rapids, Michigan

ACKNOWLEDGMENTS

We would like to start by thanking Art Jongsma for involving us in this project. It has certainly been a tremendous learning experience. We would like to express our appreciation to several important people who helped to make *The Juvenile Justice and Residential Care Treatment Planner* a reality. We'd like to acknowledge the contributions of Sue Rhoda, who provided word processing skills on the initial stages of this project. To Jen Byrne, Dr. Jongsma's project manager, for her attention to detail; to our editors at John Wiley & Sons for their support and to the many colleagues who contributed clinical wisdom and helpful references. We would also like to express our gratitude to our families and friends.

BILL, WANDA, KATE, AND MICHELL

My parents Essie and Matthew Dennis deserve the most thanks. Your love and support over the years has helped to guide me down many roads. In work and in play, your teachings and your values have always forced me to persevere and strive for excellence. A heartfelt thanks to two special friends, Dwight Hugget and Terri Oliver, on whom I have come to rely for support over the years. Thank you both for believing in my dreams. Lastly, I would like to extend a hearty thank-you to my graduate school advisor, Honore M. Hughes, PhD. You have been an excellent mentor and I have relied heavily on your "Honore-ism" in my contributions to this planner.

WANDA D. DENNIS, PH.D.

Participating in this project would not have been possible without the love and support of my husband Pierre, my mother Albertha Myers, my father Ernest Myers, and a host of family and friends. And I can't forget the patience of my son Micah. A special thanks to Vetta Sanders Thompson, Ph.D., for her professional guidance and advice.

MICHELL A. MYERS, PH.D.

I would like to thank my husband Joe Sullivan for his boundless patience, wry humor, and unconditional support. I would like to thank my son Patrick for making the past nine months one of the most special and joyous times in my life. To my family and friends, thanks for your constant love and encouragement.

KATHLEEN O'CONNELL SULLIVAN, PSY.D.

I would like to thank my wife, Lynn, for her continued love and support. I also thank my three children, Breanne, Kelsey, and Andrew, for the love and laughter that they bring into my life.

WILLIAM P. MCINNIS, PSY.D.

I dedicate this book to the administrative, clinical, and youth care staff at Wedgwood Christian Youth and Family Services. They provide deeply caring psychological services to adolescents who have been repeatedly abused, neglected, and/or abandoned by adults who were supposed to care. Blessed are the merciful.

ARTHUR E. JONGSMA, JR.

INTRODUCTION

PLANNER FOCUS

This year marks the 102nd anniversary year of the juvenile court in the United States. Guided by the spirit of the American Child Guidance movement, juvenile court judges sought professional assistance in understanding the mental health problems of children who appeared before the court. In 1909, William Healy established the Juvenile Psychoanalytic Institute, later renamed the Institute of Juvenile Research. The purpose of the Institute was to evaluate and diagnose children seen by the juvenile court. As time passed, the value of mental health professionals became more apparent, and an increasing number of clinics servicing the juvenile justice system were established. Today, the juvenile court's reliance on mental health professionals is stronger than ever. An important development has been the centralization of mental health services. Some assessment centers like Juvenile Assessment Centers (JAC), Target Cities or Treatment Alternatives for Safe Communities (TASC) provide a single point of entry for assessment and provisions for comprehensive services.

The advent of *The Juvenile Justice and Residential Care Treatment Planner* is a continuation of Wiley's Practice Planners, which are designed to provide specialized resources for professionals. To enhance the treatment resources for children and adolescents, Wiley's first step was to create a treatment planner that addressed the unique mental health needs of children and adolescents. *The Juvenile Justice and Residential Care Treatment Planner* enhances this effort by expanding on the resources available to address the treatment concerns specifically relative to children and adolescents who are involved in the legal system. *The Juvenile Justice and Residential Care Treatment Planner* blends mental health and legal concerns in a variety of ways. Chapters that highlight traditional mental health diagnoses incorporate important matters relative to delinquency within the behavioral definitions, objectives, and treatment interventions. In addition, other

1

chapters focus primarily on delinquent activities and highlight specific mental health concerns that may need to be addressed.

The Juvenile Justice and Residential Care Treatment Planner was developed to assist professionals (e.g., probation officers, case managers, therapists, etc.) who are working with youth in the juvenile justice system. However, this book is equally suited to assist professionals who work with clients in outpatient or residential settings who engage in delinquent behavior even though the client may not be formally charged or involved with the legal system. At times, professionals who use the Planner may discover the close relationship that exists between mental health concerns and the acting-out behaviors that come to the attention of the juvenile court. Many young people who interface with the juvenile court have mental health diagnoses; thus, there is overlap when considering treatment options for this population and other youth with mental health diagnoses. It is hoped that the uniqueness of this Planner will illustrate how the juvenile court client frequently requires specific interventions.

An additional goal of *The Juvenile Justice and Residential Care Treatment Planner* is to assist professionals in collaborating with one another to provide comprehensive services to this client population. It suggests a spectrum of services that may be necessary to address the needs of youth who are committing delinquent acts and who may also be involved with the juvenile court. In this way, *The Juvenile Justice and Residential Care Treatment Planner* provides a variety of professionals with useful information to inform and advance treatment decisions.

HISTORICAL BACKGROUND

Since the early 1960s, formalized treatment planning has gradually become a vital aspect of the entire health care delivery system, whether it is treatment related to physical health, mental health, child welfare, or substance abuse. What started in the medical sector in the 1960s spread into the mental health sector in the 1970s as clinics, psychiatric hospitals, agencies, and so on began to seek accreditation from bodies such as the Joint Commission on Accreditation of Healthcare Organizations (JCAHO) to qualify for third-party reimbursements. For most treatment providers to achieve accreditation, they had to begin developing and strengthening their documentation skills in the area of treatment planning. Previously, most mental health and substance abuse treatment providers had, at best, a bare-bones plan that looked similar for most of the individuals they treated. As a result, clients were uncertain as to what they were trying to attain in mental health treatment. Goals were vague, objectives were nonexistent, and interventions were applied equally to all clients. Outcome data were not measurable, and neither the treatment provider nor the client knew exactly when treatment was complete. The initial development of rudimentary treatment plans made inroads toward addressing some of these issues.

With the advent of managed care in the 1980s, treatment planning has taken on even more importance. Managed care systems *insist* that clinicians move rapidly from assessment of the problem to the formulation and implementation of the treatment plan. The goal of most managed care companies is to expedite the treatment process by prompting the client and treatment provider to focus on identifying and changing behavioral problems as quickly as possible. Treatment plans must be specific as to the problems and interventions, individualized to meet the client's needs and goals, and measurable in terms of setting milestones that can be used to chart the patient's progress. Pressure from third-party payers, accrediting agencies, and other outside parties has therefore increased the need for clinicians to produce effective, high-quality treatment plans in a short time frame. However, many mental health providers have little experience in treatment plan development. Our purpose in writing this book is to clarify, simplify, and accelerate the treatment planning process for youth involved in the juvenile justice system.

TREATMENT PLAN UTILITY

Detailed written treatment plans can benefit not only the client, therapist, treatment team, insurance community, and treatment agency, but also the overall psychotherapy profession. The client is served by a written plan because it stipulates the issues that are the focus of the treatment process. It is very easy for both the provider and the client to lose sight of what the issues were that brought the patient into therapy. The treatment plan is a guide that structures the focus of the therapeutic contract. Since issues can change as therapy progresses, the treatment plan must be viewed as a dynamic document that can and must be updated to reflect any major change of problem, definition, goal, objective, or intervention.

Clients and therapists benefit from the treatment plan, which forces both to think about therapy outcomes. Behaviorally stated, measurable objectives clearly focus the treatment endeavor. Clients no longer have to wonder what therapy is trying to accomplish. Clear objectives also allow the patient to channel effort into specific changes that will lead to the long-term goal of problem resolution. Therapy is no longer a vague contract to just talk honestly and openly about emotions and cognitions until the client feels better. Both the client and the therapist are concentrating on specifically stated objectives using specific interventions.

Providers are aided by treatment plans because they are forced to think analytically and critically about therapeutic interventions that are best suited for objective attainment for the patient. Therapists were traditionally trained to "follow the patient," but now a formalized plan is the guide to the treatment process. The therapist must give advance attention to the technique, approach, assignment, or cathartic target that will form the basis for interventions.

Clinicians benefit from clear documentation of treatment because it provides a measure of added protection from possible patient litigation. Malpractice suits are increasing in frequency, and insurance premiums are soaring. The first line of defense against allegations is a complete clinical record detailing the treatment process. A written, individualized, formal treatment plan that is the guideline for the therapeutic process, that has been reviewed and signed by the client, and that is coupled with problem-oriented progress notes is a powerful defense against exaggerated or false claims.

A well-crafted treatment plan that clearly stipulates presenting problems and intervention strategies facilitates the treatment process carried out by team members in inpatient, residential, or intensive outpatient settings. Good communication between team members about what approach is being implemented and who is responsible for which intervention is critical. Team meetings to discuss patient treatment used to be the only source of interaction between providers; often, therapeutic conclusions or assignments were not recorded. Now, a thorough treatment plan stipulates in writing the details of objectives and the varied interventions (e.g., pharmacologic, milieu, group therapy, didactic, recreational, individual therapy, etc.) and who will implement them.

Every treatment agency or institution is constantly looking for ways to increase the quality and uniformity of the documentation in the clinical record. A standardized, written treatment plan with problem definitions, goals, objectives, and interventions in every client's file enhances that uniformity of documentation. This uniformity eases the task of record reviewers inside and outside the agency. Outside reviewers, such as JCAHO, insist on documentation that clearly outlines assessment, treatment, progress, and termination status.

The demand for accountability from third-party payers and health maintenance organizations (HMOs) is partially satisfied by a written treatment plan and complete progress notes. More and more managed care systems are demanding a structured therapeutic contract that has measurable objectives and explicit interventions. Clinicians cannot avoid this move toward being accountable to those outside the treatment process.

The psychotherapy profession stands to benefit from the use of more precise, measurable objectives to evaluate success in mental health treatment. With the advent of detailed treatment plans, outcome data can be more easily collected for interventions that are effective in achieving specific goals.

HOW TO DEVELOP A TREATMENT PLAN

The process of developing a treatment plan involves a logical series of steps that build on each other, much like constructing a house. The foundation of any effective treatment plan is the data gathered in a thorough biopsychosocial assessment. As the client presents himself/herself for treatment, the clinician must sensitively listen to and understand what the client struggles with in terms of family-of-origin issues, current stressors, emotional status, social network, physical health, coping skills, interpersonal conflicts, self-esteem, and so on. Assessment data may be gathered from a social history, legal file physical exam, clinical interview, psychological testing, or contact with a client's guardian, social service worker, and/or probation officer. The integration of the data by the clinician or the multidisciplinary treatment team members is critical for understanding the client, as is an awareness of the basis of the client's struggle. We have identified six specific steps for developing an effective treatment plan based on the assessment data.

Step One: Problem Selection

Although the client may discuss a variety of issues during the assessment and court orders may request specific services, the clinician must ferret out the most significant problems on which to focus the treatment process. Usually a *primary* problem will surface, and *secondary* problems may also be evident. Some *other* problems may have to be set aside as not urgent enough to require treatment at this time. An effective treatment plan can only deal with a few selected problems; otherwise, treatment will lose its direction. *The Juvenile Justice and Residential Care Treatment Planner* offers 32 problems from which to select those that most accurately represent your client's presenting issues.

As the problems to be selected become clear to the clinician or the treatment team, it is important to include opinions from the client as to his/her prioritization of issues for which help is being sought. A client's motivation to participate in and cooperate with the treatment process depends, to some extent, on the degree to which treatment addresses his/her greatest needs.

Step Two: Problem Definition

Each individual client presents with unique nuances as to how a problem behaviorally reveals itself in his/her life. Therefore, each problem that is selected for treatment focus requires a specific definition about how it is evidenced in the particular client. The symptom pattern should be associated with diagnostic criteria and codes, such as those found in the *Diagnostic and Statistical Manual* or the *International Classification of Diseases*. The Planner, following the pattern established by *DSM-5™*, offers such behaviorally specific definition statements from which to choose or from which to serve as a model for your own personally crafted statements. You will find several behavior symptoms or syndromes listed that may characterize 1 of the 32 presenting problems.

Step Three: Goal Development

The next step in treatment plan development is that of setting broad goals for the resolution of the target problem. These statements need not be crafted in measurable terms but can be global, long-term goals that indicate a desired positive outcome to the treatment procedures. The Planner suggests several possible goal statements for each problem, but one statement is all that is required in a treatment plan.

Step Four: Objective Construction

In contrast to long-term goals, objectives must be stated in behaviorally measurable language. It must be clear when the client has achieved the established objectives; therefore, vague, subjective objectives are not acceptable. Review agencies (e.g., JCAHO), HMOs, and managed care organizations insist that psychological treatment outcome be measurable. The objectives presented in this Planner are designed to meet this demand for accountability. Numerous alternatives are presented to allow construction of a variety of treatment plan possibilities for the same presenting problem. The clinician must exercise professional judgment as to which objectives are most appropriate for a given client.

Each objective should be developed as a step toward attaining the broad treatment goal. In essence, objectives can be thought of as a series of steps that, when completed, will result in the achievement of the long-term goal. There should be at least two objectives for each problem, but the clinician may construct as many as are necessary for goal achievement. Target attainment dates should be listed for each objective. New objectives should be added to the plan as the individual's treatment progresses. When all of the necessary objectives have been achieved, the client should have resolved the target problem successfully.

Step Five: Intervention Creation

Interventions are the actions of the clinician designed to help the client complete the objectives. There should be at least one intervention for every objective. If the client does not accomplish the objective after the initial intervention, new interventions should be added to the plan.

Interventions should be selected on the basis of the client's needs and the treatment provider's full therapeutic repertoire. *The Juvenile Justice and Residential Care Treatment Planner* contains interventions from a broad range of therapeutic approaches, including cognitive, dynamic, behavioral, multisystemic, pharmacologic, family-oriented, and client-centered therapy. Other interventions may be written by the provider to reflect his/her own training and experience. The addition of new problems, definitions, goals, objectives, and interventions to those found in the Planner is encouraged because doing so adds to the database for future reference and use.

Some suggested interventions listed in the Planner refer to specific books that can be assigned to the client for adjunctive bibliotherapy. Appendix A contains a full bibliographic reference list of these materials. The books are arranged under each problem for which they are appropriate as assigned reading for clients. When a book is used as part of an intervention plan, it should be reviewed with the client after it is read, enhancing the application of the content of the book to the specific client's circumstances. For further information about self-help books, mental health professionals may wish to consult *The Authoritative Guide to Self-Help Books* (1994) by Santrock, Minnett, and Campbell (available from The Guilford Press, New York).

A list of reference resources is also provided for the professional provider in Appendix C. These books are meant to elaborate on the methods suggested in some of the chapters.

Assigning an intervention to a specific provider is most relevant if the patient is being treated by a team in an inpatient, residential, or intensive outpatient setting. Within these settings, personnel other than the primary clinician may be responsible for implementing a specific intervention. Review agencies require that the responsible provider's name be stipulated for every intervention.

Step Six: Diagnosis Determination

The determination of an appropriate diagnosis is based on an evaluation of the client's complete clinical presentation. The clinician must compare the behavioral, cognitive, emotional, and interpersonal symptoms that the client presents with the criteria for diagnosis of a mental illness condition as described in *DSM-5*. The issue of differential diagnosis is admittedly a difficult one that research has shown to have rather low interrater reliability. Psychologists have also been trained to think more in terms of maladaptive behavior than disease labels. In spite of these factors, diagnosis is a reality that exists in the world of mental health care, and it is a necessity for third-party reimbursement. (However, recently, managed care agencies are more interested in behavioral indices that are exhibited by the client than the actual diagnosis.) It is the clinician's thorough knowledge of *DSM-5* criteria and a complete understanding of the client assessment data that contribute to the most reliable, valid diagnosis. An accurate assessment of behavioral indicators will also contribute to more effective treatment planning.

HOW TO USE THIS PLANNER

Our experience has taught us that learning the skills of effective treatment plan writing can be a tedious and difficult process for many clinicians. It is more stressful to try to develop this expertise when under the pressure of increased patient load and short time frames placed on clinicians today by managed care systems. The documentation demands can be overwhelming when we must move quickly from assessment to treatment plan to progress notes. In the process, we must be very specific about how and when objectives can be achieved, and how progress is exhibited in each client. *The Juvenile Justice and Residential Care Treatment Planner* was developed as a tool to aid clinicians in writing a treatment plan in a rapid manner that is clear, specific, and highly individualized according to the following progression:

1. Choose one presenting problem (Step One) that you have identified through your assessment process. Locate the corresponding page number for that problem in the Planner's table of contents.
2. Select two or more of the listed behavioral definitions (Step Two) and record them in the appropriate section on your treatment plan form. Feel free to add your own defining statement if you determine that your client's behavioral manifestation of the identified problem is not

listed. (Note that while our design for treatment planning is vertical, it will work equally well on plan forms formatted horizontally.)

3. Select a single long-term goal (Step Three) and again write the selection, exactly as it is written in the Planner or in some appropriately modified form, in the corresponding area of your own form.

4. Review the listed objectives for this problem and select the ones that you judge to be clinically indicated for your client (Step Four). Remember, it is recommended that you select at least two objectives for each problem. Add a target date or the number of sessions allocated for the attainment of each objective.

5. Choose relevant interventions (Step Five). The Planner offers suggested interventions that are related to each objective in the parentheses following the objective statement. However, do not limit yourself to those interventions. The entire list is eclectic and may offer options that are more tailored to your theoretical approach or preferred way of working with clients. Also, just as with definitions, goals, and objectives, there is space allowed for you to enter your own interventions into the Planner. This allows you to refer to these entries when you create a plan around this problem in the future. You will have to assign responsibility to a specific person for implementation of each intervention if the treatment is being carried out by a multidisciplinary team.

6. Several *DSM-5* diagnoses are listed at the end of each chapter that are commonly associated with a client who has this problem. These diagnoses are meant to be suggestions for clinical consideration. Select a diagnosis listed or assign a more appropriate choice from the *DSM-5* (Step Six).

7. To accommodate those practitioners who tend to plan treatment in terms of diagnostic labels rather than presenting problems, Appendix B lists all of the *DSM-5* diagnoses that have been presented in the various presenting problem chapters as suggestions for consideration. Each diagnosis is followed by the presenting problem that has been associated with that diagnosis. The provider may look up the presenting problems for a selected diagnosis to review definitions, goals, objectives, and interventions that may be appropriate for their clients with that diagnosis. Congratulations! You should now have a complete, individualized treatment plan that is ready for immediate implementation and presentation to the client. It should resemble the format of the sample plan presented on the facing page.

A FINAL NOTE

One important aspect of effective treatment planning is that each plan should be tailored to the individual client's problems and needs. Treatment plans should not be mass produced, even if clients have similar problems. The individual's strengths and weaknesses, unique stressors, social network, family circumstances, and symptom patterns *must* be considered in developing a treatment strategy. Drawing upon our own years of clinical experience, we have put together a variety of treatment choices. These statements can be combined in thousands of permutations to develop detailed treatment plans. Relying on their own good judgment, clinicians can easily select the statements that are appropriate for the individuals whom they are treating. In addition, we encourage readers to add their own definitions, goals, objectives, and interventions to the existing samples. It is our hope that *The Juvenile Justice and Residential Care Treatment Planner* will promote effective, creative treatment planning—a process that will ultimately benefit the client, clinician, and mental health community.

SAMPLE TREATMENT PLAN

PROBLEM: PROBATION NONCOMPLIANCE

Definitions: Failure to obey court-ordered probationary requirements and directives.

Disobedience of reasonable directions of the caregiver.

Goals: Comply with all probationary directives.

Comply with the rules and expectations in the home,
school, work setting, and in the community on a consistent basis.

Short-Term Objectives

1. Complete psychological testing to identify factors that may contribute to probation noncompliance. (1, 2)

2. Identify obstacles to complying with the recommendations and/or requirements of the juvenile justice system. (3)

Therapeutic Interventions

1. Arrange for psychological testing of the client to assess current cognitive, social, and emotional factors that contribute to noncompliant behavior.

2. Provide feedback to the client and his/her caregiver, juvenile justice officials, and relevant school personnel regarding the assessment results and recommendations.

3. Assist the client in identifying situations or personal problems that interfere with his/her compliance with the terms of probation (e.g., family conflict, peer pressure, unresolved grief, academic skills deficits, etc.).

3. Implement a constructive problem-solving approach to obstacles to probation noncompliance. (4)

4. Teach the client problem-solving techniques (e.g., define the problem, brainstorm possible solutions, list pros and cons of each possible solution, implement action, evaluate outcome, etc.) that can be applied to personal problems that interfere with his/her probation noncompliance.

4. Verbalize an awareness of how probation noncompliance impacts family members and self. (5, 6)

5. Discuss the negative consequences for the client from his/her noncompliant behaviors (e.g., more restrictive settings, tether, tighter curfews, etc.) and the positive consequences that arise from compliant behavior (e.g., terminating probation, increased independence, less restrictive curfew, etc.).

6. Assist the client in identifying the short- and long-term consequences of violating probation for family members (e.g., prolonged involvement with legal system, disappointment and resentment, loss of trust, etc.).

5. The caregiver learns and implements appropriate and effective parenting techniques and disciplinary strategies. (7, 8, 9)

7. Recommend that the caregiver read books on effective parenting and limit setting (e.g., *The New Dare to Discipline* by Dobson; *Parents, Teens, and Boundaries* by

Bluestain; *Toughlove* by York, York, and Wachtel; or *Parents and Adolescents* by Patterson and Forgatch).

8. Teach the caregiver how to implement effective parenting techniques and disciplinary strategies including natural and logical consequences.

9. Confront the caregiver's tendency to respond to the client's behavioral problems in an overly punitive or over-protective and lax manner.

Diagnosis: Oppositional Defiant Disorder F913

ACADEMIC UNDERACHIEVEMENT/ LEARNING DISABILITIES

BEHAVIORAL DEFINITIONS

1. Reading achievement, as measured by individually administered, standardized tests of reading recognition or comprehension, is significantly below the expected level, given the client's chronological age, grade, and measured intelligence.
2. Mathematical ability, as measured by individually administered, standardized tests, is significantly below the expected level, given the client's chronological age, grade, and measured intelligence.
3. Written language skills, as measured by individually administered, standardized tests, are significantly below the expected level given the client's chronological age, grade, and measured intelligence.
4. History of academic performance that is below the expected level, given the client's measured intelligence or performance on standardized achievement tests.
5. Repeated failure to complete school or homework assignments on time.
6. Poor organization or study skills.
7. Frequent tendency to postpone doing homework assignments in favor of engaging in recreational, leisure, or social activities.
8. Recurrent pattern of engaging in acting-out, oppositional, disruptive, and negative attention-seeking behaviors when encountering frustration in learning.
9. Low frustration tolerance as manifested by tendency to give up easily when encountering difficulty with schoolwork.
10. Excessive anxiety that interferes with performance during tests and ability to complete schoolwork in a timely manner.
11. Feelings of depression, insecurity, and low self-esteem that interfere with learning and academic progress.

12. Hypersensitivity to teasing or criticism about learning problems or school performance.
13. Family history of members having academic problems, failures, or disinterest.

__. _____

_____

__. _____

_____

__. _____

_____

LONG-TERM GOALS

1. Attain and maintain a level of academic performance that is commensurate with intellectual ability.
2. Achieve the academic goals that have been identified on the client's Individualized Educational Plan (IEP) or established in therapy.
3. Perform up to the level of capability in the area of academic weakness.
4. Complete school and homework assignments on a regular and consistent basis.
5. Establish and maintain a healthy balance between achieving academic goals and meeting social, emotional, and self-esteem needs.
6. Eliminate the pattern of engaging in acting-out, oppositional, disruptive, or negative attention-seeking behaviors when confronted with frustration in learning.
7. Stabilize mood, build self-esteem, and significantly reduce the level of anxiety in order to cope effectively with the frustrations associated with academic pursuits.
8. Remove emotional impediments or resolve family conflicts and environmental stressors that will allow for improved academic performance.

__. _____

_____

__. _____

_____

__. _____

_____

SHORT-TERM OBJECTIVES

1. Complete a psychoeducational evaluation. (1, 5)

2. Complete psychological testing. (2, 5)

3. Complete a neuropsychological assessment. (3)

THERAPEUTIC INTERVENTIONS

1. Arrange for a comprehensive psychoeducational evaluation to determine whether possible learning disability or intellectual limitations are contributing to the client's lowered academic performance, angry outbursts, or acting-out and aggressive behaviors in the school system.

5. Provide feedback to the client, caregivers, school officials, and probation officer regarding assessment procedures and evaluation findings.

2. Arrange for a psychological evaluation to assess whether attention-deficit/hyperactivity disorder (ADHD) or emotional factors are interfering with the client's academic performance or contributing to his/her behavioral problems in the school setting.

5. Provide feedback to the client, caregivers, school officials, and probation officer regarding assessment procedures and evaluation findings.

3. Refer the client for a neuropsychological evaluation to rule out the presence of neurological and/or organic factors that may be contributing to the client's learning weaknesses and/or impulse control problems.

4. Caregivers and the client provide psychosocial history information. (4)

4. Gather a detailed history of academic performance and school behavioral problems that includes key developmental milestones, family history of educational achievements and failures, onset of academic problems, and frequency of behavioral problems.

5. Cooperate with a hearing, vision, or medical examination. (6)

6. Refer the client for a hearing, vision, or medical examination to rule out possible hearing, visual, or health problems that are interfering with his/her academic performance.

6. Comply with the recommendations made at the Individualized Educational Planning Committee (IEPC) regarding educational interventions. (7, 8)

7. Attend an IEPC meeting with the caregivers, teachers, and school officials to determine the client's eligibility for receiving special education services, designing educational interventions, and establishing educational goals.

8. Recommend that the client be moved to a special education classroom or receive teacher consultation services to address academic weaknesses or emotional/behavioral problems that interfere with learning.

7. Move to an appropriate classroom setting. (8)

8. Recommend that the client - be moved to a special education classroom or receive teacher consultation services to address academic weaknesses or emotional/behavioral problems that interfere with learning.

8. Establish educational goals regarding academic performance and school behavior. (9, 24)

9. Meet with the client, caregivers, teachers, and school officials to establish clear-cut educational goals regarding academic performance and school behavior.

24. Instruct the client to meet privately with school counselors or resource room teachers to receive feedback on his/her progress in achieving educational goals.

9. Caregivers and teachers implement educational strategies that focus on maximizing the client's learning strengths and compensate for learning weaknesses. (10)

10. Consult with the client, caregivers, teachers, or court officials about designing effective learning programs or intervention strategies that build on the client's strengths and compensate for his/her weaknesses.

10. Identify stressors within the school that impede academic performance and contribute to behavioral problems. (11)

11. Explore possible sources of conflict or stressors within the school setting (e.g., falling out with a friend, frequent arguments with one teacher, a demanding course load) that contribute to behavioral problems and academic failures or underachievement.

11. Comply fully with conditions of probation. (12, 13)

12. Confer with the probation officer or court officials, and recommend that the client's regular attendance at school be made a mandatory condition of probation.

13. Consult with the client, caregivers, probation officer, or court officials to establish a contingency contract by means of which the client can

reduce the length of his/her probation or amount of restitution if he/she achieves specific, educational goals.

12. Participate regularly in tutoring services to improve frustration tolerance and increase skills in the area of academic weakness. (14, 15)

14. Recommend that the caregivers seek privately contracted tutoring for the client after school to boost his/her skills in the area of his/her academic weakness (i.e., reading, mathematics, or written expression); facilitate a tutor referral.

15. Arrange through school personnel for the client to receive peer tutoring to increase skills in the area of his/her academic weakness, improve study skills, and stimulate greater interest in learning.

13. Implement effective study skills that increase the frequency of completion of school assignments and improve academic performance. (16, 17)

16. Teach the client more effective study skills (e.g., remove distractions, study in quiet places, develop outlines, highlight important details, schedule breaks, etc.).

17. Assign the client to read *13 Steps to Better Grades* (Silverman) to improve his/her organizational and study skills; process his/her reading in follow-up sessions.

14. Implement effective test-taking strategies that decrease anxiety and improve test performance. (19, 20)

19. Teach the client more effective test-taking strategies (e.g., study in smaller segments over an extended period of time, review material regularly, read directions twice, recheck work, etc.).

20. Train the client to use guided imagery or relaxation techniques to reduce anxiety before or during the taking of tests.

15. Complete large projects or long-term assignments consistently and on time. (18, 21, 22)

18. Encourage the client to use a self-monitoring checklist to increase completion of school assignments and improve academic performance. Have the client break down assignments into smaller sections and use a self-recording form to keep track of when he/she completes each section, rechecking work to avoid careless errors.

21. Direct the client and the caregivers to use planners or calendars to record school or homework assignments, to plan ahead for long-term projects, and to identify missing or incomplete assignments.

22. Assign the "Break It Down into Small Steps" program from the *Brief Adolescent Therapy Homework Planner* (Jongsma, Peterson, and McInnis) to help the client complete projects or long-term assignments on time.

16. Caregivers and client maintain regular communication (i.e., daily to weekly) with teachers. (23, 24, 25)

23. Encourage the caregivers to maintain regular (daily or weekly) communication with the teachers to help the client remain organized and keep up with school assignments.

24. Instruct the client to meet privately with school counselors or resource room teachers to receive feedback on his/her progress in achieving educational goals.

25. Recommend that the teachers send home weekly progress reports informing the caregivers about the client's academic performance, completion of school and/or homework assignments, and behavioral problems.

17. Establish a regular routine that allows time to engage in leisure or recreational activities, spend quality time with family and peers, and complete homework assignments. (26, 27)

26. Assist the client and his/her caregivers in developing a routine daily schedule at home that allows him/her to achieve a healthy balance of completing school and/or homework assignments, engaging in leisure activities, and spending quality time with family and peers.

27. Instruct the caregivers to demonstrate and/or maintain regular interest and involvement in the client's homework (i.e., attend parent-teacher conferences, review planners or calendars to see if the client is staying caught up with schoolwork).

18. Caregivers increase praise and positive reinforcement toward the client for improved academic performance and classroom behavior. (28)

28. Encourage the caregivers to offer frequent praise and positive reinforcement for the client's effort in completing school and/or homework assignments, achieving academic success, and engaging in responsible or positive social behaviors in the classroom.

19. Caregivers and teachers
    identify and utilize a variety
    of reinforcers to reward the
    client for completion of
    school and/or homework
    assignments and improved
    impulse control. (29, 30, 31)

29. Design and implement a
    reward system to reinforce
    the client's responsible
    behaviors, improved impulse
    control, completion of school
    assignments, and
    academic success.

30. Establish a contingency
    contract with the client,
    caregivers, and school
    officials that identifies the
    negative consequences for
    his/her disruptive classroom
    behaviors or failure to
    complete school and/or
    homework assignments.

31. Design and implement a token
    economy for the classroom to
    improve the client's academic
    performance, impulse control,
    and social skills in the school
    setting.

20. Identify and verbalize feelings
    associated with frustration or
    difficulty with schoolwork.
    (32)

32. Help the client identify and
    resolve painful emotions, core
    conflicts, or stressors that
    impede academic performance
    or contribute to acting-out
    behaviors in the school
    setting.

21. Increase verbalizations reflect-
    ing acceptance of the learning
    disability. (33, 34)

33. Assist the client in coming
    to an understanding and
    acceptance of the limitations
    surrounding his/her learning
    disability.

34. Assign the younger client to
    read *Many Ways to Learn:
    Young People's Guide to
    Learning Disabilities* (Stern) or

Keeping Ahead in School: A Student's Book About Learning Disabilities and Learning Disorders (Levine) to educate him/her about various learning disabilities and help develop an acceptance of his/her specific learning disability; process reading(s) in follow-up sessions.

22. Increase the frequency of on-task behaviors at school, completing school assignments without expressing the desire to give up. (35)

35. Teach the client positive coping mechanisms (e.g., relaxation techniques, positive self-talk, cognitive restructuring) to use when encountering anxiety, frustration, strong feelings of anger, or difficulty with schoolwork.

23. Increase the frequency of positive statements about school experiences and confidence to succeed academically. (36, 37, 38)

36. Reinforce the client's successful school experiences and positive statements about school.

37. Confront the client's self-disparaging remarks and expressed desire to give up when encountering difficulty or frustration with school and/or homework assignments.

38. Assign the client the task of making one positive statement daily to himself/herself about school and his/her ability and recording it in a journal or writing it on a sticky and posting it in the bedroom or kitchen.

24. Decrease the frequency and severity of acting-out or aggressive behaviors when encountering frustration with school assignments. (39, 40)

39. Teach the client meditational and self-control strategies (e.g., "stop, look, listen, and think"; count to 10; breathing and relaxation skills; positive self-talk; etc.) to inhibit the impulse to act out or engage in negative attention-seeking behaviors when encountering frustration with schoolwork.

40. Use modeling and role playing in individual sessions to help the client learn more effective ways to deal with teasing or criticism about being in special education class(es).

25. Identify and verbalize how a defensive attitude and acting-out behaviors contribute to further conflict at school. (41)

41. Challenge and discourage the client from responding in an overly defensive or physically aggressive manner to any teasing or criticism about his/her learning disability. Help the client to understand how his/her defensive or hostile responses only contribute to further conflicts or problems at school.

26. Reduce the frequency and intensity of arguments or disputes with peers or adult authority figures at school. (42)

42. Teach the client effective problem-solving strategies (i.e., identify the problem, brainstorm alternate solutions, select an option, implement a course of action, and evaluate the outcome) to help reduce conflict with peers and/orauthority figures at school.

27. Increase participation in extracurricular or positive peer group activities at school. (43)

28. Develop a list of resource people within the school setting who can be turned to for support and assistance in dealing with learning, emotional, or social problems. (44, 45)

29. Complete the assigned behaviors within the school setting that demonstrate taking on increased responsibility. (46)

30. Identify and verbalize how specific, responsible actions lead to improvements in academic performance and interpersonal relationships. (47, 48, 49, 50)

43. Encourage the client to participate in extracurricular or positive peer group activities through the school to help improve his/her self-esteem, frustration tolerance, and social skills.

44. Identify a list of individuals within the school to whom the client can turn for support, assistance, or instruction when he/she encounters frustration with learning and conflict with peers or authority figures.

45. Give the client a directive to phone a peer or classmate at least one time before the next session to seek assistance when he/she encounters problems with homework.

46. Consult with teachers or school officials to assign the client a task at school (e.g., giving announcements over the intercom, tutoring another student in his/her area of interest or strength, etc.) to demonstrate confidence in his/her ability to act responsibly.

47. Assess periods of time when the client completed schoolwork regularly and achieved academic success. Identify and encourage the client to use similar strategies to improve his/her current academic functioning.

48. Examine coping strategies that the client has used to solve other problems. Encourage the client to use similar coping strategies to overcome his/her problems in learning or to resolve interpersonal conflicts.

49. Give the client a homework assignment of identifying a hero or positive role model (e.g., a prominent athlete or politician, a friend or family member, etc.) who was able to overcome a learning disability to achieve success in life. Explore in the next sessions those factors that contributed to the hero's or role model's success; encourage the client to take similar steps to achieve academic success.

50. Give the client a homework assignment in the latter stages of treatment (i.e., approaching termination) to list and record the positive steps that he/she took to achieve his/her academic goals; process this list in the following session to encourage the client to take similar steps in the future.

31. Caregivers identify and remove all marital, parenting, or family conflicts that may be a hindrance to the client's learning. (51, 52)

51. Conduct family therapy sessions to identify any family or marital conflicts that may be interfering with the client's academic performance or contributing to acting-out behaviors in the school setting.

52. Assist the caregivers in resolving family conflicts that block or inhibit learning, and establish new positive family patterns that reinforce the client's academic achievement and responsible behaviors; refer them for marital counseling, if necessary.

32. Caregivers establish realistic expectations of the client's learning abilities. (53, 54, 55)

53. Conduct family therapy sessions to assess whether the caregivers have developed unrealistic expectations or are placing excessive pressure on the client to perform.

54. Assist the caregivers in developing realistic expectations of the client's learning potential.

55. Confront, challenge, and work through the caregivers' denial surrounding the client's learning disability so that they cooperate with the recommendations regarding placement and educational interventions.

33. Caregivers allow the client to experience the natural consequences of his/her lowered academic performance and acting-out behaviors. (56, 57)

56. Encourage the caregivers to set firm, consistent limits and to allow natural, logical, negative consequences for the client's noncompliance or refusal to do homework.

57. Encourage the caregivers not to protect the client from the natural consequences of his/her poor academic performance or behavioral problems in the classroom (e.g., loss of

credits, detention, delayed graduation, inability to take driver's training, higher cost of car insurance, etc.) and allow him/her to learn from his/her mistakes or failures.

34. Caregivers decrease the frequency and intensity of arguments with the client over issues related to school performance, homework, and behavior. (58)

58. Instruct the caregivers to avoid unhealthy power struggles or lengthy heated arguments over homework each night; use modeling and role playing to teach the caregivers conflict resolution skills.

35. Caregivers verbally recognize that their pattern of overprotectiveness interferes with the client's academic growth and assumption of responsibility. (59)

59. Assess the parent-child relationship to help determine whether the caregivers' overprotectiveness and/or overindulgence of the client contributes to his/her academic underachievement or acting-out behaviors at school.

36. Take prescribed medication as directed by the physician. (60)

60. Arrange for a medication evaluation of the client if it is determined that an emotional problem and/or ADHD are interfering with learning. Monitor the client for compliance, effectiveness, and side effects if he/she is placed on medication.

__. _____

__. _____

__. _____

__. _____

__. _____

__. _____

DIAGNOSTIC SUGGESTIONS:

ICD-9-CM	*ICD-10-CM*	*DSM-5* Disorder, Condition, or Problem
315.00	F81.0	Specific Learning Disorder With Impairment in Reading
315.10	F81.2	Specific Learning Disorder with Impairment in Mathematics
315.2	F81.2	Specific Learning Disorder With Impairment in Written Expression
V62.3	Z55.9	Academic or Educational Problem
314.01	F90.2	Attention-Deficit/Hyperactivity Disorder, Combined Presentation
314.00	F90.0	Attention-Deficit/Hyperactivity Disorder, Predominately Inattentive Presentation
300.4	F34.1	Persistent Depressive Disorder
313.81	F91.3	Oppositional Defiant Disorder
312.9	F91.9	Unspecified Disruptive, Impulse Control, and Conduct Disorder
312.89	F91.8	Other Specified Disruptive, Impulse Control, and Conduct Disorder
317	F70	Intellectual Disability, Mild
V62.89	R41.83	Borderline Intellectual Functioning
_____	_____	_____
_____	_____	_____

ASSAULTIVE/AGGRESSIVE

BEHAVIORAL DEFINITIONS

1. History of initiating numerous physical fights at home, school, or in the community.
2. Assaultive behavior or use of weapons that has resulted in serious harm or danger to other individuals.
3. Persistent pattern of destroying property or throwing objects when angry.
4. Frequent angry outbursts that are out of proportion to the degree of the precipitating event.
5. Repeated pattern of threatening, harassing, intimidating, or bullying others.
6. Excessive screaming, cursing, or use of verbally abusive language when frustrated or stressed.
7. Excessive demands and unreasonable requests that needs be met instantly.
8. Consistent failure to accept responsibility for loss of control, accompanied by a repeated pattern of blaming others for his/her anger control problems or aggressive behaviors.
9. Intense desire for revenge or retaliation against individuals who have inflicted real or perceived hurt or harm in the past.
10. Extreme fascination with weapons and/or preoccupation with movies or songs that contain highly aggressive or violent themes.
11. Suppresses anger over time until it builds to the point where anger is unleashed in an extremely aggressive or violent manner.
12. Strong feelings of alienation from peers; frequent target of harassment, ridicule, or rejection.
13. Deep-seated fears and underlying feelings of helplessness or powerlessness that contribute to aggressive behaviors.

—. _____

_____

—. _____
   _____
   _____
—. _____
   _____

LONG-TERM GOALS

1. Significantly reduce the frequency and intensity of angry verbal outbursts and assaultive/aggressive behaviors.
2. Terminate all acts of violence or cruelty toward people and destruction of property.
3. Express anger through controlled, respectful verbalizations and healthy physical outlets on a consistent basis.
4. Employ positive coping mechanisms or conflict resolution skills on a regular basis to stop escalation of anger and control aggressive impulses.
5. Interact consistently with family members, adult authority figures, and peers in a mutually respectful and nonthreatening manner.
6. Resolve the core conflicts that contribute to the emergence of assaultive or aggressive behaviors.
7. Demonstrate marked improvement in the ability to listen and respond empathetically to the thoughts, feelings, and needs of others.
8. Caregivers establish and maintain appropriate parent-child boundaries, setting firm, consistent limits when the client reacts in a verbally or physically aggressive manner.

—. _____
   _____
—. _____
   _____
—. _____
   _____

SHORT-TERM GOALS

1. Caregivers and client provide psychosocial history information. (1)

THERAPEUTIC INTERVENTIONS

1. Gather a detailed psychosocial history of the client's development and family environment to gain insight into the

emotional factors or sequence of events that contributed to the emergence of the ssaultive/aggressive behavior. Consult court and police records for more information regarding the emergence of the client's assaultive/aggressive behavior pattern.

2. Complete psychological testing. (2, 5)

2. Arrange for psychological testing of the client to assess whether emotional factors (i.e., depression, anxiety, fearfulness), psychotic features, or attention-deficit/hyperactivity disorder (ADHD) are contributing to his/her loss of control and an emergence of assaultive/aggressive behavior.

5. Provide feedback to the client, his/her caregivers, school officials, or criminal justice officials regarding findings from psychological, psychoeducational, or substance abuse evaluations.

3. Complete a psychoeducational evaluation. (3, 5)

3. Arrange for a psychoeducational evaluation to determine whether intellectual limitations or a possible learning disability are contributing to the client's loss of control or assaultive/aggressive behavior in the school setting.

5. Provide feedback to the client, his/her caregivers, school officials, or criminal justice officials regarding findings from

psychological, psychoeducational, or substance abuse evaluations.

4. Complete a substance abuse evaluation, and comply with the recommendations that are offered by the evaluation findings. (4, 5)

4. Arrange for substance abuse evaluation to assess whether substance abuse problems are contributing to the client's assaultive/aggressive behavior. Refer him/her for treatment if indicated. (See the "Substance Abuse" chapter in this Planner.)

5. Provide feedback to the client, his/her caregivers, school officials, or criminal justice officials regarding findings from psychological, psychoeducational, or substance abuse evaluations.

5. Cooperate with the recommendations or requirements mandated by the criminal justice system. (6, 7, 8)

6. Consult with criminal justice officials about the appropriate consequences for the client's destructive or assaultive/aggressive behavior (e.g., pay restitution, community service, confinement, probation, intensive surveillance, etc.).

7. Consult with the caregivers, probation officer, and other criminal justice officials about the need to place the client in an alternative setting (e.g., foster home, group home, residential program, juvenile boot camp, or juvenile detention facility) as a consequence for his/her recurrent assaultive/ aggressive behavior.

8. Encourage and challenge the caregivers not to protect the

client from the natural or legal consequences of his/her destructive or assaultive/aggressive behavior.

6. Move to an appropriate alternative setting or juvenile detention facility. (7)

7. Consult with the caregivers, probation officer, and other criminal justice officials about the need to place the client in an alternative setting (e.g., foster home, group home, residential program, juvenile boot camp, or juvenile detention facility) as a consequence for his/her recurrent assaultive/aggressive behavior.

7. Caregivers remove weapons or prevent the client's access to weapons. (9)

9. Instruct the caregivers to remove all weapons or prevent the client's access to weapons to deter or limit the chances of him/her engaging in serious, violent behavior.

8. Caregivers establish appropriate boundaries and follow through consistently with consequences for the client's assaultive/aggressive behavior. (10, 11, 12)

10. Assist the caregivers in establishing clearly defined rules, boundaries, and consequences for the client's assaultive/aggressive behavior. Have the client repeat these rules to demonstrate that he/she understands the expectations.

11. Refer the caregivers to parent-training classes to help increase their knowledge of appropriate disciplinary techniques and to learn how to manage the client's assaultive/aggressive behavior.

12. Assign caregivers to read *The Explosive Child* (Greene) to learn effective strategies on how to deal with the inflexible-explosive child who has an extremely low frustration tolerance.

9. Recognize and verbalize how anger-control problems negatively affect self and others. (13)

10. Decrease the frequency of verbalizations that project the blame for anger-control problems onto other people. (14)

11. Begin to express anger through controlled, respectful verbalizations and healthy physical outlets. (15, 16)

12. Reduce the frequency and intensity of angry, verbal outbursts when frustrated or stressed. (17, 18)

13. Confront the client firmly about the impact of his/her destructive or assaultive/ aggressive behavior, pointing out consequences for himself/herself and others.

14. Confront statements in which the client blames others for his/her loss of control and fails to accept responsibility for his/her destructive or assaultive/aggressive behavior.

15. Teach meditational and self-control strategies (e.g., "stop, look, listen, and think"; walk away; count to 10; listen to music, etc.) to help the client to express anger through appropriate verbalizations and healthy physical outlets.

16. Teach the client effective communication and assertiveness skills to express anger in a controlled fashion and to meet his/her needs through constructive actions. Encourage the client to verbalize "I" messages and to reduce the frequency of name-calling or blaming statements.

17. Use behavioral rehearsal, role playing, and modeling to teach effective ways for the client to express anger in a controlled manner.

18. Train the client to use progressive relaxation or guided imagery techniques to help calm himself/herself and to decrease the intensity of his/her angry feelings.

13. Use self-monitoring techniques to reduce anger outbursts. (19, 20)

19. Assist the client in recognizing early signs (e.g., tiredness, muscular tension, hot face, hostile remarks, etc.) that he/she is starting to become frustrated or agitated so that he/she can take steps to remain calm and cope with frustration.

20. Encourage the client to use a self-monitoring checklist at home and/or school to develop more effective anger control. Ask him/her to select a specific behavior (e.g., ignore teasing or name-calling, ask for help instead of blowing up in the classroom when frustrated, etc.) and to monitor that behavior by using a self-recording form.

14. Cooperate with a reward system that is focused on anger management. (21, 22)

21. Design a reward system and/or contingency contract to reinforce the client's effective anger control and to deter his/her destructive or assaultive/aggressive behavior.

22. Design and implement a token economy for home and/or for school that is focused on specific prosocial behaviors (e.g., speaking assertively not aggressively, walking away from confrontation, reaching out to others in respect and warmth, etc.).

15. Caregivers increase the frequency of praise and positive reinforcement of the client for demonstrating good control of anger. (23, 24)

23. Employ the "Anger Control" exercise in the *Brief Adolescent Therapy Homework Planner* (Jongsma, Peterson, and McInnis) to help the client express his/her anger in a con-

trolled manner, using a reward system and contract to reinforce good control of anger.

24. Instruct the caregivers to observe the client and to "catch" him/her showing good control of anger. Encourage the caregivers to praise the client and to specifically identify what strategies he/she used to control anger.

16. Caregivers and client identify common anger-provoking situations that contribute to loss of control and emergence of assaultive/aggressive behavior. (19, 25, 26)

19. Assist the client in recognizing early signs (e.g., tiredness, muscular tension, hot face, hostile remarks, etc.) that he/she is starting to become frustrated or agitated so that he/she can take steps to remain calm and cope with frustration.

25. Assist the caregivers and school officials in identifying specific situations or events that routinely lead to explosive outbursts or aggressive behaviors. Teach the caregivers and school officials effective coping strategies to help defuse the client's anger and to deter his/her aggressive behavior.

26. Assign the adolescent client to read *Everything You Need to Know About Anger* (Licata) to help him/her manage anger more effectively. Process the reading with the client.

17. Identify coping strategies to control anger more effectively. (27, 28)

27. Explore periods of time when the client demonstrated good anger control. Process responses and reinforce positive coping strategies that he/she used to exercise self-control and deter aggressive impulses.

28. Encourage and challenge the client to resolve conflict by using effective problem-solving strategies (i.e., identify the problem, brainstorm solutions, select an option, implement a course of action, evaluate outcome), instead of seeking revenge or retaliation through acts of aggression or violence.

18. Decrease the frequency, duration, and intensity of arguments with authority figures. (29, 30, 31)

29. Encourage and challenge the caregivers and the client to avoid becoming locked in unhealthy power struggles or lengthy arguments that cause his/her anger to escalate. Teach effective problem-solving strategies and communication skills to resolve conflict in a constructive manner and to defuse the intensity of the client's anger.

30. Encourage the caregivers to "pick their battles" with the client to prevent his/her anger from escalating and to avoid unnecessary loss-of-control episodes. Help the caregivers to identify on which battles or misbehaviors they want to consistently set limits and which behaviors (i.e., minor annoying behaviors) they are willing to ignore.

31. Confront and challenge the caregivers to cease making overly hostile, critical, or sarcastic remarks about the client or his/her behavior, which only contribute to his/her loss of control. Encourage the caregivers to

directly verbalize the positive, specific behaviors or changes they would like to see the client demonstrate.

19. Identify family issues that contribute to assaultive/aggressive behavior. (32)

32. Conduct family therapy sessions to explore the dynamics (e.g., parental modeling of aggressive behavior; sexual, verbal, or physical abuse of family members; substance abuse in the home; neglect; etc.) that contribute to the emergence of the client's assaultive/aggressive behavior.

20. Uninvolved or detached parent(s) increase time spent with the client in recreational, school, or work activities. (33, 34)

33. Instruct the caregivers to set aside between 5 and 10 minutes each day to listen to the client's concerns and to provide him/her with the opportunity to express his/her anger in an adaptive manner.

34. Give a directive to uninvolved or disengaged parent(s) to spend more time with the client in leisure, school, or work activities.

21. Identify and verbally express feelings that are associated with past neglect, abuse, separation, or abandonment. (35, 36)

35. Encourage and support the client in expressing his/her feelings associated with neglect, abuse, separation, or abandonment. (See the "Grief/Abandonment Issues," "Physical Abuse Victim," and "Sexual Abuse Victim" chapters in this Planner.)

36. Give the client permission to cry about past losses, separation, or abandonment. Educate him/her about the healing nature of crying (i.e., provides an opportunity to express

sadness, takes the edge off anger, and helps to induce calmness after crying subsides).

22. Verbalize how fears, feelings of insecurity, or other painful emotions are connected to assaultive/aggressive behaviors. (37, 38)

37. Assist the client in making a connection between underlying, painful emotions (e.g., depression, anxiety, fear, helplessness, etc.) and angry outbursts or assaultive/aggressive behavior.

38. Examine three incidents in which the client lost control of his/her anger while experiencing painful emotions (e.g., depression, anxiety, fear, etc.). Explore how he/she could have expressed painful emotions in a more adaptive manner, instead of through assaultive/ aggressive behavior.

23. Terminate all suicidal thoughts. (39)

39. Assess and monitor the client's suicide risk after a major loss-of-control episode. Refer the client for inpatient hospitalization if he/she is deemed to be at high risk for suicide. (See the "Suicidal Ideation/Self-Harm" chapter in this Planner.)

24. Caregivers verbalize the appropriate boundaries for their discipline to prevent further occurrences of abuse and ensure the safety of the client and his/her siblings. (31, 40)

31. Confront and challenge the caregivers to cease making overly hostile, critical, or sarcastic remarks about the client or his/her behavior, which only contribute to his/her loss of control. Encourage the caregivers to directly verbalize the positive, specific behaviors or changes they would like to see the client demonstrate.

40. Confront the caregivers' physically abusive or overly punitive methods of discipline. Implement the steps that are necessary to protect the client or siblings from further abuse (e.g., report the abuse to appropriate agencies, remove the client or perpetrator from the home, etc.).

25. Identify and list targets or precipitating events that produce strong feelings of anger. (41, 42, 43)

41. Direct the client to develop a thorough list of all targets of and causes for anger.

42. Ask the client to keep a daily journal in which he/she documents persons and situations that evoke strong feelings of anger. Process these excerpts from his/her journal in follow-up therapy sessions.

43. Assign the client to list significant life experiences that have produced strong feelings of anger, hurt, or disappointment.

26. Identify and verbalize unmet needs that contribute to loss of control and assaultive/aggressive behaviors. (44)

44. Assist the client in first identifying unmet needs and then expressing them to significant others.

27. Write a letter of forgiveness to a perpetrator of hurt. (45)

45. Instruct the client to write a letter of forgiveness to a target of anger in the latter stages of treatment as a step toward letting go of anger. Process the letter in a follow-up session, and discuss what to do with the letter.

28. Identify the irrational beliefs or maladaptive thoughts that contribute to the emergence of destructive or assaultive/aggressive behavior. (46)

46. Assist the client in identifying his/her irrational thoughts that contribute to the emergence of assaultive/aggressive behavior

(e.g., believing that aggression is an acceptable way to deal with teasing or name-calling, justifying acts of violence or aggression as a means to meet his/her needs or to avoid restrictions). Replace these irrational thoughts with more adaptive ways of thinking to help control anger.

29. Increase the frequency of positive statements to improve self-esteem and anger control. (47)

47. Reinforce positive self-descriptive statements by the client to improve his/her self-esteem and anger control.

30. Increase participation in extracurricular and exercise activities. (48)

48. Encourage the client to participate in extracurricular activities or engage in regular exercise to provide a healthy outlet for anger and improve self-esteem.

31. Engage in employment activities without conflict over authority issues. (49)

49. Instruct the client to seek and secure employment in order to have funds available to make restitution for destructive or aggressive acts, to assume responsibility, and to gain income to meet his/her needs in an adaptive manner.

32. Attend an anger management group. (50)

50. Refer the client to an anger management group. Direct the client to self-disclose at least one time in each group therapy session about his/her responses to anger-provoking situations.

33. Identify and engage in prosocial leadership activities. (51)

51. Assist the client in identifying more age-appropriate ways of establishing control and/or power other than intimidating or bullying others (e.g., participate in student government at school, try out for a sports team, join a debate team, etc.).

34. Increase verbalizations of empathy, kindness, and concern for other people. (52)

52. Assign the client the task of showing empathy, kindness, or sensitivity to the needs of others (e.g., assist a peer or sibling with homework, perform a cleaning task for an ailing family member, etc.) to help build positive relationships and to undo the effects of his/her aggressive behavior.

35. Express feelings of anger in play therapy or through the medium of music or art. (53, 54, 55, 56)

53. Direct the client to draw pictures of three events or situations that commonly evoke feelings of anger. Process the client's thoughts and feelings after he/she completes these drawings.

54. Instruct the client to either sing or play a song of his/her own or one that is popular that reflects feelings of anger. Talk about a time when the client felt angry about a particular issue.

55. Conduct play therapy sessions with the younger client to explore the factors contributing to his/her assaultive/aggressive behavior. Interpret the feelings expressed in play, and relate them to his/her angry feelings and aggressive behavior.

56. Use the "Angry Tower" technique (see *101 Favorite Play Therapy Techniques* by Saxe) to help the younger client identify and express feelings of anger. First, build a tower out of plastic containers. Next, place a small item (representing the object of anger) on top of

the tower. Instruct the client to throw a small fabric ball at the tower while verbalizing anger.

36. Cooperate with a physician's evaluation as to the need for psychotropic medication to reduce anger and stabilize mood. Take medication as pre-scribed. (57, 58)

57. Refer the client to a physician for a psychotropic medication evaluation to help stabilize moods and improve his/her anger control.

58. Monitor the client for pre-scribed psychotropic medica-tion compliance, side effects, and effectiveness. Consult with the prescribing physician at regular intervals.

37. Disclose past rejection and/or peer conflict experiences. (59)

59. Explore the client's experience of rejection by peers and the possible causes for this alien-ation (e.g., hostility toward them, hypersensitivity to teas-ing, target of scapegoat rejec-tion, poor social skills, etc.).

38. Identify coping strategies for peer conflict. (50, 60)

50. Refer the client to an anger management group. Direct the client to self-disclose at least one time in each group ther-apy session about his/her responses to anger-provoking situations.

60. Teach the client means of coping with and improving conflicted peer relationships (e.g., social skills training; outside intervention with bullies; conflict resolution training; reaching out to build new friendships; identifying empathic resource peers or adults in school to whom he/she can turn when hurt, lonely, or angry; etc.).

__. _____   __. _____
    _____   _____
__. _____   __. _____
    _____   _____
__. _____   __. _____
    _____   _____

DIAGNOSTIC SUGGESTIONS:

ICD-9-CM	_ICD-10-CM_	_DSM-5_ Disorder, Condition, or Problem
312.34	F63.81	Intermittent Explosive Disorder
312.9	F91.9	Unspecified Disruptive, Impulse Control, and Conduct Disorder
312.89	F91.8	Other Specified Disruptive, Impulse Control, and Conduct Disorder
312.8	F91.x	Conduct Disorder
312.9	F91.9	Unspecified Disruptive, Impulse Control, and Conduct Disorder
312.89	F91.8	Other Specified Disruptive, Impulse Control, and Conduct Disorder
314.01	F90.1	Attention-Deficit/Hyperactivity Disorder, Predominately Hyperactive /Impulsive Presentation
314.01	F90.9	Unspecified Attention-Deficit/Hyperactivity Disorder
314.01	F90.8	Other Specified Attention-Deficit/Hyperactivity Disorder
V71.02	Z72.810	Adolescent Antisocial Behavior
V61.20	Z62.820	Parent-Child Relational Problem
_____	_____	_____
_____	_____	_____

ATTENTION-DEFICIT/ HYPERACTIVITY DISORDER (ADHD)

BEHAVIORAL DEFINITIONS

1. Poor impulse control as manifested by acting without considering the consequences of his/her actions.
2. Excessive or loud talking, blurting out remarks at inappropriate times, and frequent interruptions or intrusions into others' personal business.
3. Recurrent pattern of seeking instant gratification of needs at the expense of achieving more meaningful, long-term goals.
4. Hyperactivity as evidenced by high energy level, restlessness, fidgety motor movements, and difficulty sitting still.
5. Low frustration tolerance that contributes to poor anger control and frequent, intense emotional outbursts.
6. Persistent pattern of engaging in disruptive, acting-out, aggressive, or antisocial behavior at home, school, or in the community.
7. Propensity for taking ill-advised risks and engaging in thrill-seeking or potentially dangerous behavior.
8. Poor social skills, combined with impulsivity, that places strain on interpersonal relationships and interferes with ability to establish and maintain close, meaningful friendships.
9. Short attention span, proneness to experiencing frequent lapses in level of attention and concentration.
10. Easily distracted by extraneous stimuli and/or internal thoughts.
11. Impression that he/she is not listening well.
12. Repeated failure to follow through on instructions or complete school assignments, chores, or job responsibilities in a timely manner.
13. Poor organizational skills as manifested by forgetfulness, inattention to details, and losing things that are necessary for tasks.

14. Low self-esteem and development of negative self-image (e.g., perceives self as being a troublemaker or annoying pest).
15. Difficulty accepting responsibility for actions and often projects the blame for his/her misbehavior onto others.

__. _____

_____

__. _____

_____

__. _____

_____

LONG-TERM GOALS

1. Demonstrate marked improvement in impulse control as manifested by significant reduction in the frequency and severity of disruptive, aggressive, and acting-out behavior.
2. Take medication as prescribed on a regular basis to decrease impulsivity, hyperactivity, and distractability.
3. Sustain attention and concentration for consistently longer periods of time.
4. Complete schoolwork, homework assignments, or household chores and responsibilities on a consistent basis.
5. Develop positive social skills to maintain lasting peer friendships.
6. Caregivers establish appropriate boundaries and set firm, consistent limits with disruptive, aggressive, or acting-out behavior.
7. Improve self-esteem and regularly verbalize positive self-descriptive statements.

__. _____

_____

__. _____

_____

__. _____

_____

SHORT-TERM OBJECTIVES

1. Complete psychological testing to confirm the diagnosis of ADHD and/or rule out emotional factors that may be contributing to impulsivity, hyperactivity, or inattentiveness. (1, 2, 4)

2. Complete psychoeducational evaluation to rule out learning disabilities or intellectual limitations that may be contributing to impulsivity, hyperactivity, or inattention in the school setting. (3, 4)

THERAPEUTIC INTERVENTIONS

1. Arrange for psychological testing of the client to confirm the presence of ADHD in him/her.

2. Arrange for psychological testing to rule out emotional factors or possible bipolar disorder that may be contributing to the client's impulsivity, hyperactivity, inattentiveness, or distractability.

4. Provide feedback to the client, caregivers, school officials, or criminal justice officials regarding findings from the psychological or psychoeducational evaluations.

3. Arrange for a comprehensive psychoeducational evaluation of the client to determine whether a possible learning disability or intellectual limitations are contributing to his/her poor academic performance, inattentiveness, distractability, or impulsive and disruptive behavior in the school setting.

4. Provide feedback to the client, caregivers, school officials, or criminal justice officials regarding findings from the psychological or psychoeducational evaluations.

3. Take prescribed medication as directed by the physician or psychiatrist. (5, 6)

5. Refer the client for a medication evaluation to address ADHD symptoms, improve impulse control, and/or stabilize moods.

6. Monitor the client for medication compliance, side effects, and effectiveness. Consult with the prescribing physician or psychiatrist at regular intervals.

4. Resolve and work through resistance to taking medication as prescribed. (7, 8, 9)

7. Encourage and challenge the client to take medication as prescribed. Gently but firmly confront the client when he/she talks of discontinuing the medication.

8. Explore reasons for the client's failure to take medication as prescribed. Address and work through the client's and/or his/her caregivers' resistance to taking the medication.

9. Instruct the client to list the pros and cons of staying on the medication after he/she has demonstrated improvements in his/her impulse control over a period of time (e.g., between two and three months). Process this list with the therapist.

5. Identify positive effects of taking medication as prescribed on a regular basis. (10)

10. Assist the client in identifying and listing the positive effects that have occurred in his/her life since beginning to take the medication on a regular basis.

6. Caregivers, siblings, and criminal justice officials verbalize

11. Educate the client's caregivers, siblings, probation officer, or

an increased knowledge and understanding of ADHD symptoms. (11, 12, 13)

criminal justice officials about the symptoms of ADHD.

12. Assign the caregivers to read books or materials on ADHD to educate themselves about the symptoms and learn effective treatment interventions (e.g., *Taking Charge of ADHD: The Complete, Authoritative Guide for Parents* by Barkley, *Teenagers with ADD: A Parents' Guide* by Zeigler Dendy, or *Dr. Larry Silver's Advice to Parents on Attention Deficit Hyperactivity Disorder* by Silver).

13. Refer the client's caregivers to an ADHD support group to increase their understanding of the condition, receive outside support, and learn effective strategies to manage or deal with symptoms.

7. Read educational materials to gain greater knowledge about ADHD and effective treatment interventions. (14)

14. Assign the adolescent client to read books or materials to help him/her to gain a greater understanding of ADHD and to learn effective strategies to improve impulse control, organizational abilities, and social skills (e.g., *Adolescents and Add: Gaining the Advantage* by Quinn, or *Help4Add High School* by Nadeau).

8. Cooperate with recommendations or requirements mandated by the criminal justice system. (15, 16)

15. Consult with criminal justice officials about the appropriate consequences for the client's impulsive or

antisocial behavior (e.g., pay restitution, perform community service, confinement, probation, or intensive surveillance).

16. Inform the probation officer about the presence of the client's ADHD. Recommend that the client's participation in outpatient therapy or compliance with taking his/her medication be a mandatory condition of his/her probation.

9. Move to an appropriate alternative setting or juvenile detention facility. (17)

17. Consult with caregivers, probation officer, and other criminal justice officials about the need to place the client in an alternative setting (e.g., foster home, residential program, juvenile detention facility, etc.) as a consequence for his/her antisocial behavior, to prevent future occurrences of delinquent activities, and to help him/her develop greater self-control.

10. Identify and verbalize an awareness of the negative consequences that irresponsible or antisocial behavior produce for self and others. (18)

18. Firmly confront the client's irresponsible, impulsive, and antisocial behavior, pointing out consequences for himself/herself and others.

11. Increase verbalizations of an acceptance of responsibility for own actions, and cease making excuses or blaming others for misbehavior. (19, 20)

19. Confront statements in which the client blames others for his/her impulsive behavior and fails to accept responsibility for the consequences of his/her actions.

20. Challenge the client to cease making excuses for his/her

irresponsible or antisocial behavior because he/she has ADHD. Remind him/her that the vast majority of individuals with this condition do not engage in delinquent or illegal activities.

12. Caregivers allow the client to experience the natural or legal consequences of his/her acting-out or antisocial behavior. (21)

21. Encourage and challenge the caregivers not to protect the client from the natural legal consequences of his/her impulsive actions or antisocial behavior because he/she has ADHD.

13. Caregivers establish clearly defined rules and follow through consistently with consequences for the client's impulsive or acting-out behavior. (22, 23)

22. Conduct family therapy sessions to help the caregivers establish clearly defined rules, boundaries, and consequences for the client's hyperactive, impulsive, and acting-out behavior; have the client repeat the rules and consequences to demonstrate an understanding of the expectations.

23. Teach the caregivers effective disciplinary techniques (e.g., time out, response cost, undoing, removal of privileges, use of natural consequences, etc.) to improve the client's impulse control, reduce hyperactivity, and deter acting-out behavior.

14. Caregivers increase structure at home to help the client delay the need for instant gratification in order to achieve long-term goals. (24)

24. Assist the caregivers in increasing structure at home to help the client to learn to delay his/her need for instant gratification in favor of achieving more meaningful long-term goals

(e.g., complete homework at scheduled times, perform chores before playing video games or socializing with friends, etc.).

15. Caregivers and school officials identify and utilize a variety of effective reinforcers to improve the client's self-control and increase positive behavior. (25)

25. Consult with the caregivers and school officials to identify a list of rewards to reinforce the client for exercising self-control and engaging in responsible or desired social behavior at home or school.

16. Caregivers and teachers increase praise and positive verbalizations toward the client. (26, 27)

26. Encourage the caregivers and teachers to offer frequent praise and positive reinforcement to the client when he/she exercises good self-control and engages in desired behavior.

27. Instruct caregivers and teachers to observe the client and "catch" him/her showing good self-control. Encourage caregivers and teachers to praise the client and to specifically identify what strategies he/she used to exercise good self-control.

17. Caregivers and teachers implement a reward system, contingency contract, or token economy. (28, 29)

28. Design a reward system and/or contingency contract to reinforce the client's desired positive behavior and deter impulsive or acting-out behavior.

29. Design and implement a token economy at home or school to improve the client's impulse control, social skills, and academic performance.

18. Reduce the frequency and severity of impulsive or acting-out behavior. (30, 31)

30. Teach the client mediational and self-control strategies (e.g., "stop, look, listen, and think"; walk away; count to 10; listen to music; etc.) to help inhibit impulses, decrease activity level, delay need for instant gratification, or control anger.

31. Train the client to use progressive relaxation or guided imagery techniques to help induce greater calm, inhibit his/her impulse to act out, and control his/her anger.

19. Identify and implement effective coping strategies to induce calm and exert greater self-control. (31, 32, 33, 34)

31. Train the client to use progressive relaxation or guided imagery techniques to help induce greater calm, inhibit his/her impulse to act out, and control his/her anger.

32. Instruct the client to use a self-imposed time-out to remove himself/herself from unstructured situations where there is a great deal of external stimulation. Encourage him/her to use the time-out to settle down, reduce hyperactivity, and think about behavioral alternatives and their consequences.

33. Encourage the client, caregivers, and teachers to use a signal or cue to alert the client to take steps to induce calm or regain control after he/she becomes overly restless, excitable, or impulsive.

34. Use the therapeutic game Stop, Relax and Think (Shapiro, available from Childswork/Childsplay, LLC) to assist the client in developing greater self-control.

20. Identify and implement effective problem-solving strategies. (35, 36)

35. Teach the client effective problem-solving skills (i.e., identify the problem, brainstorm alternate solutions, list pros and cons of each option, select an option, implement a course of action, and evaluate) to improve his/her impulse control and ability to resolve conflict.

36. Use the "Stop, Think, and Act" homework assignment from *The Brief Adolescent Therapy Homework Planner* (Jongsma, Peterson, and McInnis) to increase the client's ability to inhibit impulses, deter acting-out behavior, and resolve conflict more effectively.

21. Utilize self-monitoring techniques to improve impulse control, academic performance, and social skills. (37)

37. Train the client to use self-monitoring checklists to improve impulse control, social skills, and academic performance. Have him/her select a specific behavior (e.g., raising his/her hand instead of blurting out, staying on a task, complimenting others, etc.) and monitor his/her behavior by using a self-recording form.

22. Identify stressors or painful emotions that trigger an

38. Assist the client in making a connection between underlying

increase in hyperactivity, impulsivity, and antisocial behavior. (38, 39, 40, 41)

negative or painful emotions and increased impulsive or antisocial behavior.

39. Explore and identify stressful events or factors that contribute to an increase in hyperactivity, impulsivity, and antisocial behaviors. Help the client and his/her caregivers to develop positive coping strategies to manage stress more effectively.

40. Assess periods of time when the client has demonstrated improved impulse control and behaved responsibly. Process his/her responses, and reinforce the positive coping strategies that he/she used to exercise self-control and deter impulsive behavior.

41. Explore possible stressors, roadblocks, or hurdles that might cause the client's impulsive and antisocial behavior to increase in the future. Identify coping strategies (e.g., "stop, look, listen, and think"; guided imagery; using "I" messages to indicate needs; etc.) that the client and his/her family can use to cope with or overcome stressors, roadblocks, or hurdles.

23. Increase the frequency of responsible and socially appropriate behavior. (42, 43)

42. Introduce the idea that the client can change from engaging in acting-out or antisocial behavior by asking, "What will you be doing when you stop

getting into trouble with the law?" Process his/her responses, and encourage him/her to take active steps toward achieving positive behavior changes.

43. Place the client in charge of tasks at home (e.g., preparing and cooking a special dish, changing oil in the car, building shelves in the garage, etc.) to demonstrate confidence in his/her ability to act responsibly.

24. Identify and list positive ways to channel energy. (44, 45, 46, 47)

44. Give the client a homework assignment of identifying between three and five role models (e.g., responsible adult or peer) and heroes (e.g., prominent athlete, entertainment figure, etc.) who have been diagnosed with ADHD. Process this list, and reinforce with the client how these role models or heroes exercised good self-control and channeled energy in a positive direction.

45. Have the client list between 5 and 10 positive and negative ways to channel his/her energy. Review this list, and encourage him/her to channel his/her energy into responsible behavior, healthy physical outlets, or extracurricular and positive social activities.

46. Schedule a "hyper" or "blow-out" time each day or week when the client can do whatever he/she likes, provided

it is not harmful or dangerous to himself/herself or others (e.g., blasting music in the bedroom, yelling and screaming while playing basketball or dancing, eating a large bag of potato chips, etc.).

47. Identify constructive and healthy ways for the client to seek excitement and have fun (e.g., riding a roller-coaster ride at an amusement park, attending school dance, going whitewater rafting with youth group, etc.), instead of engaging in potentially dangerous or harmful thrill-seeking behavior.

25. Increase the frequency of positive interactions with caregivers, siblings, and peers. (48, 51)

48. Encourage the client and his/her caregivers to spend between 10 and 15 minutes daily in one-on-one time to increase the frequency of positive interactions and improve the lines of communication.

51. Assign the task of showing empathy, kindness, or sensitivity to the needs of others (e.g., allowing a sibling or peer to take first turn at video game, helping to raise money for school fundraiser, etc.).

26. Recognize and verbalize how affiliation with negative peer groups contributes to impulsive or antisocial behavior. (49, 50)

49. Use modeling and role-playing techniques to teach the client effective ways to resist negative peer influences and to deter his/her impulse to act out in an antisocial manner.

50. Have the client view the *Refusal Skills* video (available from Childswork/Childsplay, LLC) to teach effective assertiveness skills and to help him/her to resist negative peer influences.

27. Increase verbalizations of empathy and concern for other people. (51)

51. Assign the task of showing empathy, kindness, or sensitivity to the needs of others (e.g., allowing a sibling or peer to take first turn at video game, helping to raise money for school fundraiser, etc.).

28. Increase participation in healthy extracurricular or positive peer group activities. (52)

52. Give a homework assignment where the client identifies between 5 and 10 strengths or interests. Review this list in the following session. Encourage him/her to use strengths or interests to establish positive peer friendships.

29. Caregivers and teachers use an organized system to keep track of school assignments, chores, and work responsibilities. (53, 54, 55)

53. Assist the caregivers and teachers in developing and implementing an organizational system to increase the client's on-task behavior and completion of school assignments, chores, or work responsibilities (e.g., using calendars, charts, notebooks, and class syllabus).

54. Assist the client and his/her caregivers in developing a routine schedule to increase his/her compliance with school, household, or work-related responsibilities.

55. Encourage the caregivers and teachers to maintain regular

30. Caregivers maintain communication with the school to increase the client's compliance with completion of school assignments. (55)

31. Use effective study skills to improve academic performance. (56, 57, 58)

communication about the client's academic, behavioral, emotional, and social progress.

55. Encourage the caregivers and teachers to maintain regular communication about the client's academic, behavioral, emotional, and social progress.

56. Consult with the client's teachers to implement strategies to improve school performance (e.g., sitting in front of the class, using a prearranged signal to redirect the client back to the task, scheduling breaks between tasks, providing frequent feedback, keeping to a strict schedule, calling on the client often, etc.).

57. Teach the client more effective study skills (e.g., clearing away distractions, studying in quiet places, outlining or underlining important details, using a tape recorder, scheduling breaks in studying, etc.) to improve academic performance.

58. Teach the client more effective test-taking strategies (e.g., studying over an extended period of time, reviewing material regularly, reading directions twice, rechecking work, taking tests in resource room, etc.) to improve school grades.

32. Increase brain wave control, which results in improved impulse control and attention span. (59)

33. Express feelings through art-work. (60)

59. Use brain wave biofeedback techniques to improve the client's impulse control, attention span, and ability to relax.

60. Instruct the client to draw a picture reflecting what it feels like to have ADHD. Process the content of this drawing with the therapist.

__. _____   __. _____
_____   _____
__. _____   __. _____
_____   _____
__. _____   __. _____
_____   _____

DIAGNOSTIC SUGGESTIONS:

ICD-9-CM	_ICD-10-CM_	_DSM-5_ Disorder, Condition, or Problem
314.01	F90.2	Attention-Deficit/Hyperactivity Disorder, Combined Presentation
314.01	F90.1	Attention-Deficit/Hyperactivity Disorder, Predominately Hyperactive /Impulsive Presentation
314.00	F90.0	Attention-Deficit/Hyperactivity Disorder, Predominately Inattentive Presentation
314.01	F90.9	Unspecified Attention-Deficit/Hyperactivity Disorder
314.01	F90.8	Other Specified Attention-Deficit/Hyperactivity Disorder
312.81	F91.1	Conduct Disorder, Childhood-Onset Type
312.82	F91.2	Conduct Disorder, Adolescent-Onset Type
313.81	F91.3	Oppositional Defiant Disorder
312.9	F91.9	Unspecified Disruptive, Impulse Control, and Conduct Disorder
312.89	F91.8	Other Specified Disruptive, Impulse Control, and Conduct Disorder
296.xx	F31.xx	Bipolar I Disorder
_____	_____	_____
_____	_____	_____

CRUELTY TO ANIMALS

BEHAVIORAL DEFINITIONS

1. Intentionally inflicts pain on pets or undomesticated animals.
2. Lack of sensitivity to the needs of animals.
3. Uses a weapon to cause serious harm to animals (e.g., a bat, brick, broken bottle, knife or gun, etc.).
4. Initiates physical fights between animals for profit or pleasure.
5. Bullies, threatens, or intimidates animals for thrill-seeking purposes.
6. Forces animals into sexual activity.

__. _____
_____

__. _____
_____

__. _____
_____

LONG-TERM GOALS

1. Terminate all physically aggressive behaviors involving animals.
2. Increase capacity for concern for the welfare of animals.
3. Accept responsibility for cruel actions toward animals and experience guilt over it.
4. Demonstrate a significant improvement in impulse control.
5. Work through the emotional problems that contribute to displaced aggression toward animals.
6. Eliminate all sexual interactions with animals.

—. _____
_____

—. _____
_____

—. _____
_____

SHORT-TERM OBJECTIVES

1. Complete psychological testing. (1, 2, 3)

2. Cooperate with an evaluation by a psychiatrist to determine the possible benefits of psychotropic medication for comorbid disorders and comply with recommendations. (3, 4)

THERAPEUTIC INTERVENTIONS

1. Arrange for psychological testing of the client to assess current cognitive, social, and emotional factors that contribute to aggressive behavior toward animals.

2. Gather information regarding psychosocial stressors that influence cruelty to animals (e.g., abuse, neglect, or loss of key attachment figures due to separation, divorce, or death).

3. Provide feedback to the client and his/her caretakers and juvenile justice officials regarding the assessment results and recommendations.

3. Provide feedback to the client and his/her caretakers and juvenile justice officials regarding the assessment results and recommendations.

4. Arrange for a psychiatric evaluation of the client to assess whether a psychotic disorder is present and

whether medication might improve the client's functioning (e.g., control impulses, increase attention, improve thought disorder, and/or stabilize his/her mood).

3. Take medication as prescribed by the physician and report as to the effectiveness and side effects. (5)

5. Monitor effectiveness and side effects of prescribed medications; consult with a prescribing physician regarding medication regimen.

4. Acknowledge and accept the legal consequences for exhibiting aggression toward animals. (6, 7)

6. Discuss the legal consequences of aggressive behavior toward animals (e.g., probation, restitution, community service, placement in an alternative setting, etc.).

7. Encourage the client to identify reasons for accepting and complying with the legal consequences (e.g., probation, restitution, community service, placement in an alternative setting, etc.) for cruel and aggressive behavior involving animals.

5. Verbally acknowledge all acts of aggression involving animals. (8, 9, 10)

8. Provide the client with opportunities to disclose the details of his/her acts of aggression toward animals and acknowledge responsibility for his/her behavior.

9. Encourage the client to acknowledge patterns of aggressive acts that have resulted in harm to animals within the past month and process in session.

6. Increase the number of statements that reflect the acceptance of responsibility for aggressive behavior rather than projecting blame onto others. (11, 12, 13)

7. Decrease the frequency, severity, and duration of aggressive acts involving animals. (14, 15)

8. Caretakers verbalize and enforce clear expectations

10. Encourage the caretakers to identify behaviors or situations that have escalated into harmful acts involving animals and discuss with the client in family therapy sessions.

11. Confront statements in which the client projects blame onto others for his/her aggressive behavior and fails to accept responsibility for his/her actions.

12. Praise the client when he/she acknowledges acts of aggression involving animals and accepts responsibility.

13. Explore and discuss the underlying reasons for the client's pattern of blaming others for his/her antisocial behaviors.

14. Encourage the client to make a verbal commitment to decreasing aggressive behavior involving animals.

15. Assist the client in identifying the behaviors (e.g., engaging in abusive language toward animals or playing with pets when angry) and attitudes (e.g., pets can fend for themselves or animals don't feel pain) that must be modified in order to decrease aggression toward animals. Process this list with the client.

16. Encourage the caretakers to restrict the client's access to

regarding the client terminating cruelty to animals. (16, 17)

animals during the beginning phase of treatment.

17. Assist the caretakers in developing a behavioral contract that stipulates clear expectations for behavior at home and at school, including rewards for prosocial behavior and negative consequences for aggressive behavior involving animals.

9. Identify social interactions that frequently trigger or elicit aggressive behavior. (18, 19)

18. Encourage the client to keep a daily log of situations or social interactions that typically trigger or escalate aggressive behavior. Process this log in session.

19. Assist the client in recognizing patterns of social interaction that place him/her at risk for aggressive behavior (e.g., associating with disruptive peers, using illegal substances, provoking aggression between animals for pleasure or profit, etc.). Encourage avoidance of these social interactions.

10. Verbalize an increased awareness of how a personal history of abuse and/or loss may contribute to antisocial behaviors. (20)

20. Explore the client's background for a history of abuse (e.g., physical, emotional, or sexual) and/or loss (e.g., separation from a key attachment figure through abandonment or death) that may contribute to his/her aggressive behavior toward animals and process this in session.

11. Identify feelings related to a history of loss and/or abuse. Verbalize how these feelings may impact current functioning. (21, 22)

21. Assist the client in identifying and verbalizing feelings that are associated with abuse or loss (e.g., rejection, rage, fear, loneliness, anxiety, etc.).

22. Assist the client in identifying how the feelings resulting from the loss or the abuse (e.g., rejection, rage, fear, loneliness, anxiety, etc.) may be connected to his/her current aggressive behavior involving animals.

12. Resolve negative feelings related to a history of loss and/or abuse. (23, 24, 25)

23. Conduct individual therapy sessions to provide the client with an opportunity to work through feelings resulting from a past abuse or loss.

24. Use a therapeutic game (Talking, Feeling, and Doing Game; Furious Fred; Breaking the Chains of Anger; or From Rage to Reason) to develop more effective anger and impulse control.

25. Ask the client to complete and process an exercise from *The Me Nobody Knows* (Bean and Bennett) or *Life After Trauma* (Rosenbloom and Williams) workbook(s) to work through issues of abuse and/or loss.

13. Identify the sources of anger and powerlessness that fuel cruelty to animals. (22, 26)

22. Assist the client in identifying how the feelings resulting from the loss or the abuse (e.g., rejection, rage, fear, loneliness, anxiety, etc.) may be connected to his/her current aggressive behavior involving animals.

14. Engage in healthy roles of leadership empowerment. (27)

15. Monitor and process cognitive distortions that coincide with acts of aggression toward animals. (28, 29)

16. Develop a list of alternative ways to address problems rather than engaging in aggressive behavior toward animals. (30, 31)

26. Use play therapy techniques to explore the sources of anger and powerlessness that fuel the client's cruelty to animals.

27. Explore with the client alternative, healthier means of feeling powerful (e.g., joining an athletic team, seeking a leadership position in a school organization, taking on a teaching or tutoring role with younger children, etc).

28. Assist the client in developing an awareness of cognitive distortions that contribute to the emergence and maintenance of his/her aggressive behavior toward animals (e.g., animals like to play rough; pets can fend for themselves; he was only a stray; he's a big and strong dog, he can take it; etc.). Encourage the client to monitor his/her cognitive distortions, and process these in session.

29. Help the client to collect evidence that disputes his/her distorted thought patterns.

30. Assist the client in implementing problem-solving strategies (e.g., defining the specific problem, brainstorming alternative solutions that are safe and nonaggressive, anticipating consequences, implementing a solution, and evaluating outcome effectiveness).

31. Encourage the client to implement problem-solving strategies during the week. Work through obstacles to effective problem solving in session.

17. Use coping strategies and relaxation techniques three times per day to deter impulsive behavior, including aggressive acts toward animals. (32)

32. Teach and monitor the use of relaxation techniques (e.g., visualization, meditation, breathing, progressive muscle relaxation, etc.) and coping skills (e.g., thought stopping, positive affirmations, self-talk, etc.) to assist the client in improving impulse control.

18. Identify legal alternatives to generating money rather than engaging animals in fighting for profit. (33)

33. Assist the client in identifying legal ways to obtain money rather than engaging animals in fights for profit.

19. Increase the frequency of kind and compassionate acts involving animals by 50 percent. (34, 35, 36)

34. Refer the client to pet therapy where he/she can learn to interact with animals in a safe and appropriate manner.

35. Encourage the client to volunteer at a local animal shelter (e.g., Humane Society or the Society for the Prevention of Cruelty to Animals) to make restitution for his/her acts of aggression toward animals. Ensure that adequate supervision is provided.

36. Assign a homework task in which the client must demonstrate kindness or sensitivity to the needs of other people or animals. Process this demonstration in session.

20. Caretakers increase supervision of the client's behavior and monitor physically aggressive acts. (37, 38, 39, 40)

37. Discuss with the caretakers the importance of consistently supervising the client's interactions with animals and confronting any behavior that may lead to aggression.

38. Confront the caretakers' tendency to respond to the client's aggressive interactions in an overly punitive manner or in a passive, discounting manner.

39. Encourage the client and his/her caretakers to use monitoring checklists to develop more effective anger and impulse control in the home setting. Instruct the client and his/her caretakers to compare the checklists and discuss similarities and differences in the ratings. Process this information in family therapy sessions.

40. Encourage the caretakers to provide praise and positive reinforcement to the client when he/she exhibits responsible, prosocial behavior and good impulse control in the home setting without prompting.

21. Caretakers teach and model proper grooming and animal care to the client. (41)

41. Encourage the caretakers to teach and share appropriate grooming techniques and animal care (e.g., feeding, exercise, medical care, training techniques, etc.) with the client. Monitor the client while

he/she implements grooming techniques and animal care.

22. Disclose any bizarre or delusional thoughts regarding animals. (4, 42)

4. Arrange for a psychiatric evaluation of the client to assess whether a psychotic disorder is present and whether medication might improve the client's functioning (e.g., control impulses, increase attention, improve thought disorder, and/or stabilize his/her mood).

42. Explore the client's thought process for evidence of a psychotic process that may need intensive psychiatric intervention or hospitalization.

__. _____
_____

__. _____
_____

__. _____
_____

__. _____
_____

__. _____
_____

__. _____
_____

DIAGNOSTIC SUGGESTIONS:

ICD-9-CM	_ICD-10-CM_	_DSM-5_ Disorder, Condition, or Problem
312.81	F91.1	Conduct Disorder, Childhood-Onset Type
312.82	F91.2	Conduct Disorder, Adolescent-Onset Type
313.81	F91.3	Oppositional Defiant Disorder
312.9	F91.9	Unspecified Disruptive, Impulse Control, and Conduct Disorder
312.89	F91.8	Other Specified Disruptive, Impulse Control, and Conduct Disorder
314.01	F90.2	Attention-Deficit/Hyperactivity Disorder, Combined Presentation
312.34	F63.81	Intermittent Explosive Disorder
V71.02	Z72.810	Adolescent Antisocial Behavior
_____	_____	_____
_____	_____	_____

DECEITFUL/MANIPULATIVE

BEHAVIORAL DEFINITIONS

1. Falsifies information, misleads, and/or deviously influences others in an attempt to gain special treatment, privileges, or personal profit.
2. Attempts to con others with lies and deceptions to satisfy needs and/or for thrill seeking and pleasure.
3. Uses calculating and intimidating behavior to influence others to act in ways tended to satisfy needs and wants or to exert power.
4. Demonstrates a pattern of repetitive lying and often blurs the distinction between reality and fantasy.
5. Fails to accept responsibility for deceitful or manipulative behavior, denying any intent to mislead others.
6. Superficially charming, fun, and entertaining in an attempt to get needs and/or wants met.
7. Lacks confidence in own abilities and therefore manipulates and deceives to get needs met.
8. Pits caregivers and peers against each other in order to get desires fulfilled.
9. Uses aliases to con others and/or cover up delinquent acts.

___. _____
   _____
___. _____
   _____
___. _____
   _____

LONG-TERM GOALS

1. Eliminate manipulative and deceptive behavior.
2. Tell the truth consistently, and understand the need for trust in any meaningful relationship.
3. Clearly and directly express needs and wants in a manner that does not exploit or harm others.
4. Increase confidence in ability to meet needs without being manipulative or deceitful.
5. Develop fulfilling relationships, decreasing the need to be manipulative.
6. Take responsibility for own behavior.

—. _____
   _____

—. _____
   _____

—. _____
   _____

SHORT-TERM OBJECTIVES

1. Verbalize an understanding of deceitful and manipulative behavior. (1)

2. Identify own instances of deceitful and manipulative behavior and its effect on self and others. (2, 3)

THERAPEUTIC INTERVENTIONS

1. Help the client to define examples of deceitful and manipulative behavior.

2. Present vignettes that demonstrate different types of manipulative behavior. Ask the client to identify which types of behavior he/she exhibits. Confront denial as necessary.

3. Assist the client in identifying and writing a list of the effects of deceitful and manipulative behavior on himself/herself and others (e.g., hurting others' feelings, breaking trust, engendering anger, promoting low self-esteem, etc.).

3. Acknowledge that deceitful and manipulative behavior contributed to involvement with the juvenile justice system. (4)

4. Verbalize an awareness of and comply with the legal consequences of deceitful and manipulative behavior. (5, 6)

4. Provide information explaining to the client the legal consequences of his/her deceitful and manipulative behavior.

5. Encourage acknowledgment and acceptance of, as well as compliance with, the legal consequences.

6. Discuss with the client the potential legal problems (e.g., probation, detention, requirement to pay restitution, etc.) that may develop as a result of his/her continued use of unlawful deception and manipulation.

5. Disclose aliases and delinquent acts that are associated with each alias. (7, 8, 9)

7. Ask the client to identify aliases, and encourage him/her to confess delinquent acts that he/she carried out using the identified alias.

8. Encourage the client to relinquish all false identification cards.

9. Help the client to understand how using aliases to preserve anonymity encourages delinquency by fostering a false sense of power and invincibility.

6. Identify deceitful and manipulative behavior that has occurred over the past week. (10, 11, 12)

10. Assist the client in increasing his/her awareness of deceitful and manipulative behavior by instructing him/her to keep a log of interactions with individuals whom he/she is inclined to attempt deceiving and manipulating.

11. Give the client feedback regarding deceitful and manipulative behavior occurring during the session.

12. Ask family members and/or caregivers to make the client aware of his/her attempts to deceive and manipulate.

7. Identify situations and/or people that evoke or trigger deceitful and manipulative behavior. (13)

13. Assist the client in identifying situations or people that evoke or trigger deceitful and manipulative behavior (e.g., threat of being punished, failure, restrictions being imposed, etc.).

8. Identify prior life events that have fostered the use of deceit and/or manipulation. (14)

14. Assist the client in developing an awareness of prior life events and relationships that encouraged or fostered deceitful and manipulative behavior (e.g., a parent who lied, a caregiver who was overly punitive, an affiliation with a peer or gang that reinforced deceit, physical abuse, etc.).

9. Track thoughts that precede deceitful and manipulative behavior. (15, 16)

15. Help the client to become aware of cognitive distortions associated with deceptive and manipulative behavior by asking him/her to keep a log of his/her thoughts that precede and follow such behavior (e.g., "This person is going to take advantage of me"; "I deserve this reward without having to work for it"; "This person is weak and deserves to be taken advantage of "; "It's not my fault that others are too trusting"; etc.).

16. Process with the client his/her log of thoughts that precede and follow deceitful and manipulative behavior. Assist him/her in correcting his/her faulty cognitions.

10. Identify those feelings that are involved in the decision to deceive and manipulate. (17, 18)

17. Assist the client in labeling feelings that evoke or trigger deceptive and manipulative behavior (e.g., anger, fear, entitlement, worthlessness, anxiety, insecurity, jealousy, sadness, etc.).

18. Process the client's feelings leading to a decision to engage in deceitful and manipulative behavior.

11. Identify goals achieved by deceitful and manipulative behavior. (19)

19. Facilitate the client's identifying goals that are achieved by manipulative and deceitful behavior (e.g., getting attention, satisfying needs and/or wants, expressing anger or other feelings, etc.) by encouraging open dialog.

12. Make a list of alternative ways to achieve goals that are associated with deceitful and manipulative behavior. (20)

20. Explore with the client alternative, nonexploitive ways to achieve goals that are associated with deceitful and manipulative behavior (e.g., asking directly for what he/she wants, being assertive, using direct communication, relying on personal abilities and strengths, etc.).

13. Practice alternatives to manipulative and deceitful behavior twice per day. (21, 22)

21. Ask the client to make a list of alternative strategies that he/she would most likely use to achieve goals typically achieved by manipulation and deception.

14. Verbalize an increased sensitivity and/or empathy toward individuals being manipulated or deceived. (23, 24, 25)

15. Make amends with those who have been hurt by deception or manipulation. (26)

16. Ask for help directly when own needs cannot be met alone. (27, 28)

22. Role-play with the client alternatives to deceptive and manipulative behavior (e.g., assertive communication, etc.). Assign the client to use these alternatives on a daily basis. Process the outcome with him/her.

23. Engage the client in a perspective-taking exercise by asking him/her to describe how it might feel to be deceived and/or manipulated.

24. Implement a role-reversal technique and role-play a situation in which the client is the recipient of deceitful and manipulative behavior. Process his/her feelings.

25. Positively reinforce (e.g., implement a tangible reward system, verbally reinforce him/her, etc.) the client's behavior that is indicative of his/her sensitivity toward others (e.g., verbalizes compassion toward someone in pain, performs an act of kindness toward someone in need, tells the truth, etc.).

26. Assign the client to make amends (e.g., apologize verbally or in writing, pay restitution, etc.) to individuals whom he/she has impersonated, duped, or conned.

27. Assist the client in identifying needs that are not being met. Encourage him/her to ask for help rather than using deception and manipulation to satisfy the need.

28. Role-play the client asking for help, and assign in vivo asking-for-help exercises. Process the outcome of these in vivo exercises with him/her.

17. Acknowledge own poor self-concept (self-efficacy and self-esteem) and how it contributes to deceitful and manipulative behaviors. (29, 30)

29. Discuss the concepts of self-esteem and self-efficacy with the client, focusing on the connection between feeling that he/she is not worthy and/or capable of meeting his/her needs, and the subsequent reliance on manipulation and deception to satisfy his/her needs.

30. Explore with the client his/her underlying, negative assumptions about himself/herself that foster a reliance on deceptive and manipulative behavior.

18. Express feelings of inadequacy. (31)

31. Encourage expression of feelings and inadequacies to increase conscious awareness of feelings that lead to deceitful and manipulative behavior.

19. Acknowledge personal strengths and talents, and implement activities that use these abilities. (32)

32. Reinforce the client's talents and feelings of competence (e.g., encourage him/her to become involved in activities in which he/she can be successful; have him/her talk about or display his/her talents in a group setting; identify strengths that he/she possesses and share these in individual sessions; ask family members and/or caregivers to identify the client's strengths and to share them with him/her in a family therapy session).

20. Accept refusal of requests made to others without attempts to manipulate. (33, 34, 35)

33. Assist the client in gaining awareness of his/her response when others reject or fail to honor his/her request (e.g., anger, revenge, entitlement, self-protection, etc.).

34. Teach the client techniques that will help him/her to control the tendency to manipulate and deceive others when they disagree with his/her request (e.g., thought-stopping techniques, self-monitoring techniques, assertive communication techniques, etc.).

35. Reward the client for accepting unfavorable responses to his/her requests without attempting to manipulate or deceive.

21. Engage in direct expression and assertiveness, three times daily. (36, 37)

36. Teach assertive, honest communication techniques (i.e., teach the client the difference between assertiveness and aggressiveness; instruct the client on planning what he/she is going to say before saying it; encourage asking questions, eye contact, and honest expression of feelings; etc.).

37. Provide the opportunity for the client to practice direct communication and assertive skills in individual and group therapy sessions. Encourage this practice in his/her natural environment.

22. Cooperate with a psychological assessment to determine if underlying problems are contributing to deceit. (38)

38. Complete a psychological evaluation to determine if the client's behavior is a manifestation of a serious, underlying

problem (e.g., lying to cover drug use, academic problems, delinquency, psychiatric illness, etc.). Refer him/her for additional services as needed (e.g., medication management, drug treatment, support groups, etc.).

23. The caregivers identify behavior within the family that encourages the client to engage in manipulative behavior. (39)

39. In family therapy sessions, investigate the family dynamics that promote deception and manipulation (e.g., severe criticism or rejection of the client, modeling of deceit, abuse of the client, substance abuse by the caregiver, etc.).

24. Caregivers list consequences for the client's deceitful and manipulative behavior. (40)

40. Assist the caregivers in developing and implementing a coordinated and consistent plan of consequences that is designed to decrease the client's deceitful and manipulative behavior (e.g., identifying target behavior, establishing consequences, communicating and implementing a behavior plan, and monitoring effectiveness).

25. The family and/or caregiver refrain from responding in ways that reinforce the client's deceitful and manipulative behavior.
(41, 42, 43, 44)

41. Encourage the caregivers to withdraw attention when the client refuses to cooperate with activities or is disruptive and/or inappropriate in his/her attempt to manipulate the situation.

42. Encourage the caregivers to give attention and support to the client when he/she exhibits appropriate behavior (e.g., expressing feelings and needs, attending activities, completing chores, etc.) without deceiving and/or manipulating.

43. Urge the caregivers to establish a united front to prevent splitting by making the family and/or caregivers aware of the client's manipulative and deceitful behavior (e.g., self-pity, somatic complaints, vulgar language, teasing, flattery, inappropriate jokes, lying, etc.). Encourage the family to refrain from responding to the client's deceptive and manipulative behavior.

44. Educate the caregivers on how setting inconsistent limits encourages deception and manipulation by communicating to the client that he/she can possibly control the situation or get away with his/her misbehavior this time.

—. _____
   _____
—. _____
   _____
—. _____
   _____

—. _____
   _____
—. _____
   _____
—. _____
   _____

DIAGNOSTIC SUGGESTIONS:

ICD-9-CM	_ICD-10-CM_	_DSM-5_ Disorder, Condition, or Problem
309.81	F43.10	Posttraumatic Stress Disorder
309.24	F43.22	Adjustment Disorder, With Anxiety
309.3	F43.24	Adjustment Disorder, With Disturbance of Conduct
V71.02	Z72.810	Adolescent Antisocial Behavior
312.8	F91.x	Conduct Disorder
312.9	F91.9	Unspecified Disruptive, Impulse Control, and Conduct Disorder
312.89	F91.8	Other Specified Disruptive, Impulse Control, and Conduct Disorder
313.81	F91.3	Oppositional Defiant Disorder
_____	_____	_____
_____	_____	_____

DEPRESSION

BEHAVIORAL DEFINITIONS

1. Frequent sad, depressed, and melancholy moods.
2. Flat, constricted affect.
3. Social withdrawal and/or feelings of being alienated, misunderstood, or rejected by peers.
4. Markedly diminished interest or pleasure in nearly all activities or activities that used to bring pleasure in the past.
5. Psychomotor agitation or retardation.
6. Lack of energy, frequent complaints of feeling tired or fatigued.
7. Endogenous signs of depression (e.g., decrease in appetite, overeating, difficulty falling asleep, early morning awakenings, oversleeping, etc.).
8. Feelings of hopelessness and helplessness; strong doubts that life will improve in the future.
9. Low self-esteem, feelings of inadequacy and worthlessness.
10. Repeated thoughts of death or suicide, history of suicidal gestures or attempts.
11. Angry outbursts or frequent irritable moods that mask deeper feelings of sadness or depression.
12. Recurrent pattern of engaging in victimless antisocial behavior (e.g., truancy, curfew violations, running away, etc.) or minor acting-out behavior (e.g., school suspensions for disruptive behaviors) that serve as a cry for help.
13. Guilt or remorse about acting-out and antisocial behavior.
14. Unresolved grief or abandonment issues.

—. _____

_____

—. _____
_____
—. _____
_____

LONG-TERM GOALS

1. Significantly reduce the frequency and severity of depressed or irritable mood.
2. Stabilize mood and return to the previous level of adaptive functioning.
3. Eliminate the pattern of acting out or engaging in aggressive or antisocial behaviors when feeling sad or depressed.
4. Develop a positive self-image as manifested by consistently verbalizing positive self-descriptive statements and taking active steps to meet personal needs.
5. Demonstrate regular interest, enjoyment, or pleasure in recreational, leisure, social, or work activities at home, school, or in the community.
6. Employ positive coping mechanisms to effectively manage life stressors and avoid experiencing a relapse of depressed mood.
7. Resolve family or peer conflicts that contribute to the emergence of depressed moods or acting-out and/or antisocial behavior.
8. Successfully work through feelings of sadness or grief about past losses, abandonment, or rejection experiences.

—. _____
_____
—. _____
_____
—. _____
_____

SHORT-TERM OBJECTIVES	**THERAPEUTIC INTERVENTIONS**
1. Complete psychological testing. (1)	1. Arrange for psychological testing of the client to determine whether he/she truly has a depressive

	disorder, to assess the severity and depth of depression, and to identify the possible factors contributing to the emergence of depressed moods and acting-out behaviors. Provide feedback of the test results to the client and, with proper signed release forms, to other interested parties.
2. Provide a detailed history of past depressed moods. (2)	2. Gather detailed psychosocial history of the client's depressed moods, including age of onset, frequency and severity of depressed moods, family history of affective disorders, periods of contented or happy moods, and the precipitating events leading up to the emergence of depressed moods.
3. Cooperate with a physician's evaluation to assess possible organic causes for depression and need for medication. (3)	3. Refer the client to a physician or psychiatrist to rule out organic causes for depression, assess the need for antidepressant medication, and arrange for a prescription, if appropriate.
4. Take prescribed medication as directed by the physician. Report to the physician or appropriate professionals about the effectiveness of the medications and any side effects. (4)	4. Monitor the client for medication compliance, effectiveness, and side effects, consulting with the prescribing physician or psychiatrist at regular intervals. Explore reasons for the client's resistance if it is learned that he/she is not taking the medication as prescribed.
5. Identify sources of depressed mood. (5, 6, 7)	5. Ask the client to make a list of what he/she is depressed about

and process this list with the therapist. Explore with the client what would help him/her to feel happier or more contented.

6. Explore with the client early childhood experiences or past painful events that contribute to his/her current depressed state.

7. Develop a time line in session where the client records positive and negative life experiences or events. Identify positive life experiences that led to improvements in his/her mood and behavior. Conversely, detail past events or stressors that triggered bouts of depression or acting-out behaviors.

6. Express feelings of hurt, sadness, or depression that are related to past painful events. (8, 9)

8. Actively build the level of trust with the client in individual sessions through consistent eye contact, active listening, unconditional positive regard, and warm acceptance to improve his/her ability to identify and express sad, depressed, and angry feelings.

9. Encourage the client to share feelings of sadness about family members, peers, or significant others in order to clarify them and help gain insight into the factors contributing to the emergence of his/her depressed mood.

7. Record feelings of sadness in a daily journal. (10)

8. Specify what is missing from life to cause feelings of depression. (11)

9. Identify negative cognitive messages that contribute to or maintain feelings of depression. (12, 13)

10. Replace negative cognitive messages and self-defeating talk with positive, reality-based cognitive messages. (14)

11. Increase verbalizations of positive self-talk. (15)

10. Have the client keep a journal in which he/she records experiences or situations that evoke feelings of depression. Process the content of this journal with the client to help him/her express and work through feelings of sadness.

11. Ask the client to discuss what is missing from his/her life that contributes to his/her unhappiness.

12. Assist the client in developing an awareness of the negative cognitive messages that reinforce his/her feelings of depression, hopelessness, and helplessness.

13. Assign the client the exercise "Bad Thoughts Lead to Depressed Feelings" from *The Brief Adolescent Therapy Homework Planner* (Jongsma, Peterson, and McInnis) to teach him/her the types of distorted thinking that lead to depression.

14. Teach and reinforce positive, reality-based cognitive messages that improve self-esteem, decrease feelings of depression, and lead to adaptive behaviors.

15. Instruct the client to record in a journal on a daily basis at least five positive, affirmative statements regarding himself/herself and the future.

12. Report a reduction in suicidal thoughts and a termination of suicidal behaviors. (16, 17, 18)

16. Assess the client's risk for suicide, taking into account the extent of the ideation, the presence of primary and backup plans, past attempts, and family history.

17. Refer the client for inpatient hospitalization if he/she is deemed to be at risk for suicide or self-harm.

18. Confer with the caregivers, probation officer, attorneys, or other criminal justice officials about whether the suicidal client should be placed in a juvenile detention facility as a consequence of his/her antisocial behavior, or whether he/she should first be admitted into an inpatient psychiatric unit to eliminate suicidal risk and stabilize moods before facing legal consequences.

13. Verbally identify the connection between acting-out or antisocial behaviors and unmet needs or feelings of depression. (19, 20, 21, 22)

19. Assist the client in making a connection between acting-out or antisocial behaviors and unmet needs or underlying painful emotions (e.g., depression, anxiety, fearfulness, deprivation, rejection, etc.).

20. Assign the client the homework assignment "Surface Behavior/Inner Feelings" from *The Brief Adolescent Therapy Homework Planner* (Jongsma, Peterson, and McInnis). Process the responses to the homework to show the client the connection between his/her feelings

of hurt or sadness and acting-out behaviors.

21. Encourage and challenge the client to express openly and directly to others his/her feelings of anger, hurt, and sadness instead of channeling these emotions into acting-out or self-defeating behaviors, which fail to meet his/her deeper needs, and only serve to reinforce his/her feelings of guilt or depression.

22. Explore what needs the client is attempting to meet through his/her acting-out or antisocial behaviors. Assist the client in identifying more adaptive ways to meet his/her needs.

14. Caregivers establish appropriate boundaries and follow through consistently with consequences for antisocial behaviors. (23, 24)

23. Assist the client's caregivers in establishing clearly defined (and written) rules and consequences for antisocial or illegal behaviors. Inform the client and have him/her repeat the rules or consequences to demonstrate that he/she understands the expectations.

24. Design a reward system and/or contingency contract for the client to reinforce identified positive behaviors and deter acting-out or antisocial behaviors.

15. Caregivers increase the frequency of praise and positive reinforcement for the client's

25. Encourage the caregivers to provide frequent praise and positive reinforcement for the

prosocial or responsible behaviors. (25, 26)

client's prosocial and responsible behaviors.

26. Instruct the caregivers to observe and record between three and five positive or responsible behaviors by the client before the next therapy session. Review these behaviors in the next session with the client, and encourage him/her to continue to engage in these behaviors in the future.

16. Caregivers allow the client to experience natural or legal consequences of his/her antisocial or illegal activities. (27)

27. Encourage and challenge the caregivers to neither protect the client from the natural or legal consequences of his/her antisocial behaviors nor to allow his/her depressed moods to be used as an excuse or justification for his/her legal activities.

17. Comply with all conditions of probation or mandates from the criminal justice system. (28, 29)

28. Consult with criminal justice officials about the appropriate consequences for the client's antisocial behavior (e.g., paying restitution, performing community service, confinement, probation, intensive surveillance, etc.).

29. Inform the probation officer about the presence of the client's depressive disorder. Recommend that the client's participation in outpatient therapy and compliance with taking his/her medication be mandatory conditions of his/her probation.

18. Report a reduction in feelings of guilt after engaging in constructive or responsible actions. (30, 31, 32)

30. Consult with a probation officer or with criminal justice officials about community service projects that the client can perform to undo the effects of his/her antisocial behaviors. Reinforce the client's capacity to demonstrate empathy and caring for others after he/she completes the community service project.

31. Direct the client to offer a verbal or written apology to victim(s) or target(s) of his/her acting-out or antisocial behaviors.

32. Encourage the client to deal with his/her feelings of guilt in an appropriate manner by accepting responsibility for his/her antisocial behaviors. Identify constructive steps that he/she can take to undo past wrongdoings.

19. Move to an appropriate alternative setting to stabilize moods and deter antisocial behaviors. (33)

33. Consult with the caregivers, probation officer, and other criminal justice officials about the need to place the client in an alternative setting (e.g., foster home, residential program, inpatient psychiatric unit, juvenile detention facility, etc.) to help stabilize moods, alleviate depression, and prevent future occurrences of antisocial behavior.

20. Family members identify conflicts or stressors that contribute to the client's

34. Conduct family therapy sessions to identify possible stressors or conflict in the family

depression and/or antisocial behavior. (34, 35)

system that contribute to the emergence of the client's depression and/or antisocial behavior.

35. Explore whether the client's acting-out or antisocial behavior serves as a cry for help and a maladaptive way to gain attention from uninvolved or detached caregiver(s).

21. Increase time spent with caregiver(s) in daily conversations or recreational, leisure, school, or work activities. (36, 37)

36. Instruct the caregivers to set aside between 10 and 15 minutes daily to listen to the client's concerns and provide him/her with the opportunity to express any feelings of sadness.

37. Give a directive to the uninvolved or detached caregiver(s) to spend more time with the client in recreational, leisure, school, or work activities (e.g., attending sporting events, going to a movie together, shopping, preparing an evening meal, etc.). Monitor the caregiver's progress in making this change.

22. Caregivers cease making overly hostile or critical remarks about the client. (38, 39)

38. Conduct family therapy sessions to improve the lines of communication between the client, caregivers, and other family members. Teach effective communication skills (e.g., active listening, "I" messages, avoiding blaming statements, identifying specific positive changes that other family members can make, etc.) to help them

resolve conflict more constructively.

39. Confront and challenge the caregivers to cease making overly hostile or critical remarks about the client or his/her behavior that only contribute to his/her feelings of depression and low self-esteem. Encourage the caregivers to verbalize the positive, specific behaviors or changes that they would like to see the client make.

23. Identify and verbally express feelings that are associated with past losses, abandonment, trauma, or rejection experiences. (40)

40. Explore the client's background for a history of loss, abandonment, trauma, rejection experiences, or harsh criticism that may trigger bouts of depression. Encourage and support the client in expressing his/her painful emotions that are associated with these experiences.

24. Attend group therapy sessions that are focused on elevating mood and building self-esteem. (41)

41. Arrange for the client to attend group therapy to stabilize his/her moods, improve self-esteem, and help break his/her pattern of social withdrawal and introspective preoccupation.

25. Participate regularly in positive peer group or extracurricular activities to lift depression and decrease social isolation. (42, 43)

42. Encourage the client to participate in a positive peer group or extracurricular activities to lift depression, decrease social isolation or withdrawal, and help him/her to achieve a sense of acceptance or belonging.

43. Assist the client in finding more adaptive ways to reduce feelings of depression and

gain a sense of belonging from others (e.g., joining a school choir; attending sporting events; becoming involved in charitable activities through school, church, or community organizations; etc.) rather than acting out or engaging in antisocial behavior.

26. Identify resource people who can be relied upon for support or comfort when needed. (44)

44. Assist the client in identifying a list of resource people at school, church, or in the community to whom he/she can turn for emotional support and comfort, instead of continuing to act out in an antisocial manner as a means of gaining attention, approval, or recognition.

27. Identify more adaptive ways to reduce depression or meet needs other than through substance abuse. (45)

45. Explore the client's substance abuse pattern or arrange for an evaluation to assess whether the client's depression has contributed to the development of a substance abuse problem. Refer the client for treatment if indicated. (See the chapter entitled "Substance Abuse" in this Planner.)

28. Acknowledge sexual promiscuity and identify its relationship to depression. (46, 47)

46. Assess the client for sexual promiscuity as a way to overcome depression and to elicit nurturing or support from others.

47. Help the client to realize the potentially harmful consequences of his/her sexually promiscuous behavior for both himself/herself and for others. Identify more constructive

ways for the client to meet his/her needs or to gain support from others.

29. Identify and list coping strategies to help lift depression and deter the impulse to act out or engage in antisocial behavior. (48, 49, 50)

48. Assign the client to read *When Nothing Matters Anymore: A Survival Guide for Depressed Teens* (Cobain and Verdick) or *Adolescent Depression Workbook* (Copeland and Copans) to help him/her realize that he/she is not alone in dealing with depression and to learn more effective coping strategies to lift depression.

49. Explore periods of time when the client was not depressed and more frequently experienced contented moods. Process his/her responses and reinforce activities or positive coping strategies that he/she used in the past to experience contentment.

50. Explore the possible stressors, conflicts, or roadblocks that may cause depression and acting-out behaviors to reappear in the future. Identify positive steps that the client and/or his/her family members can take to prevent a recurrence of depressed moods or acting-out behavior.

30. Express feelings and identify needs through artwork. (51)

51. Use art therapy techniques (e.g., drawing, coloring, painting, collage, sculpture, etc.) to help the client to express depressive feelings. Use his/her artistic products as a springboard for further discussion of

his/her emotions and their causes.

31. Report that appetite and/ or sleep patterns have returned to previous normal or healthy levels. (52, 53, 54)

52. Monitor the client's food consumption. Encourage him/her to eat well-balanced meals.

53. Monitor the client's sleep patterns and the restfulness of his/her sleep.

54. Teach the client relaxation techniques to help induce calm before attempting to sleep.

__. _____   __. _____
    _____   _____
__. _____   __. _____
    _____   _____
__. _____   __. _____
    _____   _____

DIAGNOSTIC SUGGESTIONS:

ICD-9-CM	_ICD-10-CM_	_DSM-5_ Disorder, Condition, or Problem
300.4	F34.1	Persistent Depressive Disorder
296.xx	F32.x	Major Depressive Disorder, Single Episode
296.xx	F33.x	Major Depressive Disorder, Recurrent Episode
296.89	F31.81	Bipolar II Disorder
296.xx	F31.xx	Bipolar I Disorder
301.13	F34.0	Cyclothymic Disorder
309.0	F43.21	Adjustment Disorder, With Depressed Mood
310.1	F07.0	Personality Change Due to Another Medical Condition
V62.82	Z63.4	Uncomplicated Bereavement
_____	_____	_____
_____	_____	_____

DRUG SELLING

BEHAVIORAL DEFINITIONS

1. Adjudicated or waiting for a dispositional hearing due to drug selling or drug possession charges.
2. Justification of drug selling as acceptable behavior, rationalized by disillusionment and/or anger with the government, society or the "system."
3. Resorting to drug trafficking due to the inability to identify viable options for current or future sources of financial support or for obtaining material possessions.
4. Idealization of the drug trafficker's lifestyle (e.g., feelings of power, importance, wealth), resulting in a desire to sell substances.
5. Occasional participation in selling of drugs to enrich personal and/or familial financial gain.
6. Ignorance about and/or lack of fear of penalties for drug selling.
7. Minimize the harm of drug selling to self or others.
8. Demonstrates an absence of a future orientation or the belief in a foreshortened future.
9. Parental and/or family approval or a lack of visible disapproval for selling substances.
10. Selling substances to support own drug use.
11. Participation in drug selling to increase own popularity with peers (e.g.,≈ability to buy extravagant gifts, look stylish, appear streetwise, etc.).
12. Seeking a sense of belonging, resulting in joining a gang that participates in drug trafficking.

—. _____

_____

—. _____

_____

—. _____

_____

LONG-TERM GOALS

1. Discontinue the selling of substances and all other delinquent acts.
2. Identify and develop healthy, positive long-term goals.
3. Establish positive and healthy means to enrich self-esteem.
4. Eliminate the use and/or abuse of legal and illegal substances.
5. Increase moral development and sensitivity to the pain of others.
6. Increase legal financial resources.

—. _____
_____
—. _____
_____
—. _____
_____

SHORT-TERM OBJECTIVES

1. The client and the caregivers participate in the assessment of his/her prob-lems and concerns and accept the referrals or recommendations of the court. (1, 2, 3)

THERAPEUTIC INTERVENTIONS

1. Complete a comprehensive assessment that determines problems requiring intervention (e.g., scholastic difficulties, substance abuse, mental health concerns, etc.); make referrals when warranted (e.g., substance abuse treatment, job training, psychiatric evaluation, psychological testing, etc.).

2. Collaborate with others involved in the client's treatment (e.g., probation officer, case manager, teachers, family members, etc.) to ensure that he/she is receiving comprehensive services and to obtain information about further treatment.

2. Verbalize fewer statements regarding resentment for and/or resistance to treatment. (4, 5, 6)

3. Collaborate with the probation officer and/or case manager to assist the client and his/her family in understanding the legal consequences of his/her behavior and the related ramifications. Allow the client and his/her family to process their feelings regarding the recommendations of the court.

4. Encourage the client to discuss topics of interest to him/her to increase his/her comfort with treatment, reduce resistance, and to increase rapport.

5. Encourage the client to speak openly and honestly about his/her feelings related to being in treatment. Display empathic responses as a means of modeling empathy, building rapport, and reducing resistance.

6. Demonstrate respect and acceptance of the client, maintaining a nonjudgmental stance and refraining from authoritative communication.

3. Reveal the extent of involvement with drug selling as well as with other illegal behaviors. (7, 8)

7. Ask the client to reveal the history and extent of his/her criminal involvement, especially his/her drug selling.

8. Explore the client's lifestyle and to what extent the drug subculture has become a part of it (e.g., occasional selling, joining a drug gang, selling during a majority of spare time, a substance user, etc.).

4. Process the negative and positive aspects of drug selling. (9)

9. Examine the client's perceptions of the negative (e.g., court involvement, danger, disapproval by some people, etc.) and the positive (e.g., popularity, money, feeling powerful, etc.) aspects of drug selling.

5. Acknowledge involvement in a gang assembled to sell substances. Process the positive and negative aspects of participating in this group. (10, 11)

10. Assist the client in examining his/her decision to be involved in a drug gang. Process with the client positive (e.g., protection, money, "respect," etc.) and negative (e.g., paranoia, court involvement, danger, etc.) aspects of participation.

11. Refer the client to a group that focuses on diminishing gang involvement and/or seek out a former gang member to explore with the client the positive and negative aspects of gang involvement and drug selling.

6. Admit to drug use; accept a referral for substance abuse treatment. (12)

12. Inquire about the extent of the client's drug problem by asking which legal and illegal substances he/she uses, the amount of substances taken, and the route of administration. Refer the client to substance abuse treatment, if necessary. (See the chapter entitled "Substance Abuse" in this Planner.)

7. Verbalize a resolution of motivations to participate in drug selling, especially those related to feelings of powerlessness and/or anger with "society." (13, 14, 15)

13. Engage the client in a conversation about what motivated his/her decision to sell drugs. Help the client to work through any angry and/or hostile feelings that may have allowed him/her to justify his/her behavior.

14. Explore with the client the impact of media images, social class concerns, and/or shameful feelings about poverty that may have prompted his/her involvement with selling substances.

15. Help the client to discover how he/she can legally and legitimately challenge inequities in the system (e.g., racism, classism, sexism, etc.) through such activities as joining a political organization, deciding to earn a college diploma, or denouncing the influence of the media as a consumer.

8. List three beliefs that reinforce participating in drug selling and other illegal activities. (16, 17, 18)

16. Assist the client in discovering what his/her value system is by completing collages that describe himself/herself and that depict those things that are important to him/her. Process with the client the choices that he/she made when placing items on the collage and what the collage says about his/her values.

17. Investigate with the client how he/she developed his/her value system. Process with him/her the influence of the media, family members, and peers on the development of a value system.

18. Allow the client to discover how his/her value system influenced his/her decisions or feelings about selling drugs. Ask the client to discuss how his/her value system will help

or hinder him/her from completing probation.

9. Verbalize an understanding of how environment, beliefs, and behaviors can reinforce each other and contribute to rationalizing drug selling or other illegal acts. (19, 20)

19. Have the client create a fictitious character who sells drugs. Ask the client to describe certain aspects of the drug seller's environment, beliefs, and behavior (e.g., what is happening in his/her environment, what beliefs he/she develops as a result of those influences and consequently how he/she behaves, etc.). Guide the client in a discussion concerning what will happen if the character continues to believe his/her perception of the world, underscoring how negative thoughts and behaviors can be reinforced by what one seeks in his/her environment.

20. Assist the client in determining how the fictitious drug selling character could broaden his/her perspective (e.g., attempting to get input from different people and places in his/her environment, deciding to behave differently to challenge his/her thinking, etc.) and the possible benefits of doing so.

10. Actively challenge beliefs and perceptions about the world by verbalizing a decision to make a change in one's environment or behavior. (21)

21. Assist the client in examining the people, places, and things that make up his/her environment, beliefs, and behaviors. Explore the interaction between one's environment, beliefs, and actions. Process with the client how to challenge his/her perception of the

world (e.g., obtain a mentor, commit to a supervised after-school activity, decide to behave differently in a familiar situation, etc.).

11. Identify automatic thoughts and/or distorted self-talk that increase the drug selling behavior. (22, 23)

22. Assist the client in under-standing the concept of self-talk (e.g., things we tell ourselves about ourselves or others, etc.).

23. Assist the client in identifying his/her unrealistic automatic thoughts that con-tribute to or mediate his/her drug selling (e.g., Drugs don't hurt people; I need the money; This is the only way I can make money; etc.).

12. Challenge automatic thoughts or use realistic self-talk to reduce drug selling behavior. (24, 25, 26, 27)

24. Ask questions to help the client develop alternative thoughts that are more adap-tive (e.g., Drugs do hurt peo-ple; I can get a good education and then get a good-paying job; Drug selling is too risky and dangerous; etc.).

25. Encourage the client to reward himself/herself by using posi-tive self-talk when he/she avoids drug selling or related activities and to increase self-esteem.

26. Teach the client thought-stopping techniques (e.g., engage in physical activity, visualize a stop sign, snapping a rubber band on the wrist, etc.).

27. Prompt the client to recognize when he/she is resorting to negative self-talk that may lead to drug selling or related behaviors and/or diminish self-esteem. Assist him/her in learning to replace negative self-talk with positive self-statements.

13. Diminish the desire to sell drugs by setting realistic long-term goals. (28)

28. Prompt the client to establish healthy and positive goals for himself/herself.

14. Develop skills and/or resources that facilitate success in obtaining long-term goals, and terminate participation in selling substances. (29, 30)

29. Engage the client in a discussion about people, places, and situations that will interfere with goal attainment or that may contribute to his/her violation of probation (e.g., associating with peers who sell drugs or who belittle efforts toward legal forms of employment, using drugs, etc.). Assist the client in establishing alternative people, places, and situations that will provide a positive influence (e.g., joining adult-supervised after-school activities, seeking out a mentor, getting a legal job, etc.) and increase self-esteem.

30. Motivate the client to learn a variety of coping strategies (e.g., anger management, problem solving, relaxation techniques, sharpening interpersonal skills, etc.) to deal with obstacles to goal attainment. With the client's knowledge, enlist the help of supportive others (e.g., parents, teachers, mentors, etc.) to provide opportunities for the

youth to practice skills in his/her natural environment.

15. Attend a social skills training group. (31)

31. Refer the client to a group that focuses on developing inter-personal skills (e.g., conversation skills, assertiveness training, social problem solving, etc.) that will assist him/her in developing healthy, positive relationships.

16. Attend classes designed to enhance vocational and job-seeking skills. (32)

32. Assist the client in finding and/or arranging job training or a change in school placement to assist with career, financial, and/or scholastic goals.

17. The caregivers take an active role in attempting to assist the client in improving overall functioning, goal attainment, and preventing recidivism. (33, 34, 35)

33. Help the family to find resources within the community (e.g., churches, government agencies, job training and educational programs, etc.) that may help with financial and related concerns.

34. Assist the caregivers in establishing ways that they can become involved in assisting the client's efforts to improve his/her life through legal means (e.g., commiting to family therapy sessions, providing appropriate structure at home, seeking community financial resources, advocating with school officials, etc.).

35. Support the caregivers' involvement with professionals (e.g., probation officers, case managers, therapists, school officials, psychiatrists, etc.) who are assisting the client's effort to change his/her unhealthy behaviors and achieving healthy goals.

18. The caregivers supervise the client's activities and establish and explore clear rules of the home. (36, 37)

36. Encourage the caregivers to outline expectations of the client regarding rules in the home and consequences for failure to abide by these conditions. Support the caregivers' attempts at enforcing consequences.

37. Foster the caregivers appropriate monitoring of the client's activities, peers, and movement (i.e., to be informed of where the client is at all times).

19. The client and the caregivers participate in family therapy to explore family dynamics that may have influenced drug selling and related behaviors. (38, 39)

38. Encourage the caregivers, along with other family members, to participate in family therapy sessions to explore family dynamics that may contribute to the client's decision to sell drugs or participate in other delinquent activities.

39. Process with the client and his/her family the impact that his/her drug selling and other criminal activity have had on them.

20. Display a higher level of moral reasoning as evidenced by an increase in positive statements regarding morality and empathy. (40, 41, 42, 43, 44)

40. Assess the client's level of moral development by examining his/her moral reasoning and presence of empathy and guilt feelings.

41. Assist the client in creating an awareness that compassion and/or sensitivity will benefit him/her (e.g., increasing judgment, reducing conflict, influencing how others perceive him/her, etc.).

42. Prompt the client to identify people or events in history that exemplify examples of

morality, immorality, empathy, and lack of concern for others.

43. Use Kohlberg's techniques (see *Treating the Unmanageable Adolescent* by Bernstein) to increase the client's sociomoral reasoning abilities (i.e., present various problem situations and have him/her discuss his/her thoughts and attitudes and come to a consensus regarding the best solution). Challenge the client by asking questions to assist him/her in clarifying and developing his/her moral reasoning.

44. Assist the client in determining cognitive distortions that allow him/her to justify negative behavior with a lower level of moral reasoning and challenge his/her distortions.

21. Demonstrate empathy for others and express guilt related to past behavior. (45, 46, 47, 48)

45. Help the client to acknowledge how previous acts of drug selling may have caused harm to others.

46. Present vignettes (e.g., stealing from a single parent who has limited finances, attacking someone who is seen as unpopular, selling drugs in the neighborhood, etc.) to assess the client's ability to be empathic and increase his/her ability to see things from someone else's perspective.

47. Use various techniques to develop empathy in youth (e.g., playing tapes or reading letters from victims, staging a reenactment of the crime with

the perpetrator staying to observe the victim's response, using movie clips, etc.).

48. Explore examples in the client's life when he/she may have felt victimized in order to assist him/her in recognizing the victims' feelings and to begin to experience guilt related to his/her actions toward others.

22. Increase involvement in activities and places where empathy and moral behavior are considered acceptable. (49)

49. Assist the client in establishing peer relationships and places where empathy and moral behavior are considered acceptable.

__. _____
_____

__. _____
_____

__. _____
_____

__. _____
_____

__. _____
_____

__. _____
_____

DIAGNOSTIC SUGGESTIONS:

ICD-9-CM	ICD-10-CM	DSM-5 Disorder, Condition, or Problem
312.81	F91.1	Conduct Disorder, Childhood-Onset Type
312.82	F91.2	Conduct Disorder, Adolescent-Onset Type
313.81	F91.3	Oppositional Defiant Disorder
312.9	F91.9	Unspecified Disruptive, Impulse Control, and Conduct Disorder
312.89	F91.8	Other Specified Disruptive, Impulse Control, and Conduct Disorder
314.01	F90.2	Attention-Deficit/Hyperactivity Disorder, Combined Presentation
312.34	F63.81	Intermittent Explosive Disorder
V71.02	Z72.810	Adolescent Antisocial Behavior
_____	_____	_____
_____	_____	_____

ENURESIS

BEHAVIORAL DEFINITIONS

1. Repeated pattern of voluntary or involuntary voiding of urine into bed or clothes during the day or at night, after the age of five.
2. Has never achieved urinary continence (primary enuresis).
3. Developed wetting problem after a period of urinary continence (secondary enuresis).
4. Multiple incidents of nocturnal enuresis (i.e., wetting the bed more than once per night on a regular basis).
5. Family history of members having problems with primary or secondary enuresis.
6. Feelings of shame associated with enuresis that cause the avoidance of situations (e.g., overnight visits with friends) that might lead to further embarrassment.
7. Social ridicule, isolation, or ostracism by peers because of enuresis.
8. Frequent attempts to hide wet clothing or linens because of shame or fear of further ridicule, criticism, or punishment.
9. Excessive anger, rejection, or punishment by the parent(s) or caretaker(s) centering around toilet-training practices, which contributes to the child's acting-out, rebellious, or aggressive behavior.
10. Strong feelings of anger or fear, which are channeled into acts of enuresis.
11. Poor impulse control, which contributes to a lack of responsibility with toilet-training practices.

—. _____

_____

—. _____

_____

—·   _____
   _____

LONG-TERM GOALS

1. Eliminate all diurnal and/or nocturnal episodes of enuresis.
2. Resolve the underlying core conflicts contributing to the emergence of enuresis.
3. Eliminate rigid and coercive toilet-training practices by the caregivers.
4. Eradicate the hostile-dependent cycle in the family system, in which the wetting angers the caregivers, they respond in an overly critical or hostile manner, and then the client "punishes" the caregivers for their anger by wetting.
5. Express anger through appropriate verbalizations and healthy physical outlets on a consistent basis, instead of channeling anger through enuresis.
6. Increase self-esteem and successfully work through feelings of shame or humiliation associated with past enuresis.

—·   _____
   _____

—·   _____
   _____

—·   _____
   _____

SHORT-TERM OBJECTIVES

THERAPEUTIC INTERVENTIONS

1. Cooperate with a physician's evaluation of general health and possible organic causes for enuresis. (1, 2)

1. Refer the client for a medical examination to rule out organic or physical causes (e.g., urinary tract infections, nephritis, diabetes, etc.) of the enuresis.

2. Obtain medical clearance from the physician as to no organic cause for the enuresis before implementing psychological or behavioral interventions.

2. Take prescribed medication as directed by the physician. (3, 4, 5)

3. Arrange for a physician to evaluate the client's medication.

4. Monitor the client for medication compliance, side effects, and effectiveness. Consult with the prescribing physician at regular intervals.

5. Explore reasons for the client's failure to take medication as prescribed for treatment of enuresis. Address the client's and/or the caregivers' resistance to him/her taking medication as prescribed.

3. Complete psychological testing. (6)

6. Conduct psychological testing to rule out the presence of attention-deficit/ hyperactivity disorder (ADHD); impulse control disorder; or serious, underlying emotional problems. Provide feedback on the testing to the client, his/her caregivers, and to the physician.

4. Contribute data for accurate baseline of wetting behavior. (7, 8)

7. Gather a detailed history of the wetting problem: Determine the type of enuresis (i.e., primary or secondary); assess the onset and frequency of the wetting behavior; explore the family's history of problems with enuresis; inquire into what interventions have been tried in the past and their subsequent results.

8. Instruct the caregivers to obtain an accurate and detailed baseline of the current enuretic behavior prior to implementing treatment interventions.

5. Caregivers and the client verbally commit to using a urine alarm as instructed. (9, 10, 11, 12)

9. Train the client and his/her caregivers to treat nocturnal enuresis by using a urine alarm (or bell-and-pad conditioning apparatus) in which a urine-sensitive pad causes an alarm to sound when involuntary wetting occurs at night.

10. Obtain a verbal commitment from the caregivers to consistently use the urine alarm as instructed. Encourage the caregivers to provide frequent support and positive reinforcement to the client.

11. Counsel the client and his/her caregivers about the importance of his/her being fully alert or awake before turning off the alarm by himself/herself, to ensure the success of the urine alarm program.

12. Assess the client's and his/her caregivers' compliance with the use of the urine alarm. Explore whether the lack of success is due to possible misuses or failure to follow through with using the device.

6. Caregivers consistently follow through with using the urine alarm between 95 and 100 percent of the time to treat nocturnal enuresis. (10, 13)

10. Obtain a verbal commitment from the caregivers to consistently use the urine alarm as instructed. Encourage the caregivers to provide frequent support and positive reinforcement to the client.

13. Teach the caregivers that a child who is a multiple bed wetter (i.e., wets the bed more than once nightly) may take a longer time to respond to the urine alarm and/or other treatment interventions.

7. Caregivers implement a system to reward bladder control. (14)

14. Design and implement a reward system to reinforce the client for demonstrating successful bladder control.

8. Caregivers support the client in consistently using bladder retention techniques. (15, 16, 17, 18, 19)

15. Teach the client and his/her caregivers the importance of the need to increase his/her awareness of the sensation of the need to urinate.

16. Use *Full Spectrum Home Training Program* (developed by Houts, Peterson, and Wayland), which combines using the urine alarm along with cleanliness training, retention control training, and over-learning to treat primary enuresis.

17. Train the client's caregivers to use staggered awakening procedures, using a variable-interval schedule, to control nocturnal enuresis.

18. Design and implement dry-bed techniques, training the client and his/her caregivers in response inhibition, positive

reinforcement, rapid awakening, gradually increasing fluid intake, self-correction of accidents, and decreased critical parental comments about toilet-training behavior.

19. Employ the overlearning method (i.e., require that the client drink a specific amount of fluid shortly before bedtime), along with using a urine alarm in the latter stages of treatment to help prevent a relapse of nocturnal enuresis.

9. Demonstrate an increased responsibility for implementing the toilet-training practices and interventions. (20, 21, 22, 23)

20. Use "Dry Bed Training Program" in *The Brief Child Therapy Homework Planner* (Jongsma, Peterson, and McInnis) with the younger client to help him/her assume greater responsibility in managing nocturnal enuresis.

21. Encourage and challenge the client to assume active responsibility in achieving mastery of bladder control (e.g., keeping a record of wet and dry days, setting an alarm clock for voiding times, cleaning wet underwear or linens, etc.).

22. Challenge and confront the client's and his/her caregivers' lack of motivation or compliance in following through with the recommended interventions.

23. Assign the client and his/her caregivers to read *Dry All Night: The Picture Book Technique That Stops Bed Wetting* (Mack) to educate them about bed-wetting and to help the client assume an active role in overcoming nocturnal enuresis.

10. Verbalize how thoughts and fears associated with toilet-training practices are unrealistic or irrational. (24, 25)

24. Explore the client's irrational cognitive messages that produce anxiety or fear associated with toilet training (e.g., irrational fears about physical pain involved with toilet training, worries about being embarrassed while using the toilet at school or in public places, fear of growing up, etc.).

25. Assist the client in realizing that his/her thoughts and fears associated with toilet training are irrational or unrealistic.

11. Identify the negative social consequences that may occur from peers if enuresis continues. (26)

26. Identify and discuss the negative social consequences that the client may experience from peers, in order to increase his/her motivation to master bladder control.

12. Identify and implement successful strategies of bladder retention from the past. (27)

27. Inquire about what the client does differently on days when he/she demonstrates good bladder control and does not have any enuretic incidents. Process the client's responses and reinforce any effective strategies that are used to gain bladder control.

13. Identify rebellious feelings that contribute to the emergence of enuresis. (28)

28. Explore the relationship between enuresis and antisocial behaviors, assessing whether the client experiences a regressive loss of bladder control when demonstrating an increase in acting-out or antisocial behaviors. Probe the underlying dynamics of painful emotions that contribute to regression with both bladder control and rebellious behavior.

14. The client and his/her caregivers should identify family stressors that contribute to the onset or reinforcement of enuresis. (29, 30, 31)

29. Conduct family therapy sessions to assess the dynamics that contribute to the emergence or reinforcement of the client's enuresis.

30. Use a strategic family therapy approach, in which the therapist does not talk about enuresis but discusses what might surface if this problem were resolved (i.e., camouflaged or covert problems may be revealed).

31. Hold family therapy sessions to explore whether marital, family, or the client's own behavioral or emotional problems need to be addressed before implementing treatment interventions to manage enuresis.

15. Caregivers verbally recognize how rigid toilet-training practices or hostile, critical remarks contribute to the client's enuresis. (32, 33, 34)

32. Explore interactions between the caregivers and the client to assess whether the caregivers' toilet-training practices are excessively rigid or if the caregivers frequently make hostile, critical remarks about the client.

33. Confront and challenge the caregivers about making overly critical or hostile remarks that contribute to the client's low self-esteem, shame, embarrassment, and anger.

34. Challenge the caregivers to cease punishing the client for his/her wetting problem. Help the caregivers realize that punishment fails to correct the wetting problem.

16. Caregivers decrease the frequency and the severity of hostile, critical remarks regarding the client's enuretic behavior and toilet training. (33)

33. Confront and challenge the caregivers about making overly critical or hostile remarks that contribute to the client's low self-esteem, shame, embarrassment, and anger.

17. Caregivers increase empathic responses to the client's thoughts, feelings, and needs. (35, 36)

35. Counsel the client's caregivers on effective, nonabusive toilet-training practices (e.g., using praise, material reinforcers, patience, hopefulness, etc.).

36. Assign the caregivers to read *No More Bed-Wetting: How to Help Your Child Stay Dry* (Arnold) to learn effective ways to manage nocturnal enuresis.

18. Understand and verbally recognize the secondary gain that results from enuresis. (37, 38)

37. Assess the interactions between the caregivers and the client for the presence of a hostile-dependent cycle where the client's wetting angers the caregivers, the caregivers respond in an overly hostile

manner, the client seeks to punish the caregivers for their strong display of anger, and so on.

38. Assist the client and his/her caregivers in developing insight into the secondary gain (e.g., avoidance of separation from the caregivers; attention from the caregivers, physician, or counselor; etc.) received from enuresis.

19. Disengaged caregiver increases involvement in toilet-training practices. (39)

39. Assign the disengaged caregiver the responsibility of overseeing or teaching the client effective toilet-training practices (e.g., keeping a record of wet and dry days; gently awakening the client for bladder voiding; reminding or teaching the client about how to clean wet underwear, pajamas, or linens; etc.).

20. Disengaged caregiver strengthens the relationship with the client as demonstrated by increased time spent together with the client. (40)

40. Give a directive to the disengaged caregiver to spend quality time with the client (e.g., working on homework together, engaging in a sporting activity, talking one-on-one for 10 to 15 minutes daily, etc.).

21. Identify the stressors that contribute to a relapse of enuresis. (41, 42)

41. Explore whether a relapse of the client's enuresis is due to an increase in family or environmental stress.

42. Assess whether the client's enuresis is associated with separation, loss, trauma, or rejection experiences.

22. Identify and express feelings that are associated with past separation, loss, trauma, or rejection experiences, and how they are connected to enuretic behavior. (43, 44)

43. Explore whether the client's enuresis is associated with separation, loss, trauma, or rejection experiences.

44. Conduct individual play therapy sessions with the younger client to provide him/her with the opportunity to express and work through feelings that are associated with past separation, loss, trauma, or rejection experience that could contribute to the emergence of enuresis.

23. Decrease the frequency of self-descriptive statements that reflect feelings of low self-esteem, shame, or embarrassment. (45, 46)

45. Teach the client effective communication and assertiveness skills to improve his/her ability to express thoughts and feelings through appropriate verbalizations.

46. Identify and list the client's positive characteristics to help decrease feelings of shame and embarrassment. Reinforce his/her positive self-statements.

24. Increase the frequency of positive self-descriptive statements that reflect improved self-esteem. (46, 47)

46. Identify and list the client's positive characteristics to help decrease feelings of shame and embarrassment. Reinforce his/her positive self-statements.

47. Assign the client to make one positive self-statement daily, and record this in a journal. Reinforce positive self-descriptive statements.

25. Appropriately express anger verbally and physically rather than channeling emotions into enuretic behavior. (48, 49)

48. Teach the client appropriate physical outlets, which allow the expression of anger in a more constructive manner

rather than channeling his/her anger into inappropriate wetting.

49. Use a mutual storytelling technique with the younger client, in which the therapist and the client alternate telling stories through the use of puppets, dolls, and stuffed animals. The therapist should model appropriate ways for the client to express his/her feelings.

___. _____
    _____

___. _____
    _____

___. _____
    _____

___. _____
    _____

___. _____
    _____

___. _____
    _____

DIAGNOSTIC SUGGESTIONS:

ICD-9-CM	_ICD-10-CM_	_DSM-5_ Disorder, Condition, or Problem
307.6	F98.0	Enuresis
312.81	F91.1	Conduct Disorder, Childhood-Onset Type
313.81	F91.3	Oppositional Defiant Disorder
314.01	F90.2	Attention-Deficit/Hyperactivity Disorder, Combined Presentation
300.4	F34.1	Persistent Depressive Disorder
296.xx	F32.x	Major Depressive Disorder, Single Episode
296.xx	F33.x	Major Depressive Disorder, Recurrent Episode
309.81	F43.10	Posttraumatic Stress Disorder
_____	_____	_____
_____	_____	_____

FAMILY INSTABILITY/VIOLENCE

BEHAVIORAL DEFINITIONS

1. Frequent or severe incidents of domestic violence occurring in the home.
2. Ongoing conflicts between family members that result in fractional family relationships.
3. Parental separation and/or divorce has caused emotional turmoil, economic stress, and loyalty conflicts.
4. History of instability in parent partners who have come and gone in the client's life.
5. Alcohol and/or drug abuse are present in the household.
6. History of neglect and/or abuse within the family.
7. Family members make verbal threats of harm toward each other.
8. Parents display hostile or apathetic feelings toward the client.
9. Family members involved in illegal behavior and encourage or support the client's illegal behavior.
10. Lack of consistent parental employment has led to financial stress and frequent geographic moves.
11. Siblings engage in fighting, threats of violence, excessive teasing, taunting, and unhealthy rivalry.
12. Intrusive recurrent thoughts of family conflict and/or violence.
13. Frequent prolonged periods of depression, irritability, anxiety, and/or apathetic withdrawal in response to family conflict.
14. Escapes the chaos of the home environment by spending more time on the street and/or gang activity.

—. _____
   _____

—. _____
   _____

—. _____
_____

LONG-TERM GOALS

1. Parents develop skills to provide a stable, nurturing home environment free from conflict, abuse, and violence.
2. Parents establish consistency in supervision, rules, and responsible involvement in the client's life.
3. Parents terminate participation in and/or approval of the client's illegal behavior.
4. Establish residency in an alternative home setting.
5. Develop coping skills that will lead to a decrease in psychological symptoms (e.g., anxiety, depression, etc.) related to exposure to family conflict.
6. Terminate antisocial acting-out behavior in reaction to chaotic, hostile home environment.

—. _____
_____

—. _____
_____

—. _____
_____

SHORT-TERM OBJECTIVES

1. Provide a history of experience and feelings related to home and family. (1)

2. Cooperate with assessment procedures. (2)

THERAPEUTIC INTERVENTIONS

1. Explore the client's perception and experience related to his/her home environment. Probe for his/her emotional reaction.

2. Complete a psychological assessment to determine if the client is experiencing clinically significant symptoms of

depression, anxiety, posttraumatic stress disorder (PTSD), and so on.

3. Take psychotropic medications as prescribed, and report regarding its effectiveness and side effects. (3, 4)

3. Refer the client to a physician for an evaluation to determine the appropriateness of psychotropic medications to manage his/her symptoms.

4. Monitor the client's adherence to the psychotropic medication prescription, and assess for its effectiveness and side effects.

4. Cooperate with a social service agency investigation of the home and family. (5, 6)

5. Discuss with the client and his/her caregivers concerns regarding child maltreatment and the obligation to file a protective service report.

6. Report to protective service agency incidents of abuse and/or neglect of the client by caregivers.

5. Accept a transfer to a safe, stable living environment. (7, 8, 9)

7. Process with the client and his/her caregivers his/her feelings regarding the justice official's decision to place him/her in a more stable living environment.

8. Provide the opportunity for the caregivers and family members to say good-bye.

9. Suggest strategies that the client, caregivers, and family members can implement to feel connected while the client is in an alternative placement (e.g., writing letters, calling, e-mailing, keeping memorabilia, etc.).

6. Client and family members acknowledge their respective contributions to the family conflict and instability. (10, 11)

10. Help the client recognize his/her contribution to the family's conflicts and instability.

11. Confront the client's and family members' denial of responsibility, blaming, and rationalization.

7. Verbalize a plan of action to be used when threats of violence occur in the home. (12, 13, 14, 15)

12. Ask the client and the caregivers to list ways to reduce violence and conflict in the home (e.g., follow house rules, communicate respectfully, respect boundaries, contribute to the household chores, etc.).

13. Identify warning signs that conflict may become violent (e.g., clenched fist, loud arguing, violating personal space, verbal threats, raised voices, etc.) and develop plans to de-escalate conflict before it intensifies.

14. Assist the client in identifying individuals to call for help within or outside of the family when the threat of or actual violence occurs.

15. Ask the client and his/her caregivers to list options for obtaining safety and assistance (e.g., call 911, contact an identified person to seek help for the family, escape to an identified safe place, use a secret code to signify the need for help). Practice these safety strategies.

8. Define and express feel-ings relative to family violence and conflict. (16, 17)

16. Use a feelings chart to assist the client in identifying feelings experienced in response to family instability and conflict.

17. Help the client make a connection between his/her feelings about the family situation and his/her acting-out behavior.

9. Participate actively in therapy with the caregivers and family members. (18, 19, 20, 21)

18. In family therapy, ask each family member to talk about the importance of peace and mutual support in the family.

19. Ask each family member to present unresolved conflicts that he/she feels toward family members. Encourage family members to listen to each person without disagreeing or becoming defensive.

20. Assess the relationship between the client and the absent caregiver. Determine if the client would benefit from increased involvement with the absent caregiver.

21. Encourage each family member to identify how the family conflict has impacted his/her life.

10. Parents acknowledge family problems and make a commitment to changing the behaviors that contribute to family instability and conflict. (22, 23, 24)

22. Ask the client and his/her family member and/or caregiver to make a list of things that he/she would like to change in the home environment.

23. Solicit from each family member a commitment to work toward family harmony and stability.

24. Discuss with the family members the benefits of individual treatment. Refer each member to individual therapy as needed or as appropriate.

11. Recognize how family conflict and instability contribute to impairments in social, interpersonal, and academic functioning. (25, 26)

25. Assess the client's social, interpersonal, and academic functioning.

26. Assist the client in identifying how his/her personal problems (e.g., negative peer relationships, rebellion, academic failures, poor self-concept, etc.) are related to his/her family environment.

12. List new coping techniques to be implemented to avoid negative reactions to family stress. (27)

27. Use role playing, in vivo exercises, and skills training to assist the client in developing ways to cope with family stress (e.g., implementing healthy communication styles, maintaining a positive peer group for support, journaling feelings, sharing painful experiences with a supportive adult, etc.) and to avoid its negative effects on his/her social, interpersonal, and academic functioning.

13. The client and family demonstrate an improvement in the ability to respond appropriately to the thoughts, feelings, and needs of others. (28)

28. Help the client, family members, and caregivers recognize how he/she tends to respond to others in an aggressive or ineffective manner. Use modeling and behavior rehearsal to teach assertiveness, empathy, and "I" messages to improve communication.

14. Describe relationships with each household member. (29, 30)

29. Explore the client's perception of his/her relationship with his/her caregivers, siblings, and all household members. Assist him/her in identifying ways to improve his/her relationship with each member.

30. Assist the client, his/her care-givers, and family members in recognizing the frequency of negative interactions in the home environment.

15. Implement a plan to improve relationships with each house-hold member and report results. (31, 32)

31. Assist the client, his/her care-givers, and family members in planning activities to increase positive interactions.

32. Ask the client, his/her care-givers, and family members to record the intensity and fre-quency of conflicts. Compare each member's perception of family conflict.

16. Decrease the frequency and intensity and inappropriate expression of anger. (33, 34, 35)

33. Assist the client in recognizing his/her anger, identifying the source, and appropriately expressing anger.

34. Refer the client to an anger management group to learn ways to modulate anger or reduce aggression and destruc-tive acting out.

35. Teach the client and his/her family members effective ways to resolve conflict (e.g., com-munication skills, assertiveness skills, problem-solving skills, etc.).

17. Obtain employment to attain financial, emotional, and social benefits. (36)

18. Caregivers take action to reduce the financial stress and actively begin the process of obtaining employment. (37, 38)

19. The client and/or caregivers acknowledge substance abuse problems and make a commitment to substance abuse treatment. (39)

20. Caregivers cooperate with a referral for parent training. (40, 41, 42, 43)

36. Encourage the client to obtain an after-school or summer job to help him/her feel affirmed, escape the family conflict, and support the family. Teach him/her basic skills that will allow him/her to obtain and maintain employment.

37. Refer family members for job training and employment placement services.

38. Encourage the caregivers to seek family assistance from a local social service agency.

39. Assess family members for chemical dependence problems. Refer the client and/or family members to substance abuse treatment.

40. Refer the caregivers to parent-training classes or assist in developing skills that support a nurturing home environment.

41. Educate the caregivers regarding relevant developmental issues that are related to the client and age-appropriate expectations.

42. Assist the caregivers in establishing and communicating clear, realistic, age-appropriate expectations to the client.

43. Recommend that the parents read books to increase their knowledge of positive parenting techniques (e.g., *Parents*

and Adolescents by Patterson and Forgatch or *The New Dare to Discipline* by Dobson).

__. _____   __. _____
    _____   _____
__. _____   __. _____
    _____   _____
__. _____   __. _____
    _____   _____

DIAGNOSTIC SUGGESTIONS:

ICD-9-CM	*ICD-10-CM*	*DSM-5* Disorder, Condition, or Problem
309.3	F43.24	Adjustment Disorder, With Disturbance of Conduct
309.4	F43.25	Adjustment Disorder, With Mixed Disturbance of Emotions and Conduct
V61.21	Z69.011	Encounter for Mental Health Services for Perpetrator of Parental Child Neglect
V61.22	Z69.011	Encounter for Mental Health Services for Perpetrator of Parental Child Abuse
V61.22	Z69.011	Encounter for Mental Health Services for Perpetrator of Parental Child Sexual Abuse
_____	_____	_____
_____	_____	_____

FAMILY/SOCIETAL REINTEGRATION

BEHAVIORAL DEFINITIONS

1. Making transition to a less restrictive setting.
2. Ordered to cooperate with surveillance and/or psychological treatment services.
3. Successful completion of goals at the current setting, leading to a new placement.
4. Alienation from support systems and community agencies.
5. Prior failure to conform with societal rules.
6. Lack of enrollment or success in mainstream educational setting.
7. Return to a previously chaotic or unstable home environment.
8. Lack of vocational interest, skills, and/or employment.
9. Previous involvement with negative peer groups.
10. Antisocial pattern of behavior exists within the family.
11. Placement within a group or foster home necessitated by negative family environment.

__. _____
   _____
   _____
__. _____
   _____
   _____
__. _____
   _____

LONG-TERM GOALS

1. Achieve successful reintegration into the family and community environment.
2. Successfully adapt to group or foster home placement.
3. Transition to mainstream educational setting.

4. Use services offered by community agencies to obtain support for positive reintegration into home and community.
5. Create and maintain healthy, positive peer relationships.
6. Obtain skills for and/or experience in viable employment.

__. _____
     _____
     _____
__. _____
     _____
     _____
__. _____
     _____

SHORT-TERM OBJECTIVES

THERAPEUTIC INTERVENTIONS

1. Provide information for risk assessment and/or level of care prior to transition. (1)

2. Cooperate with an academic and career assessment and comply with recommendations. (2)

3. Make a verbal and a written commitment to continue outpatient and/or psychopharmacological therapy. (3)

4. Adhere to surveillance procedures, and process feelings about them. (4)

1. Complete a risk and/or level-of-care assessment that focuses on the issues of chronicity of problems, antisocial behavior, family support, and empathy and/or remorse.

2. Assess the client's abilities and interests as they relate to job placement, vocational training, or academic placement.

3. Refer the client to outpatient treatment (e.g., substance abuse, anger management, family, individual, group, etc.), and solicit a commitment for his/her consistent participation.

4. Assist the client with reframing negative thoughts regarding surveillance services (e.g., electronic monitoring and/or tethering, alcohol and drug screening, curfew checks, etc.). Process the client's feelings regarding compliance with

surveillance procedures and policies.

5. Describe situations and people that have a high risk of precipitating relapse into antisocial behavior. (5, 6, 7)

5. Discuss the client's feelings related to his/her potential for relapse and recidivism.

6. Assist the client in identifying any and all situations and relationships that have the potential to precipitate relapse.

7. Focus on identifying family conflict issues as possible contributing factors to relapse.

6. Practice coping skills that will be used to overcome situations that could lead to relapse. (8, 9, 10)

8. Use role playing and modeling to teach the client how to cope with people or situations that may lead to relapse or recidivism.

9. Emphasize the necessity for the client to avoid negative peer relationships and to work toward the formation of healthy, positive peer relationships and activities. Monitor his/her compliance with this necessary change.

10. Facilitate the initiation of family therapy to provide support for the client in dealing with conflict within the home.

7. Openly discuss thoughts and feelings regarding the transition, including obstacles, fears, and ambivalence. (11)

11. Assist the client in sorting out feelings regarding transition, and validate these as acceptable and normal.

8. Increase to once daily the use of positive self-talk that reflects self-confidence and optimism about the transition. (12)

12. Teach the client the value and nature of positive self-talk. Reinforce his/her implementation of self-endorsing statements.

9. Develop a sense of control regarding the transition and

13. Pinpoint events and situations that cause worries or fears,

reintegration by creating a list of things that one can influence and those that one cannot. (13)

10. Identify three or more coping strategies that have worked for identified problem(s), and incorporate them into a relapse prevention plan. (14, 15)

and help the client to find ways to avoid or accept them without maladaptive outcomes.

14. Explore what the client has learned in his/her present placement that can be applied to future situations (e.g., accepting authority, conflict resolution, study skills, assertiveness skills, etc.).

15. Assist the client in identifying positive coping skills that have been successfully implemented in the past. Discuss how they may be used profitably in the present transition.

11. Implement the use of problem-solving techniques. (16, 17)

16. Teach and reinforce problem solving (i.e., identify the problem, brainstorm solutions, evaluate the consequences, choose a solution, and review the success).

17. Facilitate role playing that allows the client to apply problem-solving skills to current conflicts in his/her life.

12. Explore and implement ways to relieve guilt that is related to a history of misconduct. (18, 19)

18. Explore reasons for the client to feel shame, guilt, remorse, and embarrassment, and encourage self-forgiveness.

19. Assist the client in writing a letter of apology to selected parties who have been hurt by him/her (e.g., family members, community, victims, support systems, etc.).

13. Verbalize and celebrate positive aspects of self. (12, 20)

12. Teach the client the value and nature of positive self-talk. Reinforce his/her implementation of self-endorsing statements.

20. Help the client to identify and take pride in his/her personal strengths, assets, and accomplishments.

14. Identify support systems and describe situations in which each support may be helpful. (21, 22)

21. Assist the client in creating a list of possible supportive peers, adults, and agencies, including phone numbers, addresses, and ways that they can be helpful.

22. Assist the client in contacting people who could be supportive to ensure that the identified person(s) are willing to assist him/her in transition.

15. Verbalize feelings of trust toward the caregivers. (23, 24)

23. Suggest and process ways that the client can establish and/or reestablish a trusting, supportive relationship with the caregivers (e.g., participating in recreational activities together, holding family meetings to share feelings, preparing and sharing a family meal, creating and establishing family celebrations, etc.).

24. Assist the client in making reasonable expectations regarding his/her relationship with his/her caregivers (e.g., caregivers will be fair, open to discussion, and show an interest in his/her accomplishments, but not be buddies, abusive, or neglectful).

16. Identify and practice five adaptive life skills that are necessary to successfully transition to a less restrictive setting. (25, 26)

25. Encourage the family and/or caregivers to reinforce the client's prosocial behavior.

26. Assist the client in listing at least five adaptive life skills necessary in less restrictive, more independent living settings (e.g., maintain basic hygiene, financial budgeting and satisfactory housekeeping, negotiate transportation, etc.). Monitor and reinforce their implementation.

17. Follow the rules and behave responsibly in spite of reduced supervision and more freedom. (27)

27. Implement graduated support and/or monitoring in the current setting, allowing the client increased freedom, independence, and responsibilities.

18. Report cooperative interaction with caregiver and positive feelings regarding the relationship. (23, 28)

23. Suggest and process ways that the client can establish and/or reestablish a trusting, supportive relationship with the caregivers (e.g., participating in recreational activities together, holding family meetings to share feelings, preparing and sharing a family meal, creating and establishing family celebrations, etc.).

28. Encourage increased and/or graduated social interactions with the caregivers (e.g., day, weekend, or holiday passes).

19. Engage in positive community activities at least twice weekly. (29, 30)

29. Assist the client in listing ways that he/she can increase positive involvement in the community (e.g., community service, recreational activities, athletic leagues, etc.).

30. Assist the client in processing his/her feelings and thoughts about the community, care-

givers, and/or school visits. Reinforce positive interactions and process conflicts.

20. Petition to make a transition to a less restrictive setting by completing a written self-evaluation of progress and by speaking on own behalf. (31, 32, 33)

31. Continue to encourage the client to accept responsibility for criminal behavior, and assist him/her in identifying societal consequences for such behavior.

32. Assign the client to write a self-evaluation of his/her progress and why he/she should transition to more freedom. Process this written document.

33. Hold a case conference with family members and all agencies involved, including both releasing and receiving agencies, to promote continuity of care.

21. State an understanding of potential incentives and/or consequences that may be earned through engaging in stipulated positive behaviors. (34, 35)

34. Initiate a token economy and level system in the new setting that provides an overall structure to assist the client in monitoring his/her own progress toward prosocial behavior.

35. Use strategies (e.g., point cards for positive target behaviors, etc.) to provide the client with concrete feedback regarding his/her behavior throughout the day.

22. Identify and practice social skills that are necessary to form healthy peer relationships, 75 percent of the time, during targeted activities. (9, 36)

9. Emphasize the necessity for the client to avoid negative peer relationships and to work toward the formation of healthy, positive peer relationships and activities. Monitor his/her compliance with this necessary change.

36. Reinforce core components of adaptive social skills (e.g., goal setting, problem solving, making friends, communicating effectively, sharing, managing anger, and resolving conflicts peacefully, etc.).

23. The family and/or caregivers incorporate surveillance requirements in behavior contracts. (37, 38)

37. Maintain communication regarding the client's progress in interagency case management teams (e.g., psychologist, psychiatrist, probation officers, social workers, etc.) and in contacts with family and/or caregivers.

38. Provide support to the family, and facilitate the implementation of a behavioral management program for the client.

24. Attend and complete a vocational training program. (39)

39. Enroll the client in a supported employment program with vocational training and job coaching.

25. Identify obstacles to successful reintegration in the move to the less restrictive setting and the type of assistance that will be needed. (33, 40)

33. Hold a case conference with family members and all agencies involved, including both releasing and receiving agencies, to promote continuity of care.

40. Conduct a client-needs assessment of the home and/or school environment to identify obstacles to a successful reintegration.

26. Verbalize a plan to prevent relapse into antisocial behavior patterns. (41, 42)

41. Assist the client in developing a relapse prevention plan, and

process obstacles to successful implementation.

42. Write a transitional plan that highlights important information including the following: reasons for the client's placement in a more restrictive setting, a brief summary of his/her behavior since arriving in the restrictive setting, recommendations for continued success, and an emergency plan that explains how to intervene with the client in a behavioral crisis.

27. Visit the less restrictive setting to reduce fear of the unknown and to gain an understanding of the rules and expectations. (33, 43, 44)

33. Hold a case conference with family members and all agencies involved, including both releasing and receiving agencies, to promote continuity of care.

43. Determine routines and procedures that are particular to the new setting to share with the client and current staff.

44. Take the client to visit the less restrictive setting prior to transition.

28. Participate in transitional planning by identifying short- and long-term goals and the steps needed to achieve them. (45, 46)

45. Assist the client in setting attainable, realistic short- and long-term goals in the development of a transition plan.

46. Invite the receiving staff to collaborate in developing the client's schedule, criteria, and time line for transition.

29. Participate in a group that provides information and support concerning expectations of the new setting. (47)

30. Report a decrease in anxiety regarding the transition to a new setting. (48)

31. Identify characteristics of healthy and unhealthy relationships, and categorize own existing relationships with others. (49)

32. Verbalize expectations of a successful transition. (50)

33. The caregivers and receiving agency adopt and implement any behavior and emergency plans. (51, 52)

47. Conduct an informative and supportive group that teaches the client about the transition process and prepares him/her for the variety of experiences that he/she will encounter in his/her new setting.

48. Teach the client relaxation procedures to alleviate stress and anxiety about the change and to prevent sabotage of progress.

49. Assist the client in identifying characteristics of healthy and unhealthy relationships. Process how healthy relationships will be formed in the new setting.

50. Emphasize the positive aspects of the transition, and ask the client to list positive expectations that he/she has.

51. Provide an emergency plan to assist the new setting in managing a behavioral crisis (e.g., identification of the behavior, who implements the plan, steps taken during a crisis, and steps following a crisis).

52. Ensure that behavior plans that target increasing the frequency of positive behavior (e.g., prosocial behavior, school attendance, practicing adaptive life skills, developing job skills, etc.) are implemented and that success is cel-

34. The caregivers and/or receiving agency staff attend a case conference and verbalize an understanding of techniques and strategies that have been successful for the client. (33, 53, 54)

ebrated. Recommend that the client self-monitor and record his/her own rate of positive behavior implementation.

33. Hold a case conference with family members and all agencies involved, including both releasing and receiving agencies, to promote continuity of care.

53. Increase the involvement of the receiving staff by inviting them to visit the client's current program and observe treatment strategies that work.

54. Provide the receiving staff and family and/or caregivers a summary of the techniques and strategies that have increased positive behavior for the client. Instruct the staff and the family and/or caregivers on how to implement strategies and provide feedback.

35. Make contact with the releasing agency as a support while reintegrating into the home and/or community. (55)

55. For a predetermined amount of time, arrange for the releasing agency to provide follow-up and support to the client in transition.

36. Participate in a graduation ceremony with the releasing agency by inviting key sup-

56. Plan a graduation ceremony, and award to the client a

portive people and family
and/or caregivers. (56)

diploma that signifies completion of transition.

___. _____
   _____

___. _____
   _____

___. _____
   _____

___. _____
   _____

___. _____
   _____

___. _____
   _____

DIAGNOSTIC SUGGESTIONS:

ICD-9-CM	_ICD-10-CM_	_DSM-5_ Disorder, Condition, or Problem
309.0	F43.21	Adjustment Disorder, With Depressed Mood
309.24	F43.22	Adjustment Disorder, With Anxiety
309.28	F43.23	Adjustment Disorder, With Mixed Anxiety and Depressed Mood
309.3	F43.24	Adjustment Disorder, With Disturbance of Conduct
309.4	F43.25	Adjustment Disorder, With Mixed Disturbance of Emotions and Conduct
312.81	F91.1	Conduct Disorder, Childhood-Onset Type
312.82	F91.2	Conduct Disorder, Adolescent-Onset Type
312.9	F91.9	Unspecified Disruptive, Impulse Control, and Conduct Disorder
312.89	F91.8	Other Specified Disruptive, Impulse Control, and Conduct Disorder
313.81	F91.3	Oppositional Defiant Disorder
314.01	F90.2	Attention-Deficit/Hyperactivity Disorder, Combined Presentation
315.00	F81.0	Specific Learning Disorder With Impairment in Reading
315.10	F81.2	Specific Learning Disorder with Impairment in Mathematics
315.2	F81.2	Specific Learning Disorder With Impairment in Written Expression
V61.20	Z62.820	Parent-Child Relational Problem
V61.8	Z63.8	High Expressed Emotion Level Within Family
V71.02	Z72.810	Adolescent Antisocial Behavior
Fire Setting	Pg. 1	
_____	_____	_____
_____	_____	_____

FIRE SETTING

BEHAVIORAL DEFINITIONS

1. Has set one or more fires in the past six months.
2. Strong preoccupation or fascination with fire, fireworks, or combustible substances.
3. Repeated instances of playing with matches, lighters, or combustible substances.
4. Persistent pattern of having matches, lighters, candles, and such in his/her possession.
5. History of setting fire to objects of low worth or insignificant value (e.g., paper, rags, small toys, grass, sticks, etc.).
6. Deliberate acts of setting fire to objects, material goods, or property, even when aware of potential dangers or risks involved.
7. History of setting fire(s) that resulted in a person's death, serious bodily harm, or injury or extensive destruction of property.
8. Premeditated acts of arson against individuals or societal institutions (e.g., school, juvenile court, employer, etc.) that arise out of a desire for revenge or retaliation.
9. Intense feelings of anger or rage that are channeled into fire-setting behavior.
10. Desire to seek thrills, excitement, or an adrenaline rush through fire-setting behavior.
11. Underlying feelings of depression, low self-esteem, or helplessness that contribute to desire to set fires as a means to gain control and/or power.
12. Acts of arson or fire setting committed while involved in gang-related activities or affiliating with negative peer groups.

—. _____

_____

__. _____
    _____
__. _____
    _____

LONG-TERM GOALS

1. Eliminate all inappropriate or potentially dangerous fire-setting behavior.
2. Secure the safety of the client, family, and the community.
3. Extinguish the client's fascination and preoccupation with fire.
4. Redirect the client's fascination with fire into positive social, physical, or recreational activities.
5. Express anger through controlled, respectful verbalizations or healthy physical activities on a consistent basis.
6. Establish and maintain positive self-image that provides confidence and feelings of empowerment to achieve desired goals.
7. Resolve core conflicts that contribute to the emergence of the fire-setting behavior.

__. _____
    _____
__. _____
    _____
__. _____
    _____

SHORT-TERM OBJECTIVES

1. Complete a psychological evaluation to confirm the diagnosis of attention-deficit/hyperactivity disorder (ADHD) and/or rule out emotional factors or psychotic process that may be contributing to fire-setting behavior. (1, 2)

THERAPEUTIC INTERVENTIONS

1. Conduct or arrange for a psychological evaluation to assess for the presence of ADHD, affective disorder, or psychotic process that may be contributing to fire-setting behavior.

2. Provide feedback to the client, parents, school officials, or

juvenile justice officials regarding the findings from the psychological testing.

2. Cooperate with a physician's evaluation for psychotropic medication. (3)

3. Refer the client for a psychiatric evaluation for psychotropic medication to improve impulse control, stabilize moods, and/or to treat a psychotic process.

3. Take prescribed medication as directed by the physician. (4)

4. Monitor the client for medication compliance, side effects, and effectiveness. Consult with the prescribing physician at regular intervals.

4. Provide a detailed history of past fire-setting behavior. (5)

5. Gather a detailed psychosocial history of the client's past fire-setting behavior, including age of onset, frequency, danger or harm incurred from fire setting, and precipitating events leading up to the emergence of fire-setting incidents.

5. Caregivers verbalize a commitment to increase structure and supervision. (6, 7)

6. Explore whether the caregivers' lack of supervision or structure has contributed to the client's past fire-setting behavior.

7. Counsel the client's caregivers about establishing appropriate parent-child boundaries and increasing structure or supervision to minimize the chances of his/her enga ging in future fire-setting behavior.

6. Caregivers consistently follow through with consequences for the

8. Assist the client's caregivers in establishing clearly defined rules and consequences for

client's fire setting behavior. (8, 9, 10, 11)

fire-setting behavior. Have the client repeat these rules to demonstrate that he/she understands the expectations.

9. Encourage and challenge the client's caregivers to follow through with consequences for the fire-setting behavior, even if he/she claims that he/she accidentally set the fire. Point out the importance of setting firm consequences to prevent future occurrences of fire-setting behavior.

10. Encourage and challenge the client's caregivers not to protect him/her from the natural or legal consequences of his/her fire-setting behavior.

11. Encourage the adolescent client to seek and secure employment as a means to pay for damages incurred from fire-setting behavior.

7. Comply with the recommendations or requirements that are mandated by the juvenile justice system. (12, 13, 14)

12. Consult with the caregivers, juvenile justice officials, and fire department about assigning appropriate consequences for the client's fire-setting behavior (e.g., probation, paying restitution, performing community service, undoing the effects of fire by helping to repair damage, etc.).

13. Direct the client to offer a written or verbal apology to the victim(s) of his/her fire-setting behavior.

14. Recommend to the caregivers, probation officer, and juvenile justice officials that the client write a paper identifying the dangers, harm, and risks involved in setting fires for himself/herself, others, and property. Direct the client to read the finished paper in court hearing.

8. Move to an appropriate alternative setting or juvenile detention facility. (15)

15. Consult with the caregivers, probation officer, or juvenile justice officials about the need to place the client who is a repeat offender in an alternative setting (e.g., foster home, group home, residential program, juvenile boot camp, juvenile detention facility, etc.) as a consequence for his/her fire-setting behavior, thereby reducing the chances of him/her committing further acts of fire setting.

9. Complete an interview and/or meeting with a firefighter or nurse about the dangers of setting fires. (16, 17)

16. Refer the client to a fire safety program offered through the local fire department to educate him/her about the dangers or risks involved in setting fires.

17. Direct the caregivers to arrange a meeting between the client and either a firefighter or nurse from a local burn unit to educate him/her about the potential dangers involved in setting fires. Assist the client and his/her caregivers in developing a list of questions to ask during the interview. Process this

experience and the information gathered in a follow-up therapy session.

10. Caregivers remove or greatly limit the client's access to matches, lighters, or combustible substances. (18)

18. Counsel the caregivers (particularly those who smoke) about removing or limiting the client's access to matches, lighters, or combustible substances to deter or limit the chances of him/her engaging in further fire-setting behavior.

11. Family members enact fire safety precautions in and around the home. (19, 20)

19. Confer with the caregivers about installing smoke detectors in the home and periodically testing them to ensure that they are working. Instruct the client's caregivers to enlist his/her help in installing and testing the smoke detectors.

20. Instruct the caregivers to enlist the client's help in locating and detecting fire hazards in or around the home. Encourage the client and his/her caregivers to work together to fireproof the home.

12. Recognize and verbalize how fire-setting behaviors pose danger for self and others. (21, 22)

21. Help the client to identify potential dangers involved in fire-setting behavior to himself/herself and others.

22. Assign the client and his/her caregivers to create two collages in session, one centering on positive aspects of fire, and the other focusing on the destructive aspects of fire. Discuss the positive and destructive aspects as

these collages are completed.

13. Identify the positive and destructive aspects of fire. (23)

23. Assist the client and his/her caregivers in identifying situations where it is safe for him/her to use matches or lighters (e.g., light candles, start a campfire, etc.) under adult supervision.

14. Demonstrate how to handle fire in a safe, appropriate, and respectful manner under the supervision of a parental figure. (24, 25)

24. Direct the father (or the male father figure) to teach the male client how to safely build a fire. The father emphasizes the need for strict control of and respect for the power of fire. Therapist provides materials in session for fire (i.e., matches, sticks, coffee can). Monitor and process the assignment.

25. Use the homework assignment "Fireproofing Your Home and Family" from the *Brief Child Therapy Homework Planner* (Jongsma, Peterson, and McInnis) to help the client to handle fire in a safe, respectful, and appropriate manner under the supervision of a parental figure.

15. Terminate statements of refusing to take responsibility or minimizing the seriousness of fire-setting behavior. (26)

26. Confront statements in which the client blames others for his/her fire-setting behavior and either fails to accept responsibility for his/her dangerous actions or minimizes the seriousness of his/her fire-setting behavior.

16. Report a decrease in the impulse or desire to set fires. (27, 28)

17. Client's caregivers increase praise and positive reinforcement for his/her taking fire safety precautions. (29)

18. Client's caregivers implement and consistently follow through with behavioral interventions to decrease his/her urge to set fires. (30, 31)

27. Design and implement an operant-based intervention for the family in which a parent allows the client to strike matches under supervision, noting the need for caution. Place a sum of money next to matches, and instruct the client that he/she will receive a predetermined sum of money (as well as praise) for each match left unstruck. Monitor intervention and provide redirection or feedback as needed.

28. Use a stimulus satiation intervention in which the client is given a box of matches while his/her caregivers instruct him/her how to safely strike them. Allow the client to strike as many as he/she desires. Monitor the intervention for safety and how it impacts the client's desire to set fires.

29. Encourage the caregivers to offer immediate praise and positive reinforcement for the client when he/she hands over matches, lighters, or combustible substances that were found lying around inside or outside of the home.

30. Establish a reward system in which the client is rewarded by his/her caregivers each time he/she turns in matches or lighters that were either in his/her possession or found

lying around the house. Keep a chart of how much money the client earns.

31. Design and implement a behavioral no-fire-setting contract with the client and his/her caregivers. Have the client sign this contract demonstrating his/her commitment not to light or set any fires without adult supervision. Specify the consequences if the client fails to comply with the terms of the contract. Monitor success or effectiveness.

19. Identify and list stressors within the family system that contribute to the urge to set fires. (32, 33)

32. Conduct family therapy sessions to explore dynamics within the family system that contribute to or reinforce the client's desire to set fires.

33. Assess whether the client's fire-setting behavior reflects a cry for help or a maladaptive attempt to elicit attention, nurturance, support, or supervision from his/her caregivers.

20. Increase the frequency of positive interactions with the caregivers. (34, 35)

34. Hold a family therapy session to allow the client to verbalize his/her needs for affection, affirmation, and support from his/her caregivers. Assist the client and his/her caregivers in identifying more adaptive ways for him/her to meet emotional needs.

35. Instruct the caregivers to set aside 15 minutes each day of one-on-one time with the

client to provide him/her with the opportunity to express thoughts, feelings, and needs.

21. Increase positive time spent with the father or male caregiver. (36)

36. Ask the father or male caregiver to identify between three and five activities that he can perform to facilitate a closer bond with the client. Instruct the father or male caregiver to engage in two of these activities before the next therapy session.

22. Verbalize feelings openly and directly, and tolerate others' expression of emotions. (37, 38)

37. Conduct family therapy sessions to improve the lines of communication and to assist family members in being able to better identify, express, and tolerate expressions of emotions, particularly when dealing with conflictual issues or painful events.

38. Assign each family member to complete the exercise "When a Fire Has No Fuel" from *The Brief Child Therapy Homework Planner* (Jongsma, Peterson, and McInnis) to help increase communication among all family members, to air grievances openly and directly, and to identify steps that can be taken to resolve conflict.

23. Identify and verbalize feelings that are associated with past chaos, instability, abuse, or violence within family system. (39, 40)

39. Explore the client's childhood background for a history of chaos, instability, violence, or physical abuse. Encourage and support the

client in expressing emotions (e.g., anger, hurt, fear, help-lessness, etc.) connected to painful or chaotic events.

40. Confront the caregivers' physically abusive or overly punitive methods of disci-pline that have contributed to the client's rage and desire to set fires. Implement the steps that are necessary to protect the client or siblings from further abuse. (See the chapter entitled "Physical Abuse Victim" in this Planner.)

24. Identify and verbalize painful emotions that contribute to the fire-setting behavior. (41)

41. Assist the client in making a connection between either feelings of anger and rage or painful emotions (e.g., hurt, sadness, helplessness, power-lessness, etc.) and fire-setting behavior.

25. Identify and list targets or pre-cipitating events that produce strong feelings of anger, hurt, helplessness, or powerlessness. (42, 43)

42. Instruct the client to keep a daily journal in which he/she documents people and situa-tions that evoke strong feel-ings of anger, hurt, or helplessness, and the desire to set fires. Process excerpts from this journal in follow-up therapy sessions.

43. Instruct the client to develop a thorough list of causes and targets for anger or rage. Assist him/her in identifying more adaptive ways to express or control anger (e.g., sharing feelings with his/her caregivers respectfully, but openly; being assertive, but

not aggressive, in communicating anger; identifying an alternate trustworthy adult in whom to confide; etc.) other than through fire-setting behavior.

26. Express anger through more appropriate verbalizations and healthy physical outlets. (44, 45, 46)

44. Teach mediational and self-control strategies (e.g., "stop, look, listen, and think"; count to 10; deep breathing; listen to music; etc.) to help the client to cope with anger appropriately and to use healthy physical outlets, instead of expressing anger through fire-setting behavior.

45. Assign the adolescent client to read *Everything You Need to Know about Anger* (Licata) to help him/her manage anger more effectively. Process this reading assignment with the client.

46. Use the Angry Tower technique (see *101 Play Therapy Techniques* by Saxe) to help the younger client identify and express feelings of anger. Build a tower out of plastic containers; place a small item (representing the object of anger) on top of the tower; then instruct the client to throw a small fabric ball at the tower while verbalizing anger.

27. Identify effective coping strategies to control anger and

44. Teach mediational and self-control strategies (e.g., "stop,

deter the impulse to set fire.
(44, 47, 48)

look, listen, and think";
count to 10; deep breathing;
listen to music; etc.) to help
the client to cope with anger
appropriately and to use
healthy physical outlets,
instead of expressing anger
through fire-setting
behavior.

47. Explore periods of time when
the client demonstrated good
anger control and did not
engage in any fire-setting
behavior. Process his/her
responses and reinforce
positive coping strategies
used to exercise self-control
and deter the impulse to set
fires.

48. Assist the client in identifying
more effective ways to achieve
a healthy sense of power or
control in life other than
through setting fires (e.g.,
trying out for a sports team,
participating in student
government, becoming
involved in community fund
drives, etc.).

28. Increase time spent in
non-fire-related interests or
activities. (49, 50)

49. Refer the client to Big
Brother/Big Sister organization to provide him/her with
the opportunity to establish
close, meaningful relationship
with a same-sex role model.

50. Encourage, support, and reinforce the client's interest and
involvement in non-fire-related
activities (e.g., participating on
a baseball or a soccer team,
singing with a school or
church choir, reading books or

29. Demonstrate the ability to resist negative peer influences to engage in fire-setting behavior. (51, 52)

magazines about the environment or other topics of interest, etc.).

51. Assess whether the client's fire-setting behavior or acts of arson are associated with gang-related activities. (See the chapter entitled "Gang Involvement" in this Planner.)

52. Use role-playing and modeling techniques to teach the client effective ways to resist negative peer pressures that contribute to his/her fire-setting behavior.

___. _____
_____

___. _____
_____

___. _____
_____

___. _____
_____

___. _____
_____

___. _____
_____

DIAGNOSTIC SUGGESTIONS:

ICD-9-CM	_ICD-10-CM_	_DSM-5_ Disorder, Condition, or Problem
312.8	F91.x	Conduct Disorder
313.81	F91.3	Oppositional Defiant Disorder
314.01	F90.2	Attention-Deficit/Hyperactivity Disorder, Combined Presentation
314.01	F90.1	Attention-Deficit/Hyperactivity Disorder, Predominately Hyperactive /Impulsive Presentation
312.9	F91.9	Unspecified Disruptive, Impulse Control, and Conduct Disorder
312.89	F91.8	Other Specified Disruptive, Impulse Control, and Conduct Disorder
309.3	F43.24	Adjustment Disorder, With Disturbance of Conduct
309.4	F43.25	Adjustment Disorder, With Mixed Disturbance of Emotions and Conduct
300.4	F34.1	Persistent Depressive Disorder
_____	_____	_____
_____	_____	_____

FOSTER CARE PLACEMENT

BEHAVIORAL DEFINITIONS

1. Assigned to foster care by a judge or probation officer.
2. Lack of a permanent, healthy, nurturing environment.
3. Living with a foster parent or relative for an extended period of time.
4. Permanent ward of the court as a result of the caregivers losing parental rights.
5. Victim of child neglect and/or abuse.
6. Voluntary relinquishment of parental rights by caregiver.
7. Awaiting adoption or other form of permanent placement.
8. In need of less restrictive environment following participation in a residential setting.
9. Multiple foster care placements due to oppositional, disruptive, and/or delinquent behavior.
10. Ambivalent feelings toward biological parent and/or foster parent.
11. Angry and distrustful attitude toward adults revealed in oppositional, disruptive behavior.
12. Low energy, socially withdrawn, self-disparaging comments, and other signs of hopelessness, depression, and grief.
13. Anxiety and insecurity evidenced by feeling on edge, concentration difficulties, trouble falling asleep, and a general state of irritability.

__. _____
_____

__. _____
_____

__. _____
_____

LONG-TERM GOALS

1. Maintain stable, controlled, responsible behavior with the supportive, respectful foster care placement or long-term living arrangement.
2. Adjust to a new foster home situation in a healthy manner.
3. Improve biological family functioning and stability.
4. Reunify the biological family.
5. Move into a permanent living arrangement such as an adoptive home.
6. Accept court wardship.
7. Resolve emotional turmoil that is associated with being removed from custody of the biological or foster parents and placed in an alternative setting.

__. _____

_____

__. _____

_____

__. _____

_____

SHORT-TERM OBJECTIVES	THERAPEUTIC INTERVENTIONS
1. Client, caregivers, and foster parents provide information to complete a biopsychosocial assessment. (1)	1. Gather a thorough psychosocial history from the client, his/her parents, and foster parent(s).
2. Complete psychological testing and receive feedback. (2)	2. Conduct a psychological assessment to determine placement needs and current level of functioning. Provide feedback to the client, court officials, and parents and/or guardians.
3. Cooperate with finding an appropriate academic placement to facilitate a healthy adjustment to a new environment. (3, 4)	3. Assist the client in finding an appropriate scholastic setting (e.g., vocational training, special education, alternative-choice or magnet school, etc.).

4. Explore obstacles that will make it difficult for the client to succeed scholastically (e.g., learning disabilities, negative peer influences, lack of academic enrichment in the home, lack of academic stimulation in the school, etc.), and identify solutions to these obstacles.

4. Cooperate with a medical evaluation for psychotropic medication. (5)

5. Arrange for a physician to evaluate the client to assess for the appropriateness of psychotropic medication.

5. Take prescribed medications and report on effectiveness and side effects. (6)

6. Monitor the client's use of psychotropic medication as to prescription compliance, effectiveness, and side effects.

6. Demonstrate knowledge of requirements to move from a more restrictive environment to foster care placement. (7)

7. Help the client to list requirements that must be met to move from a more restrictive setting to foster care placement (e.g., meeting curfew, attending classes, behaving respectfully, etc.), and identify solutions to these obstacles.

7. Monitor daily progress toward meeting goals to move from a more restrictive environment to foster care placement. Demonstrate appropriate behavior 90 percent of the time. (8)

8. Organize with the client a system that allows him/her to monitor his/her own progress toward meeting requirements to move to a less restrictive foster care placement.

8. Participate in a preplacement visit to meet the foster parents and the staff that will be working to help the child and/or his/her family reunite. (9, 10)

9. Facilitate for the client (and his/her parents, when appropriate) a visit to the foster care placement.

10. Encourage the client to develop a list of questions to ask the treatment team and/or foster parents regarding foster placement.

9. Acknowledge the issues that required placement in foster care. (11, 12)

11. Build trust by allowing the client to speak openly about any of his/her feelings and concerns.

12. Refer the client to individual therapy to work through issues that led to foster care placement (e.g., abandonment, neglect, abuse, delinquency, etc.).

10. Verbalize an understanding of typical emotional and cognitive responses that are associated with foster care placement, and acknowledge which responses have been enacted or felt. (13, 14)

13. Normalize the client's feelings and responses that are related to foster care placement by explaining typical responses to foster care placement (e.g., rejection of foster parents, acting out, feeling like one is betraying birth family, feeling responsible for placement, etc.).

14. Assist the client in identifying his/her negative patterns of behavior by reviewing problematic situations (e.g., identifying what happened prior to the problematic event, describing the situation itself, and discussing his/her reaction to the event).

11. Identify if the current method of coping is beneficial or harmful, and list at least three ways to cope more effectively. Monitor progress. (15, 16)

15. Guide the client in creating criteria to determine which methods of coping with foster placement are most beneficial (e.g., identify behaviors that violate expectations/limits, identify emotionally damaging or harmful responses, identify behavior that produces positive outcomes, identify when intent and outcome are incongruent, etc.).

16. Develop with the client methods to recognize when he/she is resorting to harmful behavior patterns, and suggest alternative responses for him/her to employ (e.g., thought stopping, positive self-talk, anger management techniques, etc.).

12. Foster parents outline a daily program that includes expectations and limit setting. (17)

17. Coach the foster parents to outline daily expectations and/or limits for the client and to share information with him/her in a direct, sensitive manner.

13. Foster parents target a maximum of three client behaviors to improve, incorporating new behaviors as the client shows progress. (18, 19)

18. Teach the foster parents the necessity for consistent discipline, and monitor the client's and the foster parents' use of expectations, limit setting, rewards, and consequences for the client.

19. Mediate a discussion between the client and foster parents regarding expectations, limit setting, rewards, and consequences.

14. Foster parents and foster care worker monitor the client's school attendance and progress. (20, 21, 22, 23)

20. Encourage the foster parents to act as mentors to the client by encouraging and supporting prosocial behavior.

21. Create with the client and foster parents a communication card to chart school performance that outlines each subject area and allows space for the teacher to evaluate the client's daily or weekly progress.

22. Have the treatment team participate in the school

conferences to identify strategies that may be useful for the teachers and administrators to improve the client's behavior and academic performance.

23. Coordinate and facilitate a collaborative approach among all persons who are participating with the client's care (e.g., therapists, foster care parents, foster care worker, and biological parents) regarding expectations, rewards, and consequences.

15. Identify the qualities and benefits of a positive peer relationship. (24, 25, 26)

24. Help the client to identify characteristics of positive and negative peer interactions.

25. Have the client list potential benefits (e.g., reduce risk of legal involvement, reinforce prosocial behaviors, maintain foster care placement, etc.) to establish merit of positive peer interaction.

26. Determine with the client what type of peer interactions fit in with the expectations of the foster parents and biological parents and how that differs from the client's preferences.

16. Participate in positive social activities with peers to maintain healthy socialization during foster care placement. (27, 28, 29)

27. Refer the client to a group focused on teaching interpersonal skills.

28. Role-play the practice of interpersonal skills in therapy sessions and process problematic interactions in the client's everyday life.

17. List areas in life over which control can be exercised. (30)

18. List long- and short-term goals. (31)

19. Acknowledge ambivalent feelings toward the foster parents and the parents, and give self permission to struggle with such emotions. (32, 33, 34)

20. Foster parents seek respite and support when necessary. (35, 36)

21. Identify previous and current losses that have had an emotional impact. (37)

29. Assist the client in discovering positive social activities (e.g., joining new clubs or discovering new hobbies).

30. Support the client in compiling a list of things that he/she can and cannot control in his/her life.

31. Assist the client in determining long- and short-term goals that he/she can achieve that are dependent on his/her efforts.

32. Normalize the client's feelings of ambivalence related to having positive feelings toward foster parents and/or forming an attachment with the foster parents.

33. Normalize ambivalent feelings toward the biological parents.

34. Suggest to the client the possibility of allowing him/her negative and positive feelings about the biological or foster parents to coexist, pointing out that most people are not either all bad or all good.

35. Educate the foster parents on how to recognize parental stress and how to seek respite care when necessary.

36. Refer the foster parent(s) to a support group of other foster parents.

37. Explain different types of losses to the client (e.g., significant people, places, or things that were familiar or provided comfort that are no longer

available). Explore the losses that the client has experienced.

22. List three ways that thoughts and/or beliefs, feelings, or behavior have changed as a result of losses. (38, 39)

38. Allow the client to create examples that demonstrate how people feel, behave, and think as a result of losses.

39. Assist the client in listing three ways that losses have impacted his/her thoughts, values, feelings, and behavior.

23. List three positive things that occurred as a result of foster care placement. (40)

40. Encourage the client to list at least three positive things about foster care placement.

24. Verbalize an understanding of issues related to the parents' dysfunction, and develop realistic expectations regarding the parents' abilities. (41, 42)

41. Help the client to acknowledge and understand mental illness, physical disability, addiction, and/or other serious limitations of his/her parent(s). Refer the client to a support group, if appropriate.

42. Support the client in recognizing the strengths and weaknesses of his/her parent(s).

25. Biological family members acknowledge the problems that led to the client's foster care placement and the feelings that have resulted from it. (43, 44, 45)

43. Refer the client's biological family to family therapy to discuss thoughts and feelings related to his/her foster care placement.

44. Assist the biological family to openly acknowledge the problems that led to the client's foster care placement.

45. Provide opportunities for all biological family members to express fears, doubts, and hopes regarding reunification.

26. Participate in home visits with the biological family, and verbalize strategies to improve visits. (46, 47, 48)

46. Help the biological family to develop a picture of how they want the family to function.

47. Support the biological family in finding solutions (e.g., using anger management techniques, adequate parenting skills, reasonable family rules, etc.) to obstacles that prevent healthy functioning.

48. During home visits, encourage the biological parents to monitor the client's adherence to expectations of the foster home, when appropriate, to provide consistency and assist with a successful reunification.

27. Biological parents identify three obstacles that will need to be addressed for successful reintegration, and develop coping strategies for each obstacle. (49, 50)

49. Assist the biological family to create new coping strategies as problems arise with the client's visits to the home.

50. Ask the biological parents to list problems that have to be solved before the client can return home. Process strategies to bring about solutions.

28. Express and mourn feelings related to inability to return to the home. (51)

51. Facilitate family sessions that allow the biological family to express feelings of love, sadness, regret, and disappointment when parental rights have been terminated.

29. Foster parents and the client express feelings about his/her leaving for a permanent placement. (52, 53)

52. Encourage the client and the foster parents to talk about their feelings related to the client leaving the foster home for a permanent placement such as adoption or emancipation.

53. Encourage the client to express fears and excitement related to adoption or emancipation.

30. List three positive outcomes as a result of foster care placement. (54)

31. Visit independent living quarters prior to transition from foster care placement, and discuss related feelings and concerns. (55, 56)

32. Identify three expected problems in adjusting to an independent living environment, and develop at least two healthy coping strategies for each problem expected. (57, 58, 59)

54. Challenge the client to list at least three positive outcomes that have happened as a result of him/her being in foster care.

55. Facilitate a visit by the client to his/her independent living facility.

56. Provide an opportunity for the client to discuss his/her feelings/concerns related to independent living transition from foster care placement.

57. Assist the client in developing a list of expected problems that he/she will have in adjusting to independent living. Help the client develop coping strategies for each problem expected.

58. Support the client's readiness for transition from foster care placement to independent living by listing the skills that he/she has mastered and those that will need to be developed for independent living.

59. Refer the client to a life skills group to assist with the development of functional

skills necessary for independent living.

___. _____

___. _____

___. _____

DIAGNOSTIC SUGGESTIONS:

ICD-9-CM	_ICD-10-CM_	_DSM-5_ Disorder, Condition, or Problem
309.0	F43.21	Adjustment Disorder, With Depressed Mood
309.24	F43.22	Adjustment Disorder, With Anxiety
309.28	F43.23	Adjustment Disorder, With Mixed Anxiety and Depressed Mood
309.3	F43.24	Adjustment Disorder, With Disturbance of Conduct
309.4	F43.25	Adjustment Disorder, With Mixed Disturbance of Emotions and Conduct
300.02	F41.1	Generalized Anxiety Disorder
309.81	F43.10	Posttraumatic Stress Disorder
308.3	F43.0	Acute Stress Disorder
296.xx	F32.x	Major Depressive Disorder, Single Episode
296.xx	F33.x	Major Depressive Disorder, Recurrent Episode
300.4	F34.1	Persistent Depressive Disorder
313.89	F94.1	Reactive Attachment Disorder
_____	_____	_____
_____	_____	_____

GANG INVOLVEMENT

BEHAVIORAL DEFINITIONS

1. Identified as gang member, gang affiliate, or as a member of a delinquent group or society.
2. Adopts and uses certain signs, symbols, insignia, jewelry, colors, and clothing to signify gang affiliation and collective involvement in criminal activity.
3. Resides in or frequents communities where gang involvement is prominent.
4. Involved in delinquent, destructive, or illegal gang activity such as fighting, vandalism, graffiti, robbery, weapon offenses, auto theft, drug dealing, or intimidation.
5. History of being arrested for illegal gang activity.
6. Family history of gang involvement.
7. Demonstrates one or more of the following risk factors for gang involvement: lives in poverty, cultural norms support gang behavior, lacks adult role models, parental drug use, academic failure, low commitment to school attendance, parents and/or guardians often unavailable.

—. _____
_____

—. _____
_____

—. _____
_____

LONG-TERM GOALS

1. Resist invitations, threats, intimidation, or coercion to join a gang.

2. Discontinue all gang-related behaviors.
3. Improve values and moral reasoning.
4. Improve the relationship with family members through increased contact and shared activities.
5. Improve conflict resolution skills.
6. Grieve losses resulting from gang involvement, including loss due to gang violence, loss of relationship with family members and friends not involved in gang activity, loss of freedom due to incarceration, and so forth.
7. Obtain educational and job skills.
8. Establish a positive social network.
9. Develop a sense of self-worth apart from gang membership.

—. _____

_____

—. _____

_____

_____

—. _____

_____

SHORT-TERM OBJECTIVES

THERAPEUTIC INTERVENTIONS

1. Cooperate with an assessment of gang involvement. (1)

1. Ask questions to determine the client's gang alliance (e.g., Crips, Bloods, Vice Lords, Latin Kings, Folks, People Nation, 18th Street, Female Gang, Skinheads, Taggers, etc.), the level of commitment (e.g., hard-core, affiliate, fringe, wanna-be, and interested members), and motivation and/or desire to discontinue gang involvement.

2. Identify reasons for joining a gang. (2)

2. Discuss with the client reasons why people join gangs (e.g., identity, recognition and/or status, belonging, love, money, support,

3. Recognize and resist gang recruitment tactics. (3, 4, 5)

4. Discuss willingness to leave the gang. (6, 7, 8)

acceptance, excitement, family tradition, etc.). Assist the client in identifying why he/she joined or wants to join.

3. Discuss with fringe, wanna-be, and interested gang members the negative consequences of joining a gang.

4. Provide information regarding gang recruitment tactics [e.g., fraternity style (requires that a street gang appear desirable), obligation (relies on the idea that failure to join the gang in the neighborhood constitutes a lack of respect and betrayal), and coercion (relies on intimidation and fear)].

5. Facilitate straight-talk sessions between former gang members (reformed and leading productive lives) and the client to discourage gang involvement and to encourage the pursuit of a more productive lifestyle.

6. Facilitate a scared-straight session between the client and paralyzed victims of gang violence, police, inmates, and so on.

7. Discuss whether the client is willing to leave the gang.

8. Explore the client's confidence in his/her ability to get out of a gang and live a productive life.

5. Identify how a family history of gang involvement has influenced own gang affiliation. (9)

9. Explore with the client his/her family's history of gang involvement and his/her fears associated with breaking the cycle.

6. Identify the needs that are being met through gang membership. (10)

10. Explore with the client how gang membership is currently helping him/her meet his/her needs for recognition and/or status, belonging, love, money, support, acceptance, and excitement (e.g., drug selling or stealing is meeting the need for money; holding an office is meeting the need for recognition and/or status; etc.).

7. Identify and implement alternative positive ways to meet needs currently being met by gang membership. (11)

11. Brainstorm with the client to identify positive ways for him/her to meet his/her need for recognition and/or status, belonging, love, money, support, acceptance, and excitement.

8. Discuss reluctance to engage in therapy due to loyalty concerns, fears, or other barriers. (12, 13)

12. Address the client's reluctance to engage in therapy due to loyalty concerns or fears. Explain confidentiality policies.

13. Work with the client to identify and overcome barriers to the therapeutic process.

9. Describe witnessed or committed gang-related acts of violence that are causing grief or remorse. (14, 15)

14. Explain the grieving process to the client. Help him/her to identify feelings associated with his/her loss.

15. Encourage the client to talk about memories of violence (e.g., ambushes, drive-by shootings, initiation beatings,

10. Learn and practice ways to cope with gang-related distress. (16)

11. Verbalize an understanding of how violent gang behavior affects the victim. (17, 18)

12. Identify the effects of criminal gang behavior from the vantage point of own family and the victim's family. (19, 20, 21)

violent robberies, assaults, etc.). Ask the client how his/her experiences have affected his/her life.

16. Assist the client in identifying ways to alleviate distress and/or grief associated with gang violence.

17. Encourage the client to acknowledge his/her role in the death or disabling of family members, friends, fellow gang member, or rival gang member as a result of gang violence (e.g., revenge attacks, initiations, etc.).

18. Assist the client in preparing apologies to the victim, parents, and/or community.

19. Ask the client to imagine the physical feelings, emotions, and thoughts that a victim might have before, after, and during an act of gang violence. Ask the client to imagine himself/herself being the victim. Challenge cognitive distortions.

20. Help the client to recognize how he/she tends to ignore or minimize the emotional and economic harm done to victims and their families resulting from his/her behavior.

21. When appropriate, facilitate a dialog between the client, the victim of a gang crime, parents, and/or neighbors.

13. Acknowledge an awareness of and comply with conditions of probation. (22, 23)

22. Consult with a juvenile justice official to determine the client's level and intensity of probation supervision (e.g., regular field supervision, intense supervision, curfew, electronic monitoring, etc.).

23. Assist the client in realizing the importance of complying with conditions of probation (e.g., mandatory drug test, probation supervision, home detention, therapy, electronic supervision, etc.).

14. Identify gang mentality, values, and morals that govern behavior. (24, 25, 26)

24. Discuss with the client his/her gang mentality (i.e., the three R's: Reputation, Respect, Retaliation and/or Revenge) and how his/her mentality influences his/her thoughts and behaviors.

25. Assist the client in identifying his/her gang mentality and/or attitude that may impede a successful transition out of the gang (e.g., apathy toward feelings of others, vengefulness, desire for quick money, etc.).

26. Teach self-monitoring techniques (e.g., using structured logs, journaling, reward, and punishment systems to help the client recognize and control thoughts, feelings, and behaviors that are indicative of gang affiliation).

15. Identify what is wrong with current values and morals, and change each to reflect more positive, healthier ways of thinking about self and others. (27, 28)

16. Make a commitment to avoid using the insignias that signify gang membership. (29)

17. Participate in education enhancement and job training. (30, 31, 32)

18. Verbalize an understanding and acceptance of the demands of employment and its long-term rewards. (33, 34)

27. Assist the client in evaluating his/her values and morals that support gang involvement. Help him/her to replace his/her way of thinking about himself/herself and others with more adaptive healthy thinking.

28. Help the client to understand how morals and values influence his/her behavior (i.e., people tend to behave in accordance with what they believe and value).

29. Encourage and reward the decreased use of gang insignias and other symbols of gang affiliation.

30. Refer the client for educational and job skills training.

31. Participate in observational and didactic work experiences.

32. Assist the client in obtaining legitimate job opportunities by linking him/her with job placement agencies in the community.

33. Discuss realistic constraints of the workplace (e.g., time schedule, pay schedules, tax deductions, etc.). Prompt the client to identify the most problematic and/or difficult constraints.

34. Help the client to generate reasons why jobs and training will result in employment that is more rewarding

19. Family members and the client identify problems impeding their relationship and fostering gang involvement. (35, 36, 37, 38)

long-term than life with a street gang.

35. Ask the client to identify verbal and nonverbal messages that he/she receives from his/her family and/or caregivers about his/her self-worth.

36. Assess risk factors (e.g., poverty, cultural norms supporting gang behavior, lack of adult role models, parental drug use, academic failure, low commitment to school, etc.) that contribute to the client's gang involvement and that assist the family in mobilizing resources to overcome these factors.

37. Encourage family members and/or caregivers to communicate disapproval of the client's gang involvement.

38. Assist the family and/or caregivers in implementing family meetings to improve communication.

20. Express the need for attention, love, and acceptance in a family session. (39, 40)

39. Encourage the family and/or caregivers to express an understanding of the client's need for acceptance, attention, and love.

40. Encourage family members' and/or caregivers' involvement in the client's daily activities and special occasions.

21. Family members increase time spent together in enjoyable activities. (41)

41. Assist the family and/or caregivers and the client in establishing quality bonding time (e.g., special outings, quiet time together, special meals, conjoint leisure activities, etc.).

22. Family members recognize and monitor the client's gang behavior and activity. (42, 43, 44)

42. Teach family members what to look for when assessing for gang involvement (e.g., colors, use of hand gestures and/or signs, clothing, money from unknown sources, changes in friends, etc.).

43. Provide the family and/or caregivers with information and pamphlets that identify gang paraphernalia (this may be obtained from the local police department).

44. Refer the family and/or caregivers to a support program designed to increase awareness of gang mentality culture.

23. Acknowledge and change thinking errors and distortions regarding self-respect, prestige, and status associated with gang activity. (45, 46)

45. Discuss with the client his/her understanding of self-worth, respect, prestige, and status as it relates to gang involvement. Challenge his/her thinking distortions and errors (e.g., thinking that reflects a misinterpretation of reality, minimization of harm inflicted upon others, denial of responsibility, and/or rationalization).

46. Assist the client in understanding how gang behavior fosters a false sense of

self-respect and respect from others, prestige, and self-worth.

24. Write down positive events and/or accomplishments prior to gang involvement that contributed to positive feelings toward self, others, and the future. (47)

47. Ask the client to talk about positive events and accomplishments that he/she experienced prior to gang involvement, and note how these events produced feelings of pride, self-worth, and hope.

25. Spend increasingly more time in constructive activities that promote positive self-worth, prestige, status, and respect. (48, 49, 50)

48. Ask the client to make a list of positive things that he/she can do to gain respect.

49. Encourage the client's involvement in socially acceptable groups or community activities where he/she can gain status (e.g., church, school, Boys' and Girls' Club, Big Brothers/Big Sisters, community service organization, community recreational programs, etc.).

50. Arrange for the client to speak to at-risk juveniles regarding the dangers of gang involvement.

26. Develop a relationship with a positive adult and/or mentor. (49, 51)

49. Encourage the client's involvement in socially acceptable groups or community activities where he/she can gain status (e.g., church, school, Boys' and Girls' Club, Big Brothers/Big Sisters, community service organization, community recreational programs, etc.).

27. Explore options to getting out of the gang, and begin to exercise the identified options. (52, 53, 54, 55, 56)

51. Identify and recruit successful community members to serve as role models for the client.

52. Refer the client and his/her family to social services to assist them in obtaining food, shelter, medical assistance, financial support, and so forth.

53. Process with the client his/her thoughts and feelings regarding relocating to avoid gang involvement.

54. Discuss with the caregivers the possibility of relocating out of their current neighborhood, town, or state.

55. Assist the client in generating alternatives to fade out of the gang (e.g., after-school activities, church involvement, job, etc.).

56. Encourage using agencies and community groups that provide assistance to gang-involved individuals (e.g., gang outreach centers, churches, etc.).

28. Learn and practice problem-solving techniques to resolve gang-related conflicts. (57, 58, 59, 60)

57. Teach and encourage the client to use problem-solving skills (e.g., acknowledging and/or identifying the problem, identifying the needs of those who will be affected, generating and/or brainstorming possible solutions, evaluating each option, implementing those options) when faced with gang-related conflicts.

58. Teach and encourage the client to use decision-making skills (i.e., examine the problem from several different perspectives, decide whether to take action, gather resources and/or seek support, make a plan, visualize the plan of action, take action) when faced with decisions that are related to gang involvement.

59. Use hypothetical vignettes to help the client to recognize and resolve potential conflicts. Encourage him/her to use problem-solving and decision-making techniques.

60. Ask the client to identify potential problems that he/she might encounter as a result of discontinuing gang involvement. Help him/her to employ problem-solving and decision-making techniques to resolve the anticipated conflicts.

—. _____   —. _____
    _____   _____

—. _____   —. _____
    _____   _____

—. _____   —. _____
    _____   _____

DIAGNOSTIC SUGGESTIONS:

ICD-9-CM	*ICD-10-CM*	*DSM-5* Disorder, Condition, or Problem
309.3	F43.24	Adjustment Disorder, With Disturbance of Conduct
309.4	F43.25	Adjustment Disorder, With Mixed Disturbance of Emotions and Conduct
312.81	F91.1	Conduct Disorder, Childhood-Onset Type
312.82	F91.2	Conduct Disorder, Adolescent-Onset Type
V71.02	Z72.810	Adolescent Antisocial Behavior
300.4	F34.1	Persistent Depressive Disorder
300.02	F41.1	Generalized Anxiety Disorder
300.01	F41.0	Panic Disorder
300.22	F40.00	Agoraphobia
309.81	F43.10	Posttraumatic Stress Disorder
_____	_____	_____
_____	_____	_____

GRIEF/ABANDONMENT ISSUES

BEHAVIORAL DEFINITIONS

1. Experienced loss due to sudden or traumatic death (e.g., murder, suicide, fatal accident, drug overdose, abortion, or miscarriage).
2. Feelings of ambivalence associated with the loss of an abusive or neglectful caregiver.
3. Experienced multiple losses (e.g., removal from home, school, and/or community; separation from siblings and family members; loss of freedom) resulting in feelings of emotional numbing and negativity.
4. Recurrent disturbing dreams of the deceased or preoccupation with the image of the deceased.
5. Increased risk-taking behavior (e.g., drug and alcohol abuse, fighting, and sexual promiscuity) in response to the loss.
6. Intense anger toward the deceased or individual who abandoned or left.
7. Feelings of guilt, hostility, fearfulness, apathy, self-doubt, and emptiness occurring after a significant loss.
8. Anticipatory grief (i.e., grief that occurs before the actual loss) results in significantly impaired functioning.
9. Symptoms of depression and anxiety precipitated by the loss.
10. Feelings of abandonment and grief that are associated with neglect, abuse, separation from family members and/or caregivers, or incarceration of a family member.
11. Loss of freedom due to detention or other restrictive placement, resulting in feelings of sadness, guilt, and/or loneliness.

__. _____
   _____

__. _____
   _____

—. _____
_____

LONG-TERM GOALS

1. Acknowledge and accept reality that has been created by the loss.
2. Facilitate a healthy and adaptive adjustment to new life circumstances following the loss.
3. Express and resolve feelings associated with each stage of grief.
4. Identify and use resources to adjust to the loss.

—. _____
_____

—. _____
_____

—. _____
_____

SHORT-TERM OBJECTIVES

THERAPEUTIC INTERVENTIONS

1. Identify the actual loss that precipitated feelings of grief and abandonment. (1)

1. Assist the client in discussing the nature of the loss (e.g., person, image, freedom, nurturance, opportunity, etc.), the circumstances (e.g., how, when, where, etc.), under which the loss occurred, and the significance of the loss.

2. Verbalize an understanding of the concept of death through formulating questions about the circumstances surrounding the loss and accepting answers. (2)

2. Provide the client with factual information about the loss. Solicit and answer questions to alleviate irrational guilt or confusion.

3. Identify factors that contributed to the loss. (3)

3. Assist the client in identifying negative patterns and/or

behaviors that contributed to the loss (e.g., drug selling, drug use, gang violence, reckless driving, and other delinquent acts).

4. Verbalize an increased understanding of the grief process and common reactions to loss. (4, 5, 6)

4. Provide grief-related reading material to assist the client in understanding and coping with the loss (e.g., *When Someone Very Special Dies* by Heegard, *Life Time: The Beautiful Way to Explain Death to Children* by Melloni and Ingpen, *On Death and Dying* by Kubler, *Sad Isn't Bad: A Good Grief Guide Book for Kids Dealing with Loss* by Mundey and Walley, and *The Grieving Teen: A Guide for Teenagers and Their Friends* by Fitzgerald).

5. Explain typical reactions to loss (e.g., shock and/or disbelief, guilt, unusual happenings, thoughts of suicide, sexual promiscuity, drug and/or alcohol abuse, anger, sadness, depression, denial, feelings of abandonment, hope, and/or acceptance).

6. Reframe the grief experience by assisting the client in thinking of working through grief by experiencing one's feelings, rather than escaping or avoiding the pain.

5. Participate in social or cultural memorial rituals. (7, 8, 9)

7. Educate the caregiver on the significance of the client's involvement and inclusion in the memorial of the deceased.

8. Provide a detailed explanation of what to expect at the memorial services.

9. Give the client the option of attending the memorial services.

6. Allow others to be supportive during grieving. (10)

10. Assist the client in identifying what others could do to be helpful to him/her during this time, and encourage him/her to let others know (e.g., spending time together, sharing memories of the deceased, visiting the gravesite together, engaging in some diversion activity, etc.).

7. Explore and create meaningful ways to memorialize the loss. (11, 12)

11. Assist the client in identifying positive aspects of the relationship with the lost attachment figure or significant other that can be carried into the future through healthy means (e.g., traditions, morals, values, beliefs, etc.).

12. Provide the client with suggestions for remembering the loss (e.g., carrying or wearing a linking object, creating a memory book, creating a collage, etc.).

8. Address the loss and issues related to the loss in a group therapy session. (13, 14)

13. Assist the client in establishing contact with a group therapy support group.

14. Encourage the client to use the peer support group to talk about experiences leading to juvenile justice involvement and the loss.

9. Recognize and examine feelings precipitated by the loss. (15, 16, 17, 18, 19)

15. Ask the client to share pictures of the deceased. Ask the client to talk about a special time spent with the deceased.

16. Create games that begin with "Do you remember" or "Remember when" to facilitate the client reminiscing and expressing feelings.

17. Use workbooks and games to encourage the identification and expression of feelings, including anger, fear, guilt, resentment, loneliness, and sadness (e.g., *Helping Me Say Goodbye: Activities for Helping Kids Cope When a Special Person Dies* by Silverman; *Fire in My Heart, Ice in My Veins: A Journal for Teenagers Experiencing a Loss* by Grollman; and *The Grief Game* by Searkley, Isteng, and Roehampton).

18. Ask the client to talk about any dreams he/she has had related to the deceased. Process the feelings that are associated with the dreams.

19. Encourage the client to use mock letter writing, journaling, role playing, and creative writing as means of expressing feelings.

10. Verbalize the termination of irrational feelings of guilt. (20, 21)

20. Explore irrational aspects of the client's beliefs leading to excessive feelings of guilt. Challenge these irrational beliefs.

21. Explore survivor's guilt (e.g., guilt stemming from surviving when gang members, family members, and/or friends were injured or killed) and process self-defeating, distorted thoughts.

11. Identify the source of rational guilt and appropriately accept responsibility for the loss. (3, 22, 23)

3. Assist the client in identifying negative patterns and/or behaviors that contributed to the loss (e.g., drug selling, drug use, gang violence, reckless driving, and other delinquent acts).

22. Encourage the client to deal with guilt in the appropriate manner by accepting responsibility for his/her behavior that contributed to the loss and admitting wrongdoing.

23. Encourage self-forgiveness.

12. Verbalize feelings of ambivalence regarding the death or loss of an abusive caregiver. (24)

24. Validate and assist the client in understanding and expressing his/her conflicting feelings toward an abusive or neglectful caregiver.

13. Identify five positive consequences that developed from the loss. (25)

25. Assist the client in identifying positive aspects of the loss and reasons why the loss may be beneficial in the long run (e.g., improved living situation, needs met regularly, educational assistance, deterred delinquency, etc.).

14. Express feelings of loneliness and fear of abandonment from family members, friends, and caregivers. (17, 24, 26)

17. Use workbooks and games to encourage the identification and expression of feelings, including anger, fear, guilt, resentment, loneliness, and sadness (e.g., *Helping Me Say Goodbye: Activities for Helping Kids Cope When a Special Person Dies* by Silverman; *Fire in My Heart, Ice in My Veins: A Journal for Teenagers Experiencing a Loss* by Grollman; and *The Grief Game* by Searkley, Isteng, and Roehampton).

24. Validate and assist the client in understanding and expressing his/her conflicting feelings toward an abusive or neglectful caregiver.

26. Explore the client's fears associated with the loss (e.g., fear of future abandonment, fear of being forgotten while in a detention or restrictive setting, fear of not getting needs met, etc.). Reinforce this openness.

15. Write a good-bye letter to the lost loved one. (27)

27. Assist the client in establishing closure by writing a good-bye letter to the lost loved one.

16. Use coping strategies and relaxation techniques three times daily to reduce anxiety associated with the loss. (28)

28. Teach the client relaxation techniques (e.g., visualization, meditation, breathing, progressive muscle relaxation, etc.) and coping skills (e.g., thought-stopping, positive affirmations; self-talk; etc.) to assist him/her in decreasing anxiety related to the loss.

17. Acknowledge and begin to accept pending loss. (29)

18. Discuss previous losses and identify feelings of numbness, pessimism, cynicism, fatalism, and insecurity that have developed due to the multiple loss. (30, 31, 32)

19. Decrease statements that are indicative of pessimism, cynicism, detachment, and insecurities to three daily, decreasing as time progresses. (33)

20. Identify and reduce destructive behavior patterns that have been exacerbated by the loss. (34)

29. Assist the client in acknowledging and accepting the pending loss (e.g., loss of freedom and/or detention; death of a significant other due to illness, violence, or trauma; removal from caregiver and community due to abuse and/or neglect; etc.).

30. Explore the details of the client's history of multiple losses.

31. Encourage discussion of feelings associated with any previous loss that may be reactivated particularly on the anniversary of the loss or during major developmental milestones.

32. Assist the client in creating a timeline (i.e., concrete representation of his/her losses) with losses and dates listed in chronological order. Process this timeline.

33. Educate the client on the cumulative effect (i.e., numbness, detachment, pessimism, cynicism, fatalism, and insecurity) of multiple losses (particularly traumatic losses), and assist him/her in monitoring and changing destructive cognitive patterns.

34. Encourage recognition of destructive behavior patterns (e.g., alcohol and drug usage, verbal and physical aggression, sexual promiscuity,

isolation, suicidal gestures, etc.) exacerbated by the loss. Encourage constructive expression of feelings, and provide referrals for more intensive treatment as necessary.

21. Make a list of five potential sources of positive support and establish contact. (35, 36)

35. Explore with the client ways in which his/her support systems may have changed as a result of the loss.

36. Help the client to identify currently available sources of positive support and potential new sources of positive support.

22. Decrease the time spent in isolative behavior by 50 percent. Increase the percentage as time progresses. (37)

37. Assist the client in seeking and cultivating a support system to substitute for the loss (e.g., establish contact with positive peer groups, facilitate involvement in mentoring programs, encourage involvement in after school activities, etc.).

23. Report a reduced frequency of the occurrence of intrusive traumatic images of the death. (38)

38. Instruct the client to confront traumatic images by talking, writing, and/or drawing about the details of the death, especially aspects of the loss that are most traumatic.

24. Family members and/or caregivers acknowledge and appropriately respond to the loss. (39, 40, 41)

39. In family therapy sessions encourage and facilitate family discussion related to the loss.

40. Assist the new or remaining caregiver in understanding and anticipating behavior that the client is likely to manifest

in response to the loss and/or separation (e.g., anger, isolation, anxiety, depression, increase in delinquent behavior, etc.).

41. Teach the family members and/or caregivers how to offer effective support to the client (e.g., how to tolerate upset feelings and intense emotions, how to accept the child's way of grieving, how to elicit open dialog about the loss, ways to support the client during the memorial service, etc.).

___. _____   ___. _____

_____   _____

___. _____   ___. _____

_____   _____

___. _____   ___. _____

_____   _____

DIAGNOSTIC SUGGESTIONS:

ICD-9-CM	_ICD-10-CM_	_DSM-5_ Disorder, Condition, or Problem
309.0	F43.21	Adjustment Disorder, With Depressed Mood
309.24	F43.22	Adjustment Disorder, With Anxiety
309.28	F43.23	Adjustment Disorder, With Mixed Anxiety and Depressed Mood
309.3	F43.24	Adjustment Disorder, With Disturbance of Conduct
309.4	F43.25	Adjustment Disorder, With Mixed Disturbance of Emotions and Conduct
V62.82	Z63.4	Uncomplicated Bereavement
296.xx	F32.x	Major Depressive Disorder, Single Episode

296.xx	F33.x	Major Depressive Disorder, Recurrent Episode
300.4	F34.1	Persistent Depressive Disorder
_____	_____	_____
_____	_____	_____

ISOLATED/DISTRUSTFUL/ANGRY

BEHAVIORAL DEFINITIONS

1. Pervasive pattern of social withdrawal and isolation from all types of peer or family interaction.
2. Little or no desire to establish close interpersonal relationships or lasting, meaningful friendships.
3. Poor social skills and self-centeredness that interfere with the ability to establish and maintain close, meaningful relationships.
4. Emotionally constricted as evidenced by showing little or no emotion, other than anger or hostility.
5. Guarded, defensive posture arising out of deep mistrust of others.
6. Social alienation, accompanied by feelings of being misunderstood, rejected, or ostracized by peers.
7. Frequent complaints about being the target of teasing, name-calling, harassment, or bullying from peers.
8. Persistent failure to interpret positive social cues of acceptance and approval and/or a tendency to perceive hostile or negative intentions from others.
9. History of engaging in solitary delinquent activities or crimes.
10. Lack of empathy and chronic disregard for the thoughts, feelings, and needs of other people.
11. Strong interest in or preoccupation with violence.
12. Repeated acts of violence, aggression, or destruction of property against individual(s) or societal institutions (e.g., school, places of business, government buildings, etc.).
13. Verbal or written threats (e.g., letters, anonymous notes, e-mail messages, etc.) against individual(s) or societal institutions.
14. Lack of guilt or remorse for how aggressive, destructive, or antisocial behaviors negatively impact others.
15. Impoverished moral reasoning and impaired use of judgment.

—. _____
   _____
   _____
—. _____
   _____
   _____
—. _____
   _____

LONG-TERM GOALS

1. Establish and maintain close family relations and lasting, meaningful friendships (i.e., more than six months).
2. Interact socially with peers or friends on a consistent basis.
3. Develop the essential social skills that will enhance the quality of interpersonal relationships.
4. Demonstrate empathy, concern, and sensitivity for the thoughts, feelings, and needs of others on a regular basis.
5. Resolve the core conflicts that contribute to the emergence of social isolation and emotional detachment.
6. Eliminate all delinquent and antisocial behavior.
7. Terminate all acts of violence toward people and the destruction of property.
8. The caregivers establish and maintain appropriate parent-child boundaries by combining love and affirmation with firm, consistent limits.

—. _____
   _____
   _____
—. _____
   _____
   _____
—. _____
   _____

SHORT-TERM GOALS	THERAPEUTIC INTERVENTIONS
1. The caregivers and the client provide psychosocial history information. (1, 2)	1. Gather a detailed psychosocial history of the client's development and family environment to gain insight into

the emotional factors or sequence of events that contributed to his/her social isolation or emotional detachment.

2. Explore the client's early childhood and family background for past rejection experiences, abandonment, neglect, abuse, or trauma that may have contributed to his/her social isolation, anger, and emotional detachment.

2. Complete psychological evaluation or assessment procedures. (3, 4, 6)

3. Arrange for psychological evaluation of the client to assess for the presence of an emerging antisocial personality structure or possible depressive disorder that may contribute to the emergence of social isolation or emotional detachment.

4. Conduct risk assessment to determine whether it is safe for the client to remain at his/her present school or should be transferred to another school setting after he/she has made a violent threat (e.g., bomb threat) or engaged in violent behavior.

6. Provide feedback to the client, caregivers, school officials, or juvenile justice officials about the results from the psychological evaluation or assessment procedures.

3. Complete a substance abuse evaluation, and comply with recommendations offered by evaluation findings. (5, 6)

5. Conduct or refer the client for a substance abuse evaluation to determine whether possible substance abuse is

contributing to the client's social withdrawal or emotional detachment. Refer the client for chemical dependence treatment if indicated. (See the chapter entitled "Substance Abuse" in this Planner).

6. Provide feedback to the client, caregivers, school officials, or juvenile justice officials about the results from the psychological evaluation or assessment procedures.

4. Cooperate with an assessment of amenability to various types of psychotherapeutic intervention. (7, 8, 9)

7. Conduct a thorough diagnostic interview to assess the client's openness and amenability for psychotherapy.

8. Assess in the early stages of treatment whether the client is an appropriate candidate for traditional, insight-oriented type of therapy (e.g., building relationship, exploring underlying dynamics, working through resistance, etc.) or is best suited for a behavioral approach that focuses on reinforcement principals and consequences.

9. Establish a contract with the resistant, hardened client, where he/she can attend less frequent sessions (e.g., once every two to three weeks) and eventually graduate from therapy by achieving specific treatment goals (e.g., obtain satisfactory grades, pass all

drug tests, cease all delinquent acts, engage in peer social activities, etc.).

5. Cooperate with the recommendations or requirements mandated by the juvenile justice system. (10)

10. Consult with caregivers, probation officer, or juvenile justice officials about the appropriate consequences for the client's aggressive or antisocial behavior (e.g., paying restitution, performing community service, probation, placing him/her on an electronic tether, etc.).

6. Move to an appropriate alternate setting or juvenile detention facility. (11)

11. Consult with the caregivers, probation officer, and other juvenile justice officials about whether the client should be placed in a structured, therapeutic, residential treatment program where he/she will receive direct therapeutic services, versus placing him/her in a juvenile detention facility, or boot camp, where he/she will receive greater external controls as a consequence for his/her serious antisocial behavior.

7. Offer a sincere apology to the victim(s) of the aggressive or antisocial behavior. (12)

12. Require the client to make a verbal or written apology to the victim(s) of his/her aggressive or antisocial behavior.

8. Comply with the recommendations made at the Individualized Educational Planning Committee (IEPC) regarding educational interventions. (13)

13. Attend an Individualized Educational Planning Committee (IEPC) meeting with the caregivers, teachers, and school officials to determine the client's eligibility for special education services, and design educational

interventions that will assist him/her in accomplishing academic goals and meeting social needs.

9. Caregivers and teachers implement educational strategies that will help the client meet his/her academic goals and social needs. (14)

14. Consult with teachers and school officials about ways to increase the client's socialization and interaction with others (e.g., pairing the client with a popular or well-liked peer on school projects, participating in student government, helping to tutor developmentally disabled students, etc.).

10. Cooperate with a reward system, contingency contract, or token economy that focuses on increasing positive social behavior and deters aggressive, antisocial, or insensitive behavior. (15, 16)

15. Design a reward system to reinforce the client for his/her positive social behavior and efforts to reach out to others with caring, empathy, and sensitivity.

16. Establish a contingency contract that specifies consequences that the client will receive for his/her aggressive, antisocial, exploitive, or insensitive behavior.

11. Use self-monitoring techniques to increase positive social interactions. (17)

17. Encourage the client to use a self-monitoring checklist at home and/or school to increase the frequency of his/her social interactions or prosocial behavior. Ask the client to select for implementation a specific prosocial behavior each day (e.g., complimenting others, introducing himself/her self to a new peer, initiating conversation, etc.), and monitor his/her behavior by using a self-reporting form.

12. Identify positive social skills that increase the probability of acceptance from others. (18, 19, 20)

18. Ask the client to keep a journal of both positive and negative social experiences. Process excerpts from journal to identify factors that contribute to social withdrawal and/or those that reinforce positive social experiences.

19. Instruct the caregivers and teachers to observe and record positive social behavior by the client in between therapy sessions and to reinforce and encourage him/her to continue to exhibit the positive social behavior.

20. Assess periods of time in the past when the client demonstrated greater interest and involvement with others. Process the client's responses, and reinforce his/her positive social skills that helped him/her connect with others.

13. Identify the irrational or distorted beliefs that contribute to social isolation or detachment. (21, 22)

21. Assist the client in identifying any irrational or distorted beliefs about specific individuals or people in the world in general (e.g., "I can never trust someone who has teased me"; "All jocks are insensitive"; believing that others are not to be trusted because of slightly insensitive remarks or teasing, etc.) that contribute to his/her social isolation and detachment.

22. Teach the client to replace irrational, distorted beliefs about individuals or the world with more positive, reality-based messages (e.g., "There are others whom you can trust"; "People have both positive and negative traits"; "Do not overreact to slightly insensitive remarks or teasing"; etc.).

14. Decrease the frequency of verbalizations that project the blame for insensitive or uncaring behavior onto others. (23, 24, 25)

23. Assess the client's emotional response to therapeutic confrontation or challenge about how his/her insensitive or uncaring behavior impacts others negatively. Evaluate whether confrontation is effective in increasing his/her sensitivity or only serves to reinforce his/her defensiveness or indifference.

24. Confront the client's uncaring, insensitive, aggressive, or acting-out behavior, pointing out negative consequences for himself/herself and others.

25. Confront statements in which the client blames others for his/her insensitive and uncaring behavior and fails to accept responsibility for the consequences of his/her actions.

15. Increase expressions of painful or vulnerable emotions. (26, 27, 28)

26. Explore past painful events in the client's life where significant others or peers have proven to be untrustworthy, unreliable, neglectful, or hurtful. Encourage and

support him/her in expressing feelings of anger, hurt, and sadness.

27. Affirm and reinforce the client for displaying personal strength (e.g., "I admire your honesty and strength in being able to share your hurt") when expressing painful or vulnerable emotions.

28. Assist the client in making a connection between painful emotions or unmet needs and social isolation or emotional detachment.

16. Identify and express feelings toward individuals who have caused disappointment, hurt, or betrayal in the past. (29, 30)

29. Assign the client the task of writing a letter to an individual by whom he/she has felt betrayed or rejected in the past. Process the content of this letter in a therapy session and support expression of feelings.

30. Use the empty chair technique in assisting the client in expressing and working through feelings of anger, hurt, and sadness about past rejection, abandonment, neglect, or abuse experiences.

17. Identify targets of and causes for anger. (31, 32)

31. Give the client the homework assignment of listing triggers and targets of his/her anger, rage, or emotional pain. Review this list in a follow-up therapy session.

32. Explore the client's violent fantasies to help gain insight into the underlying emotions or unmet needs that contribute to the emergence of hostile or violent urges. Help him/her identify more adaptive ways to express anger and meet unmet needs.

18. Identify more adaptive coping strategies to effectively deal with anger, rage, or painful emotions. (33)

33. Teach the client effective coping strategies to help him/her learn more adaptive ways to express anger, rage, or painful emotions (e.g., taking a self-imposed time-out, counting to 10, deep breathing, and relaxation techniques, using "I" messages to express needs, etc.).

19. Caregivers provide empathy and support for the client's expression of emotions. (34, 35)

34. Conduct family therapy sessions to provide the client with the opportunity to openly share his/her feelings of anger, hurt, and sadness. Encourage or prompt the caregivers to provide empathy and support for the client in expressing his/her emotions.

35. Counsel the caregivers on how to respond to the client's feelings of anger, hurt, or alienation (e.g., setting aside one-to-one time to talk, demonstrating active listening, responding empathetically to feelings of sadness or hurt beneath the anger, showing nonacceptance of aggressive retaliation, scheduling outings, etc.).

20. Caregivers recognize early signs that the client is beginning to feel angry, hurt, or alienated. (36)

21. Caregivers structure increased time spent with family members in enjoyable or meaningful activities. (37, 38, 39, 40)

36. Educate the caregivers about detecting the early signs that the client is beginning to feel angry, sad, hurt, or alienated (e.g., spending increasingly more time alone in his/her room, questioning whether anyone cares, frequently overreacting to minor irritants, leaving notes around the home that communicate anger or painful emotions, identifying with aggressive ideas or people, collecting weapons, etc.).

37. Examine how the caregivers prioritize time spent in different activities (e.g., work, household responsibilities, family activities, social outings, or personal time). Point out the lack of a healthy balance to time allocation.

38. Assist the caregivers in achieving a healthy balance between fulfilling work or household responsibilities and meeting the social or emotional needs of the client and his/her siblings.

39. Instruct the caregivers to initiate weekly family meetings where the client and his/her siblings are free to openly discuss any concerns, problems, or issues affecting the family.

40. Encourage the parents to hold weekly "family nights" that allow the client to spend quality time with family members and help build closer family ties.

22. Increase the frequency of positive interactions with the caregivers or siblings. (40, 41, 42)

40. Encourage the parents to hold weekly "family nights" that allow the client to spend quality time with family members and help build closer family ties.

41. Encourage the caregivers to try to build a sense of belonging or family cohesion with the client by sharing stories or warm memories from his/her past (e.g., retelling humorous stories of the client's early childhood years, viewing family photographs, visiting old neighborhood, etc.).

42. Direct the caregivers to schedule regular family outings where the client is able to invite or bring along a friend.

23. Actively participate in a social skills training group. (43)

43. Arrange for the client to attend a social skills training group to improve his/her social skills. Direct him/her to self-disclose at least twice in each group therapy session.

24. Identify and implement positive social skills. (44, 45)

44. Use *Skillstreaming: The Adolescent Kit* (available from Childswork/Childsplay, LLC) to teach the client positive social skills.

45. Use therapeutic games to improve the client's social

skills, empathy, and morals reasoning (e.g., Odyssey Islands Game or the Helping, Sharing, Caring Game available from Childswork/ Childsplay, LLC).

25. Increase verbalizations and actions of empathy and sensitivity to the thoughts, feelings, and needs of others. (46, 47, 48, 49, 50)

46. Teach the client the value of demonstrating empathy and caring for others as a means to build lasting meaningful relationships.

47. Use the exercise entitled "Headed in the Right Direction" from *The Brief Adolescent Therapy Homework Planner* (Jongsma, Peterson, and McInnis) to increase the client's empathy and sensitivity to the thoughts, feelings, and needs of others.

48. Use role-playing and role-reversal techniques to help the client understand how his/her insensitive or acting-out behavior negatively affects others and to increase his/her empathy for another person's point of view.

49. Praise and reinforce the client when he/she is able to express tender emotions or demonstrate sensitivity to the thoughts, feelings, and needs of others.

50. Direct the client to engage in three altruistic acts (e.g., reading to developmentally disabled student, mowing an elderly neighbor's lawn, playing video games with a

younger sibling, etc.) before the next session to increase his/her empathy and sensitivity to the thoughts, feelings, and needs of others.

26. Initiate social interactions with peers on a regular basis. (51, 52, 53, 54)

51. Use the exercise entitled "Greeting Peers" from *The Brief Adolescent Therapy Homework Planner* (Jongsma, Peterson, and McInnis) to reduce the client's social isolation and to help him/her to begin to take steps toward establishing peer friendships.

52. Assign the client the task of initiating one social contact per day.

53. Give the client the homework assignment of initiating three phone calls weekly to different individuals to increase social interactions.

54. Give the client a directive to invite a friend for an overnight visit and/or to set up an overnight visit at friend's home. Process this experience with the client.

27. Identify and employ personal strengths or interests that help build connections with peers. (55, 56, 57)

55. Assign the exercise entitled "Show Your Strengths" from *The Brief Adolescent Therapy Homework Planner* (Jongsma, Peterson, and McInnis). Instruct the client to first iden-tify between 5 and 10 strengths or interests. Review this list in the following ses-sion, and encourage him/her

to use the strengths to initiate peer contacts and begin to establish friendships.

56. Instruct the client to create a collage or photo album, entitled *Who I Am,* that includes pictures of him/her engaging in different activities or interests. Review the album and encourage him/her to engage in similar interests or activities with family members or peers to feel more accepted.

57. Identify ways in which the client is both similar and different from peers. Reinforce positive ways that he/she is unique, while also encouraging him/her to share similar talents or interests with peers to deter social isolation and begin to establish meaningful relationships.

28. Identify constructive ways to build bridges to relationships with peers. (58)

58. Explore the client's fantasies about ways in which he/she would like to gain acceptance, affirmation, or recognition from peers. Identify constructive ways to gain acceptance and affirmation (e.g., complimenting others, actively participating in classroom discussions, attending pep rallies or extracurricular activities, etc.).

29. Identify effective strategies to cope with teasing, name-calling, harassment, or bullying from peers. (59, 60, 61)

59. Teach the client more adaptive coping strategies to deal with teasing, name-calling, or criticism from peers other than withdrawal or isolation for

long periods of time (e.g., ignore teasing and initiate conversation with other peers, talk privately with a peer who continuously teases him/her, use a school counselor or mediator to help resolve differences, etc.).

60. Challenge the client in gentle but firm manner not to over-personalize teasing or name-calling. Point out how overreacting or responding in an overly sensitive manner proves to be self-defeating and actually elicits further teasing or criticism from peers.

61. Help the client to realize that it is normal for all individuals to receive some teasing, name-calling, or criticism. Encourage him/her not to overreact or withdraw when he/she is the target of mildly insensitive or sarcastic remarks from peers.

30. Cooperate with an evaluation by a physician for psychotropic medication. (62)

62. Refer the client to a physician for a psychotropic medication evaluation to help stabilize moods and reduce depression, anxiety, or irritability.

31. Take medication as prescribed. (63)

63. Monitor the client for psychotropic medication compliance, effectiveness, and side effects.

___. _____   ___. _____
      _____   _____
___. _____   ___. _____
      _____   _____
___. _____   ___. _____
      _____   _____

DIAGNOSTIC SUGGESTIONS:

ICD-9-CM	_ICD-10-CM_	_DSM-5_ Disorder, Condition, or Problem
312.8	F91.x	Conduct Disorder
313.81	F91.3	Oppositional Defiant Disorder
296.xx	F32.x	Major Depressive Disorder, Single Episode
296.xx	F33.x	Major Depressive Disorder, Recurrent Episode
300.4	F34.1	Persistent Depressive Disorder
311	F32.9	Unspecified Depressive Disorder
311	F32.8	Other Specified Depressive Disorder
300.23	F40.10	Social Anxiety Disorder (Social Phobia)
V71.02	Z72.810	Adolescent Antisocial Behavior
995.53	T74.22XA	Child Sexual Abuse, Confirmed, Initial Encounter
995.53	T74.22XD	Child Sexual Abuse, Confirmed, Subsequent Encounter
V61.22	Z69.011	Encounter for Mental Health Services for Perpetrator of Parental Child Abuse
_____	_____	_____
_____	_____	_____

LOW SELF-ESTEEM

BEHAVIORAL DEFINITIONS

1. Feelings of inadequacy, insecurity, or worthlessness.
2. Low frustration tolerance; tendency to give up easily when frustrated or unsure of self.
3. Recurrent pattern of engaging in acting-out, aggressive, or antisocial behavior when self-esteem is challenged or threatened.
4. Associates with a negative peer group or gang as a means of seeking acceptance.
5. Projects an image of bravado and braggadocio to cover up feelings of insecurity.
6. Trouble asserting self, saying no to others, or resisting negative peer influences.
7. Frequent disparaging or negative comments about self.
8. Pervasive lack of confidence in abilities in several different areas of life.
9. Seeks excessive reassurance from others that he/she is liked, accepted, or admired.
10. Difficulty in accepting compliments from others.
11. Marked reluctance to assume healthy risks or take on responsibilities because of fear of failure or rejection.
12. Self-perception of being physically or socially unattractive.
13. Poor eye contact and excessive shrinking or avoidance of other adults and peers in social situations.
14. Acts out in negative ways to draw attention upon self or to elicit support from family members, peers, or significant others.
15. Defensively blames others for own faults, shortcomings, or failures and refuses to accept responsibility for misbehavior.

__. _____
   _____
__. _____

—. _____

   _____

   _____

LONG-TERM GOALS

1. Verbalize positive and affirmative self-descriptive statements on a regular basis and reduce the frequency of self-disparaging or self-doubting remarks.
2. Resist negative peer influences by effectively asserting self and refusing to become involved in acting-out or antisocial behaviors.
3. Terminate self-defeating behaviors that only serve to reinforce feelings of low self-esteem.
4. Resolve the core conflicts contributing to the feelings of low self-esteem and insecurity.
5. Establish and maintain a positive self-image.
6. Eliminate pattern of acting out or engaging in antisocial behaviors when self-esteem is challenged or threatened.
7. Develop the essential social skills that will enhance the quality of interpersonal relationships and maintain lasting friendships.

—. _____

   _____

   _____

—. _____

   _____

—. _____

   _____

SHORT-TERM OBJECTIVES

1. Establish a close, trusting relationship with the therapist and significant others, demonstrated by an open sharing of feelings. (1, 2)

THERAPEUTIC INTERVENTIONS

1. Actively build the level of trust with the client in individual sessions through consistent eye contact, active listening, unconditional positive regard, and warm acceptance to

improve his/her ability to identify and express feelings of inadequacy and insecurity or other painful emotions.

2. Encourage and support the client in sharing feelings of insecurity or other painful emotions in therapy sessions or around family members, peers, or close, trusted individuals to clarify them and help gain insight into the factors contributing to the emergence of his/her low self-esteem.

2. Verbalize reasonable and attainable personal goals. (3)

3. Assist the client in establishing reasonable and attainable personal goals that will help to improve his/her self-esteem.

3. Identify sources of low self-esteem and feelings of insecurity. (4, 5, 6)

4. Ask the client to make a list of what he/she feels insecure about. Review this list and identify the steps or specific actions that the client can take to overcome feelings of insecurity and increase confidence in self.

5. Explore past mistakes or failure experiences that contribute to feelings of low self-esteem. Help the client to realize how he/she can learn from past mistakes to build positive self-image and achieve success.

6. Instruct the client to keep a journal in which he/she records experiences or situations that produce feelings of low self-esteem, inadequacy, or insecurity. Process the content and help him/her express and work through feelings of inadequacy or insecurity.

4. Recognize and verbalize positive changes that are goals for self. (7, 8)

7. Design an action plan that identifies specific steps the client can take to achieve personal goals and improve self-esteem.

8. Use the homework assignment entitled "Three Ways to Change Yourself " from *The Brief Adolescent Therapy Homework Planner* (Jongsma, Peterson, and McInnis) to identify specific changes that the client would like to make with himself/herself. Help the client to identify steps that he/she can take to produce desired changes in self.

5. Identify and list strengths, interests, or positive attributes. (9, 10)

9. Give the client a homework assignment of identifying between 5 and 10 unique strengths, interests, or positive attributes. Review this list with the client in the following therapy session, and encourage him/her to utilize his/her strengths, interests, or positive attributes to build positive self-image.

10. Assign the client the homework assignment entitled "Symbols of Self-Worth" from *The Brief Adolescent Therapy Homework Planner* (Jongsma, Peterson, and McInnis). First, instruct the client to take an inventory of his/her strengths, interests, or accomplishments. Next, instruct him/her to bring objects or symbols to the next therapy session that represent his/her strengths or interests. Encourage him/her to use

strengths or interests to build self-esteem.

6. Identify and implement effective strategies to improve self-esteem. (11, 12)

11. Assign the client to view the video entitled *10 Ways to Boost Low Self-Esteem* (available from The Guidance Channel) to learn effective strategies to elevate self-esteem and increase confidence in self.

12. Instruct the client to complete the exercise entitled "Self-Esteem—What Is It? How Do I Get It?" from *Ten Days to Self-Esteem* (Burns) to help increase his/her self-esteem.

7. Increase the frequency of positive self-descriptive statements. (13, 14)

13. Encourage the client to use positive self-talk (e.g., I am capable; I can do this; I can be kind; I can dance well; etc.) as a means of increasing his/her confidence and developing positive self-image.

14. Instruct the client to make three positive statements about himself/herself daily and record them in a journal. Review and reinforce these journal entries in follow-up therapy sessions.

8. Verbally acknowledge and accept compliments from others. (15)

15. Challenge the client to cease the pattern of denying his/her personal strengths or minimizing his/her accomplishments when others offer verbal praise and compliments. Reinforce his/her acceptance of compliments.

9. Decrease the frequency of self-disparaging or self-doubting remarks. (16)

16. Assist the client in developing an awareness of how his/her frequent disparaging or doubting remarks about himself/her-

self are self-defeating, as they reinforce feelings of low self-esteem and cause others to view him/her in a negative light.

10. Verbalize a healthy acceptance and tolerance for personal weaknesses, imperfections, limitations, and failures. (17, 18, 19)

17. Inform the client that he/she is not alone in experiencing feelings of insecurity and that all individuals feel some insecurity from time to time.

18. Use modeling and role-playing techniques to demonstrate how the client can face his/her insecurities and successfully manage his/her problems or stressors. Help the client to realize that self-esteem improves when one faces insecurities and successfully manages life's stressors.

19. Assist the client in developing a healthy acceptance or tolerance of his/her weaknesses, imperfections, limitations, or failures.

11. Increase eye contact with others. (20)

20. Draw attention to the client's poor eye contact. Encourage him/her to display good eye contact to convey confidence in himself/herself and to show interest in or caring for others.

12. Verbally identify the connection between acting-out or antisocial behaviors and unmet needs or feelings of low self-esteem, inadequacy, and insecurity. (21, 22)

21. Explore what needs the client is attempting to meet through his acting-out or antisocial behavior. Assist him/her in identifying more adaptive ways to meet his/her needs other than through engaging in acting-out or antisocial behavior.

22. Help the client to discover for himself/herself how involvement in antisocial behavior proves to be self-defeating as it fails to meet deeper needs and only serves to reinforce his/her feelings of low self-esteem because of the negative consequences that antisocial behavior produces for himself/herself and others.

13. Use mediational and self-control strategies to reduce the frequency of acting-out or antisocial behaviors. (23)

23. Teach mediational and self-control strategies (e.g., "stop, look, listen, and think"; count to 10; relaxation; deep breathing techniques, etc.) to help the client to control impulses to act out or engage in antisocial behavior when self-esteem is challenged or threatened.

14. Caregivers establish clearly defined rules and follow through consistently with consequences for antisocial behavior. (24, 25, 26)

24. Assist the client's caregivers in establishing clearly defined (and written) rules and consequences for acting-out and antisocial behavior. Inform the client and have him/her repeat the rules or consequences to demonstrate that he/she understands the expectations.

25. Design a reward system and/or contingency contract for the client to reinforce positive behaviors that help to build self-esteem and deter acting-out or antisocial behavior.

26. Encourage and challenge the caregivers not to protect the client from the natural or legal consequences of his/her antisocial behavior or allow his/her feelings of low self-esteem to be used as an excuse

15. Caregivers increase the frequency of praise and positive reinforcement for the client's prosocial or responsible behaviors. (27, 28)

or justification for his/her illegal activities.

27. Encourage the caregivers and teachers to provide frequent praise and positive reinforcement for the client's prosocial and responsible behavior to help him/her develop a positive self-image.

28. Instruct the caregivers to observe and record between three and five positive responsible behaviors by the client before the next therapy session. Review these behaviors in the next session, and encourage the client to continue engaging in these behaviors to boost his/her self-esteem.

16. Comply with all conditions of probation or mandates from the criminal justice system. (29, 30)

29. Consult with the probation officer and criminal justice officials about the appropriate consequences for the client's antisocial behavior (e.g., paying restitution, community service, probation, confinement in detention center, etc.).

30. Inform the probation officer about the presence of the client's low self-esteem. Recommend that the client's participation in outpatient therapy or compliance with taking his/her medication to stabilize moods or improve impulse control be a mandatory condition of his/her probation.

17. Offer apologies to the victim(s) of antisocial behavior. (31)

31. Direct the client to offer a verbal or written apology to the

18. Report a reduction in feelings of guilt after engaging in constructive or responsible actions. (32)

victim(s) or target(s) of his/her acting-out or antisocial behavior.

32. Encourage the client to deal with his/her feelings of guilt in an appropriate manner by accepting responsibility for his/her antisocial behaviors, and identify constructive steps that he/she can take to undo past wrongdoings.

19. Family members identify conflicts or stressors that contribute to the client's low self-esteem and/or antisocial behavior. (33, 34, 35)

33. Conduct family therapy sessions to identify possible sources of stress or conflict in the family system that contribute to the emergence of the client's low self-esteem and acting-out or antisocial behavior.

34. Use a family sculpting technique in which the client defines the roles of each family member in a scene of his/her choosing to assess possible family dynamics that may contribute to his/her feelings of low self-esteem and acting-out behavior.

35. Hold family therapy sessions to explore whether caregivers' overly rigid style of parenting (e.g., criticalness, overprotectiveness, setting harsh or severe limits for minor offences, refusal to allow the client a healthy degree of autonomy, etc.) contributes to his/her feelings of low self-esteem and the desire to rebel against rigid rules or boundaries.

20. Caregivers establish realistic expectations of the client's abilities. (36)

36. Observe parent-client interactions to determine whether the caregivers have developed unrealistic expectations and/or are placing excessive pressure on the client to perform. Assist the caregivers, if necessary, in establishing more realistic expectations of the client's abilities in different areas (e.g., academics, athletics, musical, artistic activities, etc.).

21. Caregivers cease making overly hostile, critical remarks, and increase positive messages to the client. (37, 38)

37. Confront and challenge the caregivers to cease making overly hostile or critical remarks about the client or his/her behavior that only reinforce his/her feelings of low self-esteem. Encourage the caregivers to verbalize the positive, specific behaviors or changes that they would like to see the client make.

38. Teach the client and his/her caregivers effective communication skills (e.g., active listening, "I" messages, avoid blaming statements, identify specific positive changes that other family members can make, etc.) to improve the lines of communication, facilitate closer family ties, and resolve conflict more constructively.

22. Increase time spent with the uninvolved or detached caregivers in recreational, leisure, school, or work activities. (39, 40, 41)

39. Assess whether the client's acting-out or antisocial behavior serves as a cry for help and maladaptive way to gain attention from uninvolved or detached caregivers.

40. Give a directive to the uninvolved or detached caregiver(s) to spend more time with the client in recreational, leisure, school, or work activities (e.g., going on an outdoor hike, attending a community festival, preparing and serving dessert for other family members, etc.). Monitor the caregiver's progress in making this change.

41. Encourage the caregivers to involve the client in extracurricular or social activities (e.g., sports, music, church youth groups, enrichment programs, experiential camps, etc.) that help to build his/her self-esteem and deter him/her from engaging in acting-out or antisocial behaviors.

23. Attend group therapy sessions focused on building social skills and self-esteem. (42)

42. Refer the client for group therapy to improve self-esteem and social skills. Give the client a directive to self-disclose at least twice at each group therapy session.

24. Participate regularly in positive peer group or extracurricular activities to improve self-esteem, and deter involvement in acting-out or antisocial behavior.
(43, 44, 45, 46)

43. Teach the client positive social skills (e.g., demonstrating active listening, complimenting others, verbalizing empathy or concern for others' problems, etc.) to help him/her achieve a sense of acceptance or belonging with peers.

44. Assist the client in identifying more constructive ways to earn peer approval and acceptance other than affiliating

with negative peer groups who influence him/her to act out or engage in antisocial behavior (e.g., trying out for school play, attending a school dance, joining a school choir, attending weekend sporting events, etc.).

45. Encourage the client to attend an experiential camp or participate in structured outdoor activities (e.g., canoeing, whitewater rafting, rock climbing, camping, etc.) to provide him/her with an opportunity to build self-esteem, develop increased confidence in himself/herself, and establish trust in others.

46. Help the client to identify healthy risks that he/she can take in the near future to improve his/her self-esteem (e.g., trying out for a sports team, attending new social functions or gatherings, initiating conversations with unfamiliar people, etc.). Challenge the client to take three healthy risks before the next therapy session.

25. Identify resource people who can be relied on for support or comfort when needed. (47)

47. Help the client to identify a list of resource people at school, church, or in the community to whom he/she can turn for emotional support and comfort instead of continuing to act out in an antisocial manner as a means to gain attention, approval, or recognition.

26. Express feelings and identify needs through artwork or music. (48, 49)

48. Employ art therapy techniques (e.g., drawing, painting, sculpting, etc.) to help the client express feelings about himself/herself and identify his/her needs.

49. Have the client sing a song, play an instrument, or bring in a recording of a song that reflects his/her feelings of insecurity or inadequacy. Use this song as a springboard to discuss factors that contribute to his/her feelings of insecurity and/or identify effective ways to improve self-esteem.

27. Complete evaluation or assessment procedures. (50, 51)

50. Arrange for psychological testing to assess the client's self-esteem and determine whether he/she has a depressive or anxiety disorder that contributes to feelings of insecurity or acting-out behavior. Provide feedback on evaluation findings to the client, caregivers, probation officer, or court officials.

51. Explore the client's substance abuse pattern or arrange for an evaluation to assess whether the client's feelings of low self-esteem have contributed to the development of a substance abuse problem. Refer the client for treatment if indicated. (See the chapter

entitled "Substance Abuse" in this Planner.)

—. _____   —. _____
     _____   _____
—. _____   —. _____
     _____   _____
—. _____   —. _____
     _____   _____

DIAGNOSTIC SUGGESTIONS:

ICD-9-CM	*ICD-10-CM*	*DSM-5* Disorder, Condition, or Problem
300.4	F34.1	Persistent Depressive Disorder
296.xx	F32.x	Major Depressive Disorder, Single Episode
296.xx	F33.x	Major Depressive Disorder, Recurrent Episode
311	F32.9	Unspecified Depressive Disorder
311	F32.8	Other Specified Depressive Disorder
300.02	F41.1	Generalized Anxiety Disorder
300.23	F40.10	Social Anxiety Disorder (Social Phobia)
314.01	F90.1	Attention-Deficit/Hyperactivity Disorder, Predominately Hyperactive /Impulsive Presentation

312.8	F91.x	Conduct Disorder
313.81	F91.3	Oppositional Defiant Disorder
317	F70	Intellectual Disability, Mild
V62.89	R41.83	Borderline Intellectual Functioning
_____	_____	_____
_____	_____	_____

PEER CONFLICT

BEHAVIORAL DEFINITIONS

1. Physical fighting or acts of aggression with peers.
2. Persistent pattern of taunting, intimidating, or threatening peers.
3. Frequent arguments or disputes with peers.
4. Antagonistic, annoying, and provocative behavior (e.g., incessant teasing, name-calling, negative attention-seeking behavior, etc.) that places strain on peer relationships.
5. Repeatedly exploits, manipulates, or cons peers to meet own needs.
6. Poor frustration tolerance; easily angered or annoyed by minor stressors or irritants involving peers.
7. Acts of violence or aggression toward peers that arise out of gang involvement or affiliation with negative peer groups.
8. Poor social skills; repeated failure to perceive important social cues or interpersonal nuances that are needed to establish friendships.
9. Self-centeredness, sense of entitlement, and extreme braggadocio that interferes with the ability to establish and maintain friendships.
10. Displays lack of empathy and cool indifference to the thoughts, feelings, needs, and rights of others.
11. Repeated pattern of blaming others for interpersonal problems and/or unwillingness to examine his/her role or contribution to any disputes or conflict with peers.
12. History of harboring grudges and being spiteful or vindictive.
13. Numerous complaints of being mistreated, criticized unfairly, or ostracized by peers.

—. _____
   _____
—. _____
   _____

—. _____
    _____

LONG-TERM GOALS

1. Interact consistently with peers in a mutually respectful and cooperative manner.
2. Significantly reduce the frequency of annoying, antagonistic, or manipulative behavior toward peers.
3. Eliminate all acts of physical aggression, violence, or cruelty toward peers.
4. Develop healthy coping mechanisms and problem-solving skills that lead to the successful resolution to conflict and disputes with peers.
5. Demonstrate a marked improvement in the ability to listen and respond emphatically to the thoughts, feelings, and needs of others.
6. Terminate involvement with gang-related or negative peer group activities.

—. _____
    _____

—. _____
    _____

—. _____
    _____

SHORT-TERM OBJECTIVES

1. Share thoughts and feelings about peer relationships. (1, 2)

THERAPEUTIC INTERVENTIONS

1. Explore the client's perception of the nature of his/her peer relationships, as well as areas of conflict. Assess the degree of the client's denial regarding conflict and projection of responsibility for conflict onto others.

2. Gather a detailed psychosocial history of the client's

development, family environment, and interpersonal relationships to gain insight into the factors contributing to the emergence of his/her strained or conflictual peer relationships.

2. Keep a journal of experiences with peers. (3)

3. Ask the client to keep a daily journal where he/she records both positive and negative experiences with peers that evoked strong emotions. Process excerpts from this journal in follow-up sessions to uncover factors that contribute to peer conflict, as well as identify strengths that the client can use to build positive peer relationships.

3. Caregivers and teachers establish clearly identified rules and consequences for the client's annoying, antagonistic, aggressive, or manipulative behavior. (4, 5, 6)

4. Instruct the caregivers to maintain regular communication with school officials to monitor the client's relationship with peers. Encourage the caregivers to follow through with firm, consistent limits if the client engages in annoying, antagonistic, or aggressive behavior with peers at school.

5. Assist the caregivers and teachers in establishing clearly defined rules and consequences for the client's annoying, antagonistic, aggressive, or manipulative behavior. Have the client repeat the rules to demonstrate that he/she understands the expectations.

4. Caregivers and teachers implement a reward system or contingency contract to reinforce the client's prosocial behavior and deter annoying, aggressive, or manipulative behavior. (7, 8)

6. Establish a contingency contract with the client, caregivers, and teachers that clearly defines the consequences the client will receive if he/she engages in annoying, aggressive, or manipulative behavior.

7. Encourage the caregivers and teachers to offer frequent praise and positive reinforcement to the client when he/she exercises good self-control or engages in prosocial behavior (e.g., verbalizing empathy or concern, complimenting others, and demonstrating acts of kindness).

8. Assist the caregivers in designing and implementing a reward system to reinforce the client's positive social behavior and deter impulsive, antagonistic, or aggressive behavior toward peers.

5. Decrease the frequency of annoying, antagonistic, aggressive, or manipulative behavior. (9, 10, 11, 12)

9. Teach the client to use a self-monitoring checklist at school to improve peer relationships and to deter the impulse to annoy or antagonize peers. Ask the client to select a specific behavior (e.g., name-calling, teasing, taunting, etc.), and monitor behavior by using a self-recording form.

10. Direct the caregivers and teachers to assign a consequence where the client performs an act of kindness or assumes a responsibility for a peer to undo the effects of

his/her annoying, antagonistic, aggressive, or manipulative behavior.

11. Disrupt the pattern of the client annoying or antagonizing peers by prescribing the symptom. Allow the client to exhibit the annoying or antagonistic behavior for five minutes daily without suffering consequences. Intervention seeks to reduce the client's need to annoy or antagonize others.

12. Provide feedback to the client on any negative social behavior that interferes with his/her ability to establish and maintain friendships.

6. Identify the negative consequences that annoying, antagonistic, aggressive, or manipulative behavior has on self and others. (13, 14)

13. Have the client list be-tween 5 and 10 negative consequences that his/her annoying, antagonistic, aggressive, or manipulative behavior has had on others.

14. Firmly confront the client about the impact of his/her annoying, antagonistic, aggressive, or manipulative behavior, pointing out consequences for himself/herself and others.

7. Increase the number of statements that reflect an acceptance of responsibility for negative social behavior. (15, 16)

15. Confront the statements in which the client blames other peers for his/her annoying, antagonistic, or aggressive behavior and fails to accept responsibility for his/her actions.

16. Challenge and confront statements by the client that minimize the effect of his/her annoying, antagonistic, or aggressive actions on others.

8. Offer an apology to peers for annoying, antagonistic, or aggressive behavior. (17)

17. Instruct the client to apologize to peer(s) for his/her annoying, antagonistic, aggressive, or manipulative behavior.

9. Implement effective coping strategies to help induce calm, control anger, or resist urge to tease or antagonize peers. (18, 19, 20)

18. Teach mediational and self-control techniques (e.g., "stop, look, listen, and think"; count to 10; walk away; listen to music, etc.) to help the client express anger through appropriate verbalizations or resist the urge to tease or antagonize others.

19. Train the client in the use of progressive relaxation or guided imagery techniques to help him/her induce calm, establish greater self-control, or decrease the intensity of angry feelings when irritated by peers.

20. Use role-playing, modeling, or behavioral rehearsal techniques to teach the client more effective ways to meet his/her needs or resolve conflict with peers.

10. Identify and implement effective conflict-resolution strategies. (21, 22, 23, 24)

21. Explore previous arguments with peers or siblings that the client was able to resolve successfully without yelling, screaming, cursing, or fighting. Process the client's positive experiences and

encourage him/her to use similar coping strategies to resolve current conflicts or disputes with peers.

22. Teach the client effective conflict resolution skills (i.e., identify the problem, brainstorm solutions, select an option, implement a course of action, and evaluate) to help decrease the frequency and intensity of arguments with peers.

23. Use The Social Conflict Game (Berg) to teach the client effective conflict resolution skills.

24. Use therapeutic games (e.g., The Angry Monster Machine by Shapiro or Anger Control by Berg) to help the younger client learn to express anger through more appropriate verbalizations and healthy physical outlets.

11. Identify peaceful resolutions or compromises to end ongoing arguments or disputes with peers. (25, 26, 27, 28, 29)

25. Assign the client to view the video entitled *Classroom Conflicts: Teen Guide to Resolving Disputes and Arguments* (available through the Guidance Channel) to teach him/her effective strategies to resolve conflict with peers.

26. Instruct the client to complete the homework assignment entitled "Negotiating a Peace Treaty" from *The Brief Adolescent Therapy Homework Planner* (Jongsma, Peterson, and McInnis) to help him/her to learn more

effective ways to resolve conflict with peers and siblings using compromise.

27. Teach the client the value of seeking compromise as a way to peacefully resolve differences with peers.

28. Praise and reinforce the client when he/she is able to resolve conflict and/or reach compromises with peers without responding in a verbally or physically aggressive manner.

29. Recommend that school officials use a mediator (e.g., social worker, school psychologist, guidance counselor, teacher, etc.) to hold a meeting with the client and other peer(s) with whom he/she has experienced ongoing conflict. Meeting seeks to terminate ongoing conflict by allowing each individual to express his/her feelings in a controlled manner and offer solutions to problems.

12. Identify and express feelings that are associated with past abuse, trauma, or rejection experiences. (30, 31, 32, 33)

30. Assist the client in making a connection between underlying, painful emotions (e.g., depression, anxiety, helplessness, insecurity, etc.) and antagonistic, aggressive, or manipulative behavior with peers.

31. Probe the client's background for past history of abuse,

trauma, or rejection experiences. Encourage and support him/her in expressing his/her feelings about the past painful experiences.

32. Encourage and support the client in expressing feelings or sharing memories about past violent acts that he/she has experienced or observed at home or in the community (e.g., physical abuse, spousal abuse, drive-by shootings, violent robberies, etc.). Assist him/her in making a connection between painful emotions and his/her bullying or aggressive behavior toward peers and others. (See the chapter entitled "Family Instability/Conflict" in this Planner.)

33. Assign the client the task of writing a letter to past perpetrators of violence, or use the empty chair technique to assist him/her in expressing feelings of anger, hurt, and sadness about past violent incidents.

13. Recognize and list causes of alienation or rejection by peers. (34, 35)

34. Examine the client's past rejection experiences by peers and the possible causes of rejection or alienation (e.g., hypersensitivity to teasing, target of scapegoating, poor social skills, etc.).

35. Use role-playing and modeling techniques with the client

who feels alienated and rejected to teach effective ways to deal with criticism, name-calling, or teasing from peers.

14. Attend and regularly partici- pate in group therapy sessions that are focused on learning social skills. (36, 37)

36. Refer the client for group therapy to improve social skills. Direct him/her to self- disclose at least two times in each group therapy session about his/her peer relation- ships.

37. Refer the client to a behavioral contracting group where he/she and other group members develop contracts each week to increase the frequency of positive peer interactions. Review progress with the contracts each week, and praise the client for achieving goals regarding peer interactions.

15. Identify and implement posi- tive social skills that will help to improve peer relationships. (38, 39, 40)

38. Teach positive social skills (e.g., compliment others, ignore teasing, use "I" messages when dealing with conflict, verbalize empathy and concern for others, etc.) to improve peer relationships.

39. Use *Skillstreaming: The Adolescent Kit* (available from Childswork/Childsplay, LLC) to teach the client positive social skills.

40. Play The Odyssey Islands Game (available from Childswork/Childsplay, LLC) in therapy session to improve

the client's social, moral, and problem-solving skills.

16. Increase involvement in positive social activities or community organizations. (41, 42)

41. Encourage the client to become involved in positive peer groups or community activities where he/she can gain acceptance and status (e.g., church or synagogue youth group, school clubs, Boys Clubs or Girls Club, Big Brothers or Big Sisters, etc.). Direct the client to use facilities in the community to provide opportunity to engage in enjoyable or meaningful social activities (e.g., playing basketball in high school gym, joining Boys Club or Girls Club, attending YWCA or YMCA functions, etc.).

42. Explore periods of time in the past when the client established positive peer relationships and participated in meaningful social activities. Process the client's responses, and encourage him/her to engage in social behavior or activities to establish peer friendships in the present.

17. Identify and list resource people to whom the client can turn for support, comfort, and guidance. (43)

43. Help the client to identify a list of resource people, both peer and adult, at school or in the community to whom he/she can turn for support, comfort, or guidance when faced with interpersonal conflict or rejection by peers.

18. Increase verbalizations of empathy and concern toward peers. (44, 45, 46)

44. Use the Helping, Sharing, Caring Game (Gardner) in therapy sessions to improve the client's empathy and sensitivity to thoughts, feelings, and needs of others.

45. Use the exercise entitled "Headed in the Right Direction" from *The Brief Adolescent Therapy Homework Planner* (Jongsma, Peterson, and McInnis) to increase the client's empathy and sensitivity to the thoughts, feelings, and needs of others.

46. Give the client a homework assignment of engaging in three altruistic or benevolent acts with peers before the next therapy session. Process how others responded to acts of kindness, and encourage the client to engage in similar behavior in the future.

19. Identify and implement positive ways to meet needs other than through gang involvement. (47, 48)

47. Brainstorm with the client more adaptive ways for him/her to meet needs for recognition/status, acceptance, money, and excitement other than through his/her involvement with gangs or gang activity. (See the chapter entitled "Gang Involvement" in this Planner).

48. Assign the client to view the video entitled *Handling Peer Pressure and Gangs* (part of Peace Talks series available through the Guidance

Channel) to help the client
resist negative peer influences
or pressure to join a gang.

—. _____   —. _____
   _____   _____
—. _____   —. _____
   _____   _____
—. _____   —. _____
   _____   _____

DIAGNOSTIC SUGGESTIONS:

ICD-9-CM	_ICD-10-CM_	_DSM-5_ Disorder, Condition, or Problem
313.81	F91.3	Oppositional Defiant Disorder
312.8	F91.x	Conduct Disorder
312.9	F91.9	Unspecified Disruptive, Impulse Control, and Conduct Disorder
312.89	F91.8	Other Specified Disruptive, Impulse Control, and Conduct Disorder
314.01	F90.1	Attention-Deficit/Hyperactivity Disorder, Predominately Hyperactive /Impulsive Presentation
314.01	F90.9	Unspecified Attention-Deficit/Hyperactivity Disorder
314.01	F90.8	Other Specified Attention-Deficit/Hyperactivity Disorder
V71.02	Z72.810	Adolescent Antisocial Behavior
_____	_____	_____
_____	_____	_____

PHYSICAL ABUSE VICTIM

BEHAVIORAL DEFINITIONS

1. Confirmed self-report or account by others of having been assaulted (e.g., hit, burned, kicked, slapped, or tortured) by an older person.
2. Physical signs of abuse (e.g., bruises, cuts, lacerations, or broken bones).
3. Recurrent and intrusive distressing recollections, accompanied by flashbacks, of the physical abuse.
4. Pronounced disturbance of mood and affect (e.g., frequent and prolonged periods of depression, irritability, or anxiety).
5. Sleep disturbance (e.g., difficulty falling asleep, early morning awakenings, refusal to sleep alone, night terrors, recurrent distressing nightmares, etc.).
6. Marked fearfulness and feelings of helplessness or powerlessness when coming into contact with the perpetrator.
7. Significant increase in the frequency and severity of aggressive, acting-out, or antisocial behavior after the onset of the physical abuse.
8. Intense feelings of anger and rage about the physical abuse.
9. Strong interest in or preoccupation with violence or aggression.
10. Deep mistrust of others as manifested by social withdrawal and problems with establishing and maintaining close interpersonal relationships.
11. Appearance of regressive behaviors (e.g., thumb sucking, infantile or childlike talk, bed wetting, etc.).
12. Running away from home to avoid further physical abuse.

—. _____

_____

—. _____

—. _____

   _____

   _____

LONG-TERM GOALS

1. Terminate all physical abuse.
2. Escape from the environment where the abuse is occurring and move to a safe haven.
3. Rebuild a sense of self-worth and overcome the overwhelming feelings of fear, helplessness, or vulnerability.
4. Caregivers establish limits on the punishment of the client such that no physical harm can occur and respect for his/her rights is maintained.
5. Resolve the feelings surrounding the physical abuse, resulting in an ability to establish and maintain close interpersonal relationships.
6. Terminate pattern of engaging in aggressive, acting-out, or antisocial behavior.
7. Client and his/her family eliminate denial, placing responsibility for the abuse on the perpetrator and allowing the client to feel supported.
8. Build self-esteem and a sense of empowerment as manifested by an increased number of positive self-descriptive statements and greater participation in extracurricular activities.

—. _____

   _____

—. _____

   _____

—. _____

   _____

SHORT-TERM OBJECTIVES

1. Tell the entire account of the history of the physical abuse. (1, 2, 3)

THERAPEUTIC INTERVENTIONS

1. Actively build the level of trust in individual sessions through consistent eye

contact, active listening, unconditional positive regard, and warm acceptance to help increase his/her ability to identify and express feelings that are connected to the physical abuse.

2. Gather a detailed psychosocial history of the client's physical abuse, including age of onset, frequency, severity, precipitating stressors, sequence of events leading up to the abuse, and extent of physical abuse within the family system. Allow the client to express feelings while sharing relevant details.

3. Explore, encourage, and support the client in verbally expressing and clarifying the facts that are associated with the abuse.

2. Agree to the need for protective boundaries for protection from further abuse. (4, 5, 6, 7)

4. Assess whether the perpetrator or the client should be removed from the home.

5. Implement the necessary steps (e.g., removal of the client from the home, removal of the perpetrator from the home) to protect the client and other children in the home from future physical abuse.

6. Empower the client by identifying the steps (e.g., phone numbers to call, safe place to go, asking for temporary alternate placement, etc.) that may be taken to protect himself/herself from future occurrences of physical abuse.

7. Reassure the client repeatedly of the concern and caring on the part of the therapist and others who will protect him/her from any further abuse.

3. Perpetrator complies with court mandates about whether to leave or remain in the home. (5)

5. Implement the necessary steps (e.g., removal of the client from the home, removal of the perpetrator from the home) to protect the client and other children in the home from future physical abuse.

4. Identify and express thoughts and feelings connected to the abuse. (8, 9, 10, 11, 12)

8. Explore, encourage, and support the client in expressing thoughts and feelings about perpetrator, himself/herself, and physical abuse.

9. Use the homework assignment entitled "Take the First Step" from *The Brief Adolescent Therapy Homework Planner* (Jongsma, Peterson, and McInnis) to identify steps that the client can take to protect himself/herself from abuse, share thoughts and feelings about how physical abuse has affected his/her life, and begin to reduce feelings of anger, shame, or guilt.

10. Assign the client the homework assignment entitled "My Thoughts and Feelings" from *The Brief Adolescent Therapy Homework Planner* (Jongsma, Peterson, and McInnis) to help establish rapport in the beginning stages of therapy and to

facilitate the expression of feelings about family members or individuals associated with the physical abuse.

11. Encourage the nonabusive caregiver to provide opportunities (e.g., family meetings) to allow the client and his/her siblings to express feelings about the physical abuse and subsequent changes that have occurred within the family system.

12. Give the client a homework assignment of listing how physical abuse has impacted his/her life. Process this list in follow-up therapy sessions.

5. Verbalize and list the ways in which physical abuse has impacted life. (9, 12)

9. Use the homework assignment entitled "Take the First Step" from *The Brief Adolescent Therapy Homework Planner* (Jongsma, Peterson, and McInnis) to identify steps that the client can take to protect himself/herself from abuse, share thoughts and feelings about how physical abuse has affected his/her life, and begin to reduce feelings of anger, shame, or guilt.

12. Give the client a homework assignment of listing how physical abuse has impacted his/her life. Process this list in follow-up therapy sessions.

6. Affirm the perpetrator as being responsible for the physical abuse. (13, 14, 15)

13. Actively confront and challenge denial about the physical abuse by the perpetrator within the entire family system.

14. Challenge or confront statements by the perpetrator, caregiver(s), or family members that project the blame or responsibility for the physical abuse onto the client or other siblings.

15. Reinforce any and all statements by the client that place the responsibility for the abuse clearly on the perpetrator, regardless of any misbehavior by the client.

7. Terminate verbalizations of excuses for the perpetrator. (15, 16, 17, 18)

15. Reinforce any and all statements by the client that place the responsibility for the abuse clearly on the perpetrator, regardless of any misbehavior by the client.

16. Challenge and confront statements by the client where he/she makes excuses for the perpetrator's abuse and accepts blame for it.

17. Reassure the client that he/she did not deserve the physical abuse, but that he/she deserves respect and a controlled response, even when behavior warrants discipline or punishment.

18. Use the homework assignment entitled "Letter of Empowerment" from *The Brief*

Adolescent Therapy Homework Planner (Jongsma, Peterson, and McInnis) to help the client express his/her feelings toward the perpetrator. Process this letter in a follow-up therapy session, and empower the client by affirming the perpetrator as being responsible for the physical abuse.

8. The perpetrator takes responsibility for the abuse. (19, 20, 21)

19. Conduct family therapy sessions where the caregivers affirm the client and his/her siblings as not being responsible for the physical abuse. Assist the client and other family members in verbalizing that the perpetrator is responsible for abuse.

20. Hold a family therapy session where the client and/or therapist confront the perpetrator with the abuse.

21. Conduct an apology session where the perpetrator identifies himself/herself as being responsible for the physical abuse, apologizes to the client and/or other family members, and pledges respect for disciplinary boundaries.

9. The perpetrator pledges respect for disciplinary boundaries. (21)

21. Conduct an apology session where the perpetrator identifies himself/herself as being responsible for the physical abuse, apologizes to the client and/or other family members, and pledges respect for disciplinary boundaries.

10. The perpetrator agrees to seek treatment. (22)

22. Require the perpetrator to attend anger management group or classes. Make cooperation with treatment a requirement of the court.

11. The caregivers verbalize the establishment of appropriate parent-child boundaries and use of effective, nonharmful disciplinary techniques. (23, 24, 25)

23. Counsel the client's caregivers about establishing appropriate parent-child boundaries and using effective, nonharmful disciplinary techniques.

24. Assign readings to the caregivers that teach effective and nonharmful ways to discipline the client and siblings (e.g., *Common Sense Parenting: A Proven Step-By-Step Guide for Raising Responsible Kids and Creating Happy Families* by Burke and Herron; *1-2-3 Magic* by Phelan; *Parenting Teens with Love and Logic* by Fay and Cline; and *Good Kids, Difficult Behavior: A Guide to What Works and What Doesn't* by Divinyi and Fallon).

25. Ask the caregivers to list appropriate means of discipline or correction. Reinforce reasonable actions and appropriate boundaries that reflect the rights and feelings of the client.

12. Family members identify dynamics, stressors, or precipitating events that contributed to the emergence of physical abuse. (26, 27)

26. Conduct family therapy sessions to assess the dynamics, stressors, or precipitating events that contributed to the emergence of the physical abuse.

27. Construct a multigenerational family genogram that identifies physical abuse within the extended family to help the perpetrator recognize the cycle of violence.

13. The nonabusive caregiver and other key family members provide consistent support, affirmation, and nurturance for the client. (28, 29)

28. Hold individual therapy sessions with the nonabusive caregiver to explore possible reasons for failing to detect early signs of physical abuse or taking steps to protect the client and his/her siblings from ongoing abuse.

29. Elicit and reinforce support and nurturance for the client from other key family members.

14. Nonabusive parent spends more quality time with the client. (29, 30)

29. Elicit and reinforce support and nurturance for the client from other key family members.

30. Direct the disengaged, nonabusive caregiver to spend more time with the client in leisure, school, or household activities to stabilize the client's moods and improve his/her behavior.

15. Express feelings regarding the physical abuse through journaling, psychodrama, and letter writing. (31, 32, 33, 34)

31. Instruct the client to keep a journal where he/she expresses thoughts and feelings about the physical abuse. Process excerpts from this journal in follow-up therapy sessions to provide the client with the opportunity to express painful emotions, decrease the intensity of feelings, and stabilize moods.

32. Use the empty chair technique to assist the client in expressing and working through his/her myriad of feelings toward the perpetrator and other family members or key figures connected to the physical abuse.

33. Use psychodrama techniques whereby the client creates a scene of his/her choosing in a therapy session to verbalize feelings of anger, hurt, and sadness toward the perpetrator about how physical abuse has impacted his/her life.

34. Instruct the client to write an angry letter to the perpetrator to help decrease the intensity of his/her hostility or rage. Process this letter in a therapy session.

16. Express feelings about physical abuse through mutual storytelling techniques and play therapy interventions. (35, 36, 37)

35. Use the Angry Tower technique (see *101 Play Therapy Techniques* by Saxe) to help the younger client identify and express feelings of anger about physical abuse—build a tower out of plastic containers, place a small item (representing the perpetrator) on top of the tower, then instruct the client to throw a small fabric ball at the tower while verbalizing anger.

36. Employ the Color-Your-Life technique (O'Connor) to improve the younger client's ability to identify and verbalize feelings associated with physical abuse. Ask the client

to match colors to different emotions (e.g., red—anger, purple—very angry, blue—sad, black—very sad, etc.) and then fill up a blank page with colors that reflect his/her feelings about physical abuse.

37. Use a mutual storytelling technique where the younger client and therapist alternate telling stories through the use of puppets and stuffed animals. The therapist first models constructive steps to take to protect himself/herself and feel empowered, then the client follows by creating a story with similar characters or themes.

17. Express feelings about physical abuse through art therapy techniques. (38, 39, 40)

38. Employ art therapy techniques (e.g., drawing, painting, sculpting, etc.) to help the client identify and express his/her feelings toward the perpetrator.

39. Instruct the client to create a drawing or sculpture that reflects how physical abuse has impacted his/her life and feelings about himself/herself.

40. Ask the client to draw pictures of his/her own face that represent how he/she felt about himself/herself before, during, and after the abuse occurred.

18. Express forgiveness of the perpetrator and others connected with the physical abuse, while insisting on respect for own right to safety in the future. (41)

41. Assign the client to write a forgiveness letter and/or complete a forgiveness exercise in which he/she verbalizes forgiveness to the perpetrator

19. Decrease the statements of being a victim while increasing statements that reflect personal empowerment. (42, 43)

20. Attend and actively participate in group therapy with other victims of physical abuse. (44)

21. Identify a list of trustworthy individuals who can be relied upon for support, guidance, and affirmation. (45, 46)

22. Increase the level of trust of others as shown by increased socialization and a greater number of friendships. (46, 47, 48)

and/or significant family members while asserting the right to safety. Process this letter in therapy sessions.

42. Instruct the client to perform a letting-go exercise in which a symbol of the physical abuse is disposed of or destroyed. Process this experience.

43. Instruct the client to record daily in a journal at least five positive, affirmative statements regarding himself/herself to build self-esteem and provide a sense of empowerment.

44. Refer the client to a victim support group with other children or adolescents to assist him/her in realizing that he/she is not alone in experiencing abuse and can gain a sense of empowerment.

45. Develop a list of resource people outside of the family to whom the client can turn for support, guidance, and affirmation.

46. Teach the client the share-check method of building trust in which the degree of shared information is related to a proven level of trustworthiness.

46. Teach the client the share-check method of building trust in which the degree of shared information is related to a proven level of trustworthiness.

47. Facilitate the client in expressing the loss of trust in adults, and relate this loss to the perpetrator's abusive behavior and the lack of protection provided.

48. Assist the client in making discriminating judgments that allow for the trust of some people rather than distrust of all.

23. Participate regularly in healthy physical or extracurricular activities. (49)

49. Encourage the client to participate in healthy physical, social, or extracurricular activities (e.g., exercising daily, trying out for school sports team, participating in an outdoor adventure or experiential camp with peers, etc.) to help build positive body image, achieve a feeling of mastery or accomplishment, and decrease feelings of helplessness or vulnerability.

24. Identify and verbalize the painful emotions that contribute to aggressive, acting-out, or antisocial behavior. (50)

50. Encourage and challenge the client to openly and directly express his/her feelings of anxiety, fear, sadness, or anger to others about physical abuse instead of channeling the painful emotions into aggressive, acting-out, or antisocial behavior. Point out to the client how involvement in acting-out behavior or illegal activities is self-defeating and fails to meet his/her deeper needs or allow him/her to work through feelings about physical abuse.

25. Reduce the frequency of aggressive, acting-out, or anti-social behavior. (50, 51, 52)

50. Encourage and challenge the client to openly and directly express his/her feelings of anxiety, fear, sadness, or anger to others about physical abuse instead of channeling the painful emotions into aggressive, acting-out, or antisocial behavior. Point out to the client how involvement in acting-out behavior or illegal activities is self-defeating and fails to meet his/her deeper needs or allow him/her to work through feelings about physical abuse.

51. Explore whether the client's hostile or aggressive stance toward others masks deeper feelings of helplessness or powerlessness. Assist the client in identifying more adaptive ways to achieve a healthy sense of power.

52. Use role-playing and role-reversal techniques to sensitize the client to how his/her aggressive behavior negatively impacts others.

26. Complete a substance abuse evaluation, and comply with the recommendations offered by the evaluation findings. (53, 54)

53. Assess and monitor the client's use of alcohol or drugs. Arrange for substance abuse evaluation and/or treatment if he/she has turned to alcohol or drugs as a maladaptive coping mechanism to deal with painful emotions about physical abuse. (See the chapter entitled "Substance Abuse" in this Planner.)

54. Contract with the client to terminate the use of all mood-altering substances.

27. Parents comply with recommendations regarding psychiatric or substance abuse treatment. (55)

55. Assess the parents for the possibility of having a psychiatric disorder and/or substance abuse problem. Refer the parents for psychiatric or substance abuse evaluation and/or treatment if it is found that they have psychiatric disorders or substance abuse problems.

28. Cooperate with a physician's evaluation for psychotropic medication. (56)

56. Arrange for a physician to perform a medication evaluation for the client to help stabilize his/her mood and reduce the intensity of anger and rage.

29. Take medication as prescribed by the physician. (57)

57. Monitor the client for compliance, side effects, and overall effectiveness of the medication.

__. _____
   _____

__. _____
   _____

__. _____
   _____

__. _____
   _____

__. _____
   _____

__. _____
   _____

DIAGNOSTIC SUGGESTIONS:

ICD-9-CM	_ICD-10-CM_	_DSM-5_ Disorder, Condition, or Problem
995.54	T74.12XA	Child Physical Abuse, Confirmed, Initial Encounter
995.54	T74.12XD	Child Physical Abuse, Confirmed, Subsequent Encounter
309.81	F43.10	Posttraumatic Stress Disorder
308.3	F43.0	Acute Stress Disorder
296.xx	F32.x	Major Depressive Disorder, Single Episode
296.xx	F33.x	Major Depressive Disorder, Recurrent Episode
311	F32.9	Unspecified Depressive Disorder
311	F32.8	Other Specified Depressive Disorder
300.4	F34.1	Persistent Depressive Disorder
300.02	F41.1	Generalized Anxiety Disorder
307.47	F51.5	Nightmare Disorder
312.8	F91.x	Conduct Disorder
313.81	F91.3	Oppositional Defiant Disorder
300.6	F48.1	Depersonalization/Derealization Disorder
300.15	F44.89	Other Specified Dissociative Disorder
300.15	F44.9	Unspecified Dissociative Disorder
———	———	———————————————
———	———	———————————————

PROBATION NONCOMPLIANCE

BEHAVIORAL DEFINITIONS

1. Failure to obey court-ordered probationary requirements and directives.
2. Violation of federal laws, state laws, or ordinance of the municipality.
3. Disobedience of reasonable directions of the caregivers.
4. Truancy from school or disobedience of school regulations.
5. Behavior and verbalizations reflect an attitude of hostile defiance or detached indifference.
6. Leaving the home without the consent of the caregiver or failure to return home.
7. Violating legal curfew or an earlier curfew that has been mutually agreed upon by the caregivers or probation officer.
8. Failure to make restitution either financially or through community service.
9. Use of illegal, mood-altering drugs or alcohol.
10. Failure to submit to court-ordered drug screening, assessment, or treatment.
11. Traveling outside the state borders without consent.
12. Failure to adhere to the conditions of the tether.

__. _____
   _____
   _____
__. _____
   _____
   _____
__. _____
   _____

LONG-TERM GOALS

1. Comply with all probationary directives.
2. Comply with the rules and expectations in the home, school, work setting, and in the community on a consistent basis.
3. Demonstrate a significant improvement in impulse control.
4. Resolve the emotional problems that contribute to or exacerbate conduct problems.
5. Eliminate all illegal behaviors.

—. _____

_____

—. _____

_____

—. _____

_____

SHORT-TERM OBJECTIVES

1. Complete psychological testing to identify factors that may contribute to probation noncompliance. (1, 2)

2. Complete a psychoeducational evaluation to determine the need for additional educational services. (2, 3)

THERAPEUTIC INTERVENTIONS

1. Arrange for psychological testing of the client to assess current cognitive, social, and emotional factors that contribute to noncompliant behavior.

2. Provide feedback to the client and his/her caregivers, juvenile justice officials, and relevant school personnel regarding the assessment results and recommendations.

2. Provide feedback to the client and his/her caregivers, juvenile justice officials, and relevant school personnel regarding the assessment results and recommendations.

3. Cooperate with an evaluation by a physician to determine the possible benefits of psychotropic medication, and comply with recommendations. (4)

4. Take medication as prescribed by the physician, and report as to the effectiveness and side effects. (5)

5. Complete a substance abuse evaluation, and comply with the recommendations offered by the evaluation findings. (2, 6, 7)

6. Comply with the move to an appropriate alternative set-

3. Arrange for a psychoeducational evaluation of the client to rule out the presence of a learning disability that may contribute to truancy and probation noncompliance.

4. Arrange for a physician to evaluate the client to assess whether medication might improve the client's impulse control and stabilize his/her mood.

5. Monitor the client's use of psychotropic medications as to prescription compliance, effectiveness, and side effects.

2. Provide feedback to the client and his/her caregivers, juvenile justice officials, and relevant school personnel regarding the assessment results and recommendations.

6. Explore the client's substance abuse and its negative effects on his/her behavior and interactions with others. Urge termination of substance abuse and the seeking of chemical dependence treatment.

7. Arrange for a substance abuse evaluation and/or treatment for the client, including random drug screens.

8. Consult with the caregivers, school officials, and juvenile

ting or juvenile detention facility. (8, 9)

justice officials about the need to place the client in a more restrictive or alternative setting (e.g., foster home, group home, day treatment program, residential program, juvenile detention facility, etc.).

9. Process with the client the reasons for placement in a more restrictive or alternative setting.

7. Acknowledge and accept legal consequences of violating probation. (10, 11)

10. Collaborate with juvenile justice officials to determine appropriate consequences for the client's noncompliant behaviors (e.g., tether, increased level of supervision, probation violation, etc.) and relay this information to the client and his/her caregivers.

11. Teach the client the legal consequences for violating probation. Ask him/her to write a list summarizing these consequences.

8. Identify obstacles to complying with the recommendations and/or requirements of the juvenile justice system. (12)

12. Assist the client in identifying situations or personal problems that interfere with his/her compliance with the terms of probation (e.g., family conflict, peer pressure, unresolved grief, academic skill deficits, etc.).

9. Implement constructive problem-solving approach to obstacles to probation compliance. (13)

13. Teach the client problem-solving techniques (e.g., define the problem, brainstorm possible solutions,

list pros and cons of each possible solution, implement action, and evaluate the outcome) that can be applied to personal problems that interfere with his/her probation compliance.

10. Verbalize an awareness of how probation violation impacts family members and self. (14, 15)

14. Discuss the negative consequences that arise for the client from his/her noncompliant behaviors (e.g., more restrictive settings, tether, tighter curfews, etc.) and the positive consequences that arise from compliant behavior (e.g., terminating probation, increased independence, less restrictive curfew, etc.).

15. Assist the client in identifying the short- and long-term consequences of violating probation for family members (e.g., prolonged involvement with legal system, disappointment and resentment, loss of trust, etc.).

11. Increase by 50 percent the number of statements that reflect the acceptance of responsibility for noncompliant behavior rather than projecting blame onto others. (16, 17)

16. Confront statements in which the client projects blame and fails to take responsibility for his/her actions.

17. Encourage the client to acknowledge responsibility for his/her misbehavior.

12. Identify recent behavioral choices that have contributed to probation violation. (18, 19)

18. Encourage the caregivers to identify behaviors or situations that place the client at risk for probation violation. Assist the client in

identifying solutions to these concerns.

19. Prompt the client to identify specific situations in which he/she engaged in noncompliant behavior at home, in the school, and in the community.

13. Identify patterns in social interactions that frequently trigger or coincide with noncompliant behavior. (20, 21)

20. Assist the client in identifying seemingly unimportant decisions that resulted in probation noncompliance (e.g., arguing with authority figures, socializing with substance abusing peers, skipping classes, etc.).

21. Assist the client in recognizing patterns of social interaction (e.g., associating with gangs, frequenting drug-infested neighborhoods, associating with peers who engage in illegal behaviors, etc.) that place him/her at risk for noncompliant behavior. Encourage avoidance of these social interactions.

14. Make a commitment to avoid potential obstacles to successfully completing probation. (18, 22)

18. Encourage the caregivers to identify behaviors or situations that place the client at risk for probation violation. Assist the client in identifying solutions to these concerns.

22. Identify and process the obstacles to successfully completing probation (e.g., failure to maintain sobriety, comply with curfew and travel constraints, consistently

attending school) and develop coping strategies to deal with each obstacle (e.g., utilizing scare-yourself imagery, engaging in positive self-talk, attending support groups, etc.).

15. Decrease the frequency and intensity of negative, confrontational, and defiant interactions with the caregivers, school officials, or juvenile justice officials. (23, 24, 25)

16. Monitor and process thoughts and feelings that coincide with noncompliant behavior. (26, 27, 28)

23. Identify situations when the client is interacting with others in a negative, confrontational, and defiant manner, and assist the caregivers and/or school officials in creating a plan to redirect the client's acting-out behavior.

24. Ask the client to complete and process a workbook exercise from *Don't Be Difficult* (Shapiro and Shore) or *How I Learned to Think Things Through* (Shapiro).

25. Ask the client to read the book *Girls and Boys Book about Good and Bad Behavior* (Gardner) and to process key concepts with the therapist.

26. Assist the client in developing an awareness of internal messages that reinforce negativity and/or noncompliant behavior.

27. Assist the client in developing an awareness of cognitive distortions (e.g., "They were asking for it"; "I deserve this"; or "I'm not hurting anybody") that contribute to the emergence and mainte-

nance of noncompliant behavior. Assist the client in replacing distortions with realistic and positive self-talk.

28. Encourage the client to identify and verbalize the feelings that elicit noncompliant behavior (e.g., anger, fear, frustration, hurt, anxiety, etc.). Teach the client alternative ways to cope with these emotions (e.g., talking to a respected adult, sharing with a counselor, writing the feelings in a journal, etc.).

17. Identify the underlying goals of the noncompliant behavior. (29)

29. Explore what the client hopes to accomplish through his/her noncompliant behavior (e.g., to communicate anger and frustration, to increase independence, to avoid dealing with difficult or painful feelings, etc.).

18. Brainstorm and implement safe and appropriate ways to address problems, rather than engaging in noncompliant behavior. (13, 30, 31)

13. Teach the client problem-solving techniques (e.g., define the problem, brainstorm possible solutions, list pros and cons of each possible solution, implement action, and evaluate the outcome) that can be applied to personal problems that interfere with his/her probation compliance.

30. Assist the client in identifying safe and appropriate ways to accomplish his/her goals of noncompliant behavior (e.g., communicating

feelings directly, earning increased independence, using coping skills, etc.).

31. Use therapeutic games to help the client explore alternative ways to have needs met without resorting to noncompliant behavior (e.g., *Don't Be Difficult* or *The Good Behavior Game* from The Center for Applied Psychology).

19. Increase compliance with rules at home and in school by 50 percent. (32, 33)

32. Prompt the client to demonstrate a verbal understanding of the expectations within the home and school setting.

33. Praise the client's increased compliance with rules at home and in the school setting.

20. The caregivers and school officials clearly communicate expectations for behavior as well as consequences for noncompliance. (34)

34. Educate the caregivers and school personnel on the importance of establishing appropriate boundaries, firm expectations, and implementing consistent consequences.

21. The caregivers learn and implement appropriate and effective parenting techniques and disciplinary strategies. (35, 36, 37, 38)

35. Teach the caregivers how to implement effective parenting techniques and disciplinary strategies including natural and logical consequences.

36. Refer the caregivers to a didactic group focused on teaching effective parenting techniques.

37. Recommend that the caregivers read books on effective parenting and limit setting (e.g., *The New Dare to Discipline* by Dobson; *Parents, Teens, and Boundaries* by Bluestein; *Toughlove* by York, York, and Wachtel; or *Parents and Adolescents* by Patterson and Forgatch).

38. Confront the caregiver's tendency to respond to the client's behavioral problems in an overly punitive or overprotective and lax manner.

22. The caregivers and/or school officials establish and implement a behavioral contract with the client. (39)

39. Develop and facilitate the implementation of a behavioral contract that stipulates clear expectations for the client's behavior at home and at school, including rewards for compliance and negative consequences for noncompliance.

23. The caregivers and school officials increase the frequency of praise and positive reinforcement when the client complies with expectations. (40, 41)

40. Encourage the caregivers to provide frequent praise and positive reinforcement for the client's prosocial and compliant behaviors.

41. Teach the caregivers and school personnel to use contingency management techniques to shape the client's behavior.

24. The caregivers allow the client to accept responsibility for and consequences of his/her behavior. (42, 43)

42. Encourage the caregivers to help the client accept responsibility for his/her noncompliance and deter them from

protecting him/her from the legal consequences of his/her behavior.

43. Confront the caregivers' efforts to sabotage limit setting and redirection provided by school personnel, employment supervisors, or juvenile justice officials.

25. Establish and maintain employment to deter impulsive and acting-out behaviors. (44, 45)

44. Refer the client to vocational training programs to develop job skills and find employment opportunities.

45. Reinforce the client's awareness of and respect for the expectations of the work setting, including the authority of the supervisor.

26. Enroll in organized extracurricular activities, and increase participation with positive peer group activities. (46, 47)

46. Encourage the client to participate in organized extracurricular activities to provide positive peer interactions in a structured setting.

47. Refer the client to group therapy in order to work on his/her socialization skills.

27. Participate in a mentoring program. (48)

48. Refer the client to a mentoring program to provide interaction with a positive adult role model (e.g., Big Brothers/Big Sisters, Police Athletic League, or the Juvenile Mentoring Program).

28. Use coping strategies and relaxation techniques three times daily to deter impulsive behavior. (49)

49. Teach and monitor the use of relaxation techniques (e.g., visualization, meditation, breathing, progressive muscle relaxation, etc.) and coping skills (e.g., thought stopping,

positive affirmations, self-talk, etc.) to assist the client in improving impulse control.

__. _____   __. _____
   _____   _____
__. _____   __. _____
   _____   _____
__. _____   __. _____
   _____   _____

DIAGNOSTIC SUGGESTIONS:

ICD-9-CM	*ICD-10-CM*	*DSM-5* Disorder, Condition, or Problem
312.81	F91.1	Conduct Disorder, Childhood-Onset Type
312.82	F91.2	Conduct Disorder, Adolescent-Onset Type
313.81	F91.3	Oppositional Defiant Disorder
312.9	F91.9	Unspecified Disruptive, Impulse Control, and Conduct Disorder
312.89	F91.8	Other Specified Disruptive, Impulse Control, and Conduct Disorder
314.01	F90.2	Attention-Deficit/Hyperactivity Disorder, Combined Presentation
V71.02	Z72.810	Adolescent Antisocial Behavior
V61.20	Z62.820	Parent-Child Relational Problem
_____	_____	_____
_____	_____	_____

RUNAWAY/STREET LIVING

BEHAVIORAL DEFINITIONS

1. Has been forced to leave home by caregivers without the option of returning ("pushouts or throwaways").
2. Living on the streets to escape psychological, physical, or sexual abuse at home.
3. Living on the streets as a result of being evicted from residence.
4. Death of the caregiver resulting in homelessness.
5. Living on the streets to support drug and alcohol addiction.
6. Living on the street as an expression of creativity and individuality.
7. Absence from home or place of legal residence for an extended period of time or permanently.
8. Leaving home to escape long-term family conflicts and chaos.
9. Has a history of running away and living on the streets and is currently expressing a desire to return to living on the streets.

__. _____
   _____

__. _____
   _____

__. _____
   _____

LONG-TERM GOALS

1. Reunite with the caregivers or another responsible, caring adult.
2. Transition to a healthy and protective living environment (e.g., foster care, group home, caring relative, etc.).

3. Learn the skills that are necessary to establish a self-supportive independent life.
4. Eliminate risky behaviors (e.g., substance abuse, promiscuity, illegal activities, etc.).
5. Learn to express individuality in more safe and constructive ways.
6. Develop coping skills to deal with family stress.
7. Begin the process of healthy separation from the caregivers.

__. _____

_____

__. _____

_____

__. _____

_____

SHORT-TERM OBJECTIVES

THERAPEUTIC INTERVENTIONS

1. Cooperate with a medical examination, and adhere to all recommendations resulting from the evaluation. (1, 2)

1. Refer the client for a medical evaluation.

2. Support the client in obtaining ongoing medical treatment for identified medical issues (e.g., pregnancy, fatal diseases, curable diseases, injuries, chronic illness, etc.).

2. Cooperate with a psychological assessment. (3)

3. Complete a psychological assessment to determine if underlying emotional, cognitive, or behavioral problems are present (e.g., depression, anxiety, thought disorder, drug addiction, etc.).

3. Acknowledge and verbalize an understanding of psychological symptoms and current diagnosis. Adhere to all recommendations resulting from the evaluation. (4, 5)

4. Provide the client with reading material that explains and normalizes his/her thoughts and feelings related to his/her current symptoms and diagnosis.

5. Assist the client and the care-givers and the juvenile justice official in understanding the nature of the identified psychological disorder (e.g., impairments, course of treatment, prognoses, etc.).

4. Identify and discuss problems precipitating the decision to run away and live on the streets. (6, 7)

6. Actively build trust with the client in one-to-one sessions through consistent contact, positive self-disclosure, non-verbal behavior, eye contact, acceptance, empathy, active listening, and adoption of a nonjudgmental attitude to help increase his/her ability to self-disclose.

7. Ask the client to identify problems precipitating his/her decision to run away and live on the street.

5. Express feelings of rejection, insecurity, and fear that triggered the choice to live on the street. (6, 8, 9)

6. Actively build trust with the client in one-to-one sessions through consistent contact, positive self-disclosure, non-verbal behavior, eye contact, acceptance, empathy, active listening, and adoption of a nonjudgmental attitude to help increase his/her ability to self-disclose.

8. Assist the client in identifying feelings (e.g., anger, fear, resentment, hurt, etc.) that motivated street living.

9. Assist the client in preparing a mock letter to his/her care-givers that expresses concern about living in the home.

6. Identify negative feelings toward self that motivates street living. (10)

7. Identify positive feelings towards self, and participate in self-enhancing activities. (11, 12, 13)

8. Discuss abuse and/or neglect issues occurring in the home prior to running away and/or while living on the street. (6, 14, 15, 16)

10. Assist the client in recognizing his/her negative self-concept and how his/her self-concept influenced his/her decision to live on the streets.

11. Prompt the client to identify personal strength or attributes.

12. Help the client to identify resilient qualities that he/she possesses, and that will assist him/her in recovering from living on the streets.

13. Introduce to the client exercises and/or activities to improve his/her self-concept (e.g., positive affirmations, reading motivational books, sports, music, academics, positive self-talk, volunteering, etc.).

6. Actively build trust with the client in one-to-one sessions through consistent contact, positive self-disclosure, nonverbal behavior, eye contact, acceptance, empathy, active listening, and adoption of a nonjudgmental attitude to help increase his/her ability to self-disclose.

14. Encourage the client to talk about his/her experience of sexual and/or physical abuse in the home or on the street.

15. Ask the client to talk about how traumatic events experienced in the home or on the street have impacted his/her life.

16. Help the client to recognize reoccurring patterns of traumatic experiences (e.g., how the identified traumas of the street are similar to traumas experienced in his/her home).

9. Identify the destructive nature of many of the street relationships. (17)

17. Assist the client in recognizing destructive relationships with certain people whom he/she identified as support persons while living on the street (e.g., pimps, people manufacturing and selling underage pornography, people soliciting sex from minors, drug dealers, etc.).

10. Acknowledge a desire for independence and separation from the caregivers. (18, 19)

18. Explore the client's need for autonomy and assist him/her in beginning the process of healthy separation from his/her caregiver.

19. Discuss with the client and his/her caregivers the need to balance his/her need for increased independence with the caregivers' need to provide continued supervision.

11. Verbalize acceptance of some responsibility for conflict with the caregivers. (20)

20. Assist the client in accepting responsibility for his/her contribution to conflict with his/her caregivers.

12. Identify and implement ways to express individualism that do not involve living on the street. (21, 22, 23)

21. Help the client to identify unique strengths and abilities (e.g., artistic abilities, academic gifts, athletic ability, etc.) that he/she possesses and that can be used to promote his/her individuality.

22. Work with the client to develop healthy ways to express his/her individuality (e.g., painting, writing, drawing, oral expression, etc.).

23. Help the client to find activities, clubs, and/or hobbies that support his/her special talent or interest.

13. Acknowledge the danger of street living and the need to accept safe shelter. (24, 25)

24. Help the client to recognize that his/her current means of survival is dangerous.

25. Refer the client to a social services agency to obtain food, safe shelter, bus tickets home, and so on.

14. Accept a referral to education and training programs to increase employment, social, and problem-solving skills. (26, 27, 28, 29)

26. Refer the client to a transitional living program (e.g., group home) that provides the skills that are necessary for independent living (e.g., money management, home maintenance, transportation skills, etc.).

27. Refer the client to education and/or job training programs to assist him/her in deceasing his/her reliance on the street economy (e.g., drug trade, prostitution, theft, etc.) for survival.

28. Facilitate the client gaining reentry to his/her school, and encourage him/her to obtain a high school diploma or equivalent.

29. Refer the client to a social skills training group or teach him/her social skills that are necessary to obtain and main-

tain employment (e.g., oral communication skills, assertiveness skills, nonverbal communication skills, etc.).

15. Disclose high-risk behaviors. (24, 30)

24. Help the client to recognize that his/her current means of survival is dangerous.

30. Encourage the client to disclose his/her high-risk behavior (e.g., substance abuse, sexual promiscuity, unprotected sex, living with strangers, arm assaults, vandalism, etc.).

16. Report a decrease in the frequency and intensity of high-risk behaviors. (31, 32, 33)

31. Prompt the client to identify short- and long-term consequences of high-risk behaviors (e.g., promiscuity, drug use, sleeping on the streets, etc.).

32. Process the client's perceived obstacles to decreasing risky behavior.

33. Establish a contract with the client that prohibits all risky behavior. Encourage him/her to commit to the contract.

17. Identify and establish contact with support groups or individuals. (34, 35, 36)

34. Provide the client with information and phone numbers for a local and the national runaway shelter, support, and help.

35. Assist the client in identifying potential individuals who can provide positive support, validation, protection, and emotional connection.

36. Refer the client to a support group for runaways.

18. Identify the basis for and results of a trusting relationship. (37)

19. Increase communication and activity with a trusted adult. (38, 39, 40)

20. Acknowledge substance addiction in self and/or family and commit to substance abuse treatment. (41, 42, 43, 44)

21. Discuss reluctance to return to the caregivers' home, and verbalize the improbability of reunification. (45, 46, 47, 48)

37. Ask the client to identify what he/she thinks are characteristics of a trusting relationship (e.g., honesty, openness, respect, mutual caring, relaxed comfortableness, etc.).

38. Ask the client to make a list of positive adults (e.g., parents, caregivers, relatives, etc.) whom he/she would like to include in his/her treatment.

39. Facilitate therapy sessions with the client and an adult whom he/she has identified as trustworthy.

40. Ask the client and the trusted adult to schedule and complete activities outside of the therapy session and process the meetings during session.

41. Assess whether the client's addiction precipitated or preceded his/her running away and living on the street.

42. Explore with the client the existence of a family history of substance abuse. Explore how the abuse affected the client.

43. Discuss with the client his/her use of alcohol and/or drugs as a means of reacting to the home environment or coping with living on the street.

44. Refer the client for drug and alcohol detoxification and treatment.

45. Assist the client in listing reasons why he/she does not want to return home. Process this list.

46. Ask the client to contrast living on the streets to living at home.

47. Discuss how the emotional attachment to the family has deteriorated, and assess the client's desire to improve the relationship.

48. Acknowledge parental bonds that have been damaged beyond repair, and determine alternative options for safe living (e.g., foster care, group home, caring relative, friend's home, etc.).

22. Communicate with the caregivers and make plans to reunite. (49, 50, 51)

49. Assist the client in constructing a message for his/her caregivers that communicates his/her desire to return home.

50. Role-play the delivery of the message to caregiver about the desire to reunite.

51. Process possible responses that the client may receive from the caregiver.

23. The client and his/her caregivers make a list of desired changes in the caregivers' home for successful reunification and implement realistic changes. (52, 53, 54)

52. Assist the client and the caregiver in constructing a list of desired changes in the caregiver home necessary for successful reunification.

53. Assist the client and caregiver in developing realistic expectations regarding his/her legal home environment.

54. Identify how the caregiver and the client can implement realistic changes necessary for successful reunification.

24. Actively participate in family sessions after reunification has occurred. (55, 56)

55. Assist the client and the caregiver in identifying potential long- and short-term obstacles to a successful reunification.

56. Conduct frequent postreunification sessions with the client and caregiver. Encourage the client and caregiver to speak freely about any issues that may threaten the longevity of the reunification.

__. _____
_____

__. _____
_____

__. _____
_____

__. _____
_____

__. _____
_____

__. _____
_____

DIAGNOSTIC SUGGESTIONS:

ICD-9-CM	_ICD-10-CM_	_DSM-5_ Disorder, Condition, or Problem
309.3	F43.24	Adjustment Disorder, With Disturbance of Conduct
309.4	F43.25	Adjustment Disorder, With Mixed Disturbance of Emotions and Conduct
314.01	F90.2	Attention-Deficit/Hyperactivity Disorder, Combined Presentation
312.81	F91.1	Conduct Disorder, Childhood-Onset Type
312.82	F91.2	Conduct Disorder, Adolescent-Onset Type
V71.02	Z72.810	Adolescent Antisocial Behavior
V61.21	Z69.011	Encounter for Mental Health Services for Perpetrator of Parental Child Neglect
995.54	T74.12XA	Child Physical Abuse, Confirmed, Initial Encounter
995.54	T74.12XD	Child Physical Abuse, Confirmed, Subsequent Encounter
995.53	T74.22XA	Child Sexual Abuse, Confirmed, Initial Encounter
995.53	T74.22XD	Child Sexual Abuse, Confirmed, Subsequent Encounter
_____	_____	_____
_____	_____	_____

SEXUAL ABUSE VICTIM

BEHAVIORAL DEFINITIONS

1. Self-report of being sexually abused.
2. Physical signs of sexual abuse (e.g., red or swollen genitalia, blood in the underwear, a tear in the vagina or rectum, venereal disease).
3. Strong interest in or curiosity about issues related to sexuality.
4. Pervasive pattern of promiscuity or the sexualization of relationships with same-age or older peers.
5. Significant increase in the frequency and severity of aggressive, acting-out, or antisocial behavior after the onset of the sexual abuse.
6. Pronounced disturbance of mood and affect (e.g., frequent and prolonged periods of depression, irritability, anxiety, and fearfulness).
7. Marked distrust of others as manifested by social withdrawal and problems with establishing and maintaining close relationships.
8. Excessive use of alcohol or drugs as a maladaptive coping mechanism to avoid dealing with painful emotions connected to sexual abuse.
9. Feelings of guilt, shame, and low self-esteem.
10. Sexualized or seductive behavior with younger children (e.g., sexualized kissing, provocative exhibition of genitalia, fondling, mutual masturbation, anal or vaginal penetration).

—. _____
_____

—. _____
_____

—. _____
_____

LONG-TERM GOALS

1. Obtain safety from all further sexual victimization.
2. Work successfully through the issue of sexual abuse with consequent understanding and control of feelings and behavior.
3. Resolve the issues surrounding the sexual abuse, resulting in an ability to establish and maintain close interpersonal relationships.
4. Establish appropriate boundaries and generational lines in the family to greatly minimize the risk of sexual abuse ever occurring in the future.
5. Termination of denial in all family members, placing responsibility for the abuse on the perpetrator and allowing the survivor to feel supported.
6. Terminate pattern of engaging in aggressive, acting-out, or substance abuse behavior when experiencing painful emotions about sexual abuse or after having exposure to sexual topics or reminders of abuse.
7. Eliminate all promiscuous or inappropriate sexual behavior.
8. Build self-esteem and a sense of empowerment as manifested by increased number of positive self-descriptive statements and greater participation in peer or extracurricular activities.

—. _____
   _____

—. _____
   _____

—. _____
   _____

SHORT-TERM OBJECTIVES	THERAPEUTIC INTERVENTIONS
1. Identify the perpetrator, nature, frequency, severity, and duration of the abuse. (1, 2, 3, 4)	1. Actively build the level of trust with the client in individual sessions through consistent eye contact, active listening, unconditional positive regard, and warm acceptance to help increase his/her ability to identify and express feelings that are connected to the sexual abuse.

2. Explore gently the sexual abuse experience while taking precautions not to place excessive pressure on the client to disclose the facts or press too early for unnecessary details.

3. Gather a detailed psychosocial history of the client's sexual abuse, including age of onset, frequency, severity, precipitating stressors, sequence of events leading up to abuse, and extent of sexual abuse within the family system. Allow the client to express feelings while sharing relevant details.

4. Use anatomically detailed dolls or puppets to have the younger client tell and show how he/she was abused. Take great caution not to lead the client.

2. Identify and express thoughts and feelings connected to the abuse. (5, 6)

5. Encourage and support the client in verbally expressing his/her thoughts and feelings associated with the sexual abuse.

6. Assign exercises from the therapeutic workbook *The Me Nobody Knows: A Guide for Teen Survivors* (Bean and Bennett) to help the client work through feelings that are associated with the sexual abuse.

3. Submit to an evaluation by legal and medical personnel. (7, 8)

7. Report sexual abuse and refer the client to the appropriate child protection agency,

criminal justice officials, or medical professionals for evaluation.

8. Consult with a physician, criminal justice officials, or child protection case managers to assess the veracity of the sexual abuse charges.

4. Agree to the need for boundaries for protection from further abuse or retaliation. (9, 10, 11, 12)

9. Consult with a physician, criminal justice officials, and child protection case managers to develop appropriate treatment interventions and safety precau- tions.

10. Assess whether a recommendation should be made to legal authorities for the perpetrator to be barred from entering the home.

11. Implement the necessary steps to protect the client and other children in the home from future sexual abuse.

12. Assess whether the client is safe while remaining in the home or should be removed.

5. Family members identify and take steps necessary to ensure protection for the client and siblings. (11)

11. Implement the necessary steps to protect the client and other children in the home from future sexual abuse.

6. Perpetrator complies with court mandates about being barred from entering the home. (10, 13)

10. Assess whether a recommendation should be made to legal authorities for the perpetrator to be barred from entering the home.

13. Instruct the client to write a letter to criminal justice officials (e.g., probation officer,

lawyer, judge) expressing feelings about sexual abuse, describing how abuse has impacted his/her life, and identifying consequences that he/she would like the perpetrator to receive.

7. Decrease secrecy in the family by informing key members about the abuse. (14, 15)

14. Facilitate conjoint sessions to reveal the sexual abuse to key family members or caregivers.

15. Actively confront and challenge denial and secrecy within the family system.

8. Increase the openness to talk about sexual abuse in the family. (16, 17)

16. Elicit and reinforce support and nurturance for the client from other key family members.

17. Encourage caregiver(s) to provide opportunities (e.g., family meetings) to allow the client and siblings to express feelings about the sexual abuse and subsequent changes that have occurred within the family system.

9. Decrease expressed feelings of shame and guilt, and affirm self as not being responsible for the sexual abuse. (18, 19, 20)

18. Challenge or confront statements by the perpetrator, caregiver(s), or family members that project the blame or responsibility for the sexual abuse onto the client or other siblings.

19. Hold family therapy sessions where the parent(s) affirm the client and his/her siblings as not being responsible for the sexual abuse. Assist the client and other family members in verbalizing that the perpetrator is responsible for abuse.

20. Use the exercise entitled "You Are Not Alone" from *The Brief Adolescent Therapy Homework Planner* (Jongsma, Peterson, and McInnis) to help the client express his/her feelings connected to the sexual abuse and decrease his/her feelings of guilt and shame.

10. Verbally identify the perpetrator as being responsible for the sexual abuse. (19, 21)

19. Hold family therapy sessions where the parent(s) affirm the client and his/her siblings as not being responsible for the sexual abuse. Assist the client and other family members in verbalizing that the perpetrator is responsible for abuse.

21. Reinforce the client for clear identification of the perpetrator as being responsible for the sexual abuse.

11. The caregivers establish and adhere to appropriate intimacy boundaries within the family. (22, 23)

22. Counsel the family members about appropriate privacy and intimacy bound- aries.

23. Empower the client by identifying and reinforcing the steps necessary to protect himself/herself from further sexual abuse.

12. Nonabusive parent and other key family members provide consistent support, affirmation, and nurturance for the client. (16, 24, 25)

16. Elicit and reinforce support and nurturance for the client from other key family members.

24. Assign the client's caregivers and significant others to read books to assist them in understanding how they can help him/her recover from the sexual abuse (e.g., *Allies in Healing* by Davis).

25. Direct the disengaged, nonabusive parent to spend more time with the client in leisure, school, or household activities to stabilize the client's moods and facilitate a sense of belonging within the family.

13. Family members identify stressors and other boundary-breaking or denial factors that contributed to the sexual abuse. (26, 27, 28)

26. Conduct individual therapy sessions with the nonabusive parent to explore possible reasons for failing to detect earlier signs of sexual abuse or take steps to protect the client or his/her siblings from the ongoing abuse.

27. Assess the family dynamics and identify the stress factors or precipitating events that contributed to the emergence of the abuse.

28. Construct a multigenerational family genogram and identify sexual abuse within the extended family to help the client realize that he/she is not the only one abused and to help the perpetrator recognize the cycle of boundary violation.

14. Verbalize and list the ways in which sexual abuse has impacted life. (29)

29. Ask the client to make a list of the way sexual abuse has impacted his/her life.

Process this list in follow-up therapy sessions.

15. Express feelings regarding the abuse through journaling, role playing, letter writing, and/or guided imagery. (30, 31, 32, 33)

30. Instruct the client to keep a journal where he/she expresses thoughts and feelings about the sexual abuse. Process the journal contents in follow-up therapy sessions to provide the client with the opportunity to further express painful emotions, decrease the intensity of feelings, and stabilize moods.

31. Use the empty chair technique to assist the client in expressing and working through his/her myriad of feelings toward the perpetrator and other family members or key figures connected to the sexual abuse.

32. Instruct the client to write an angry letter to the perpetrator to help decrease the intensity of his/her hostility or rage. Process it with the therapist.

33. Use guided-fantasy and imagery techniques to help the client express suppressed thoughts, feelings, and unmet needs associated with the sexual abuse.

16. Express feelings about sexual abuse through artwork and mutual storytelling techniques. (34, 35, 36)

34. Employ art therapy techniques (e.g., drawing, painting, sculpting, etc.) to help the client identify and express his/her feelings toward the perpetrator, himself/herself, and the future.

35. Employ the Color-Your-Life technique (see *Play Therapy Handbook* by O'Connor and Schaeffer) to improve the younger client's ability to identify and verbalize feelings associated with abuse. Ask client to match colors to different emotions (e.g., red—anger, blue—sad, black—very sad, yellow—happy) and then fill up a blank page with colors that reflect his/her feelings about sexual abuse.

36. Use a mutual storytelling technique in which the younger client and therapist alternate telling stories through the use of puppets, dolls, or stuffed animals. The therapist first models constructive steps to take to protect himself/herself and feel empowered, then the client follows by creating a story with similar characters or themes.

17. Perpetrator verbalizes responsibility for the abuse. (37, 38)

37. Hold a therapy session with the client and/or the therapist confronting the perpetrator with the abuse.

38. Conduct an apology session where the perpetrator identifies himself/herself as being responsible for the sexual abuse and apologizes to the client and/or other family members.

18. Perpetrator agrees to attend group therapy treatment. (39)

39. Require the perpetrator to participate in group therapy treatment of sexual offenders.

19. Verbalize a desire to begin the process of forgiveness of the perpetrator and others connected with the abuse. (40, 41)

40. Assign the client to write a forgiveness letter and/or complete a forgiveness exercise in which he/she verbalizes forgiveness to the perpetrator and/or significant family members. Process the letter.

41. Assign the client a letting-go exercise in the latter stages of treatment where a symbol of the abuse is disposed of or destroyed. Process this experience.

20. Decrease the statements of being a victim while increasing statements that reflect personal empowerment as a survivor. (42, 43)

42. Ask the client to identify the positive and negative consequences of being a victim versus being a survivor. Compare and process the lists.

43. Introduce the idea in later stages of therapy that the client can survive sexual abuse by asking, "What will you be doing in the future that shows you are happy and have moved on with your life?" Process the client's responses and reinforce any positive steps that the client can take to work through issues related to victimization.

21. Attend and actively participate in group therapy with other sexual abuse survivors. (44)

44. Refer the client to a survivor group with other individuals who have been victimized to assist him/her in realizing that he/she is not alone in having experienced sexual abuse.

22. Identify a support system of key individuals who will

45. Develop a list of resource people outside of the family to

provide encouragement, guidance, and affirmation. (45)

23. Increase the level of trust of others as shown by increased socialization and a greater number of friendships. (46, 47)

24. Identify and verbalize the painful emotions that contribute to aggressive, anti-social, or sexually promiscuous behavior. (48)

25. Reduce the frequency of aggressive, acting-out, or anti-social behavior. (49, 50)

whom the client can turn for support, guidance, and affirmation.

46. Teach the client the share-check method of building trust in which the degree of shared information is related to a proven level of trustworthiness.

47. Identify appropriate and inap-propriate forms of touching and affection. Encourage the client to accept and initiate appropriate forms of touching with trusted individuals.

48. Assist the client in making a connection between underly-ing, painful emotions (e.g., anxiety, fear, sadness, anger, etc.) about the sexual abuse and acting-out behavior or sexual promiscuity.

49. Encourage and challenge the client to openly and directly express feelings of anxiety, fear, sadness, or anger to others about sexual abuse instead of channeling the painful emo-tions into aggressive, antisocial, or sexually promiscuous behav-ior. Point out to the client how involvement in acting-out behavior or illegal activities is self-defeating and fails to meet his/her deeper needs or allow him/her to work through feelings about abuse.

50. Give the client a homework assignment of listing healthy

and unhealthy ways of expressing emotions about sexual abuse or meeting unmet needs. Process this list in a follow-up therapy session, and encourage the client to express his/her feelings or meet his/her needs in a healthy manner other than through acting-out or sexually promiscuous behavior.

26. Increase the frequency of positive self-descriptive statements. (51, 52)

51. Use the therapeutic game Survivor's Journey (available through Courage to Change) to provide the client with the opportun-ity to express and work through feelings pertaining to the abuse while also learning how to build self-esteem and reestablish trust with others.

52. Instruct the client to record daily in a journal at least five positive, affirmative statements regarding himself/herself to build self-esteem and provide sense of empowerment.

27. The caregivers set limits on and give consequences for the client's acting-out behavior. (53)

53. Encourage and challenge the caregivers not to allow guilt feelings about the client's victimization to interfere with the need to impose consequences for his/her aggressive, acting-out, or antisocial behavior.

28. Verbalize the risks involved with sexually promiscuous behavior. (54)

54. Provide sex education and discuss the health, reputation, and self-esteem risks involved with sexually promiscuous or seductive behavior.

29. Complete a substance abuse evaluation and comply with the recommendations offered by the evaluation findings. (55)

55. Assess and monitor the client's use of alcohol or drugs. Arrange for substance abuse evaluation and/or treatment if indicated. (See the chapter entitled "Substance Abuse" in this Planner).

—. _____

_____

—. _____

_____

—. _____

_____

—. _____

_____

—. _____

_____

—. _____

_____

DIAGNOSTIC SUGGESTIONS:

ICD-9-CM	_ICD-10-CM_	_DSM-5_ Disorder, Condition, or Problem
995.53	T74.22XA	Child Sexual Abuse, Confirmed, Initial Encounter
995.53	T74.22XD	Child Sexual Abuse, Confirmed, Subsequent Encounter
309.81	F43.10	Posttraumatic Stress Disorder
308.3	F43.0	Acute Stress Disorder
296.xx	F32.x	Major Depressive Disorder, Single Episode
296.xx	F33.x	Major Depressive Disorder, Recurrent Episode
309.21	F93.0	Separation Anxiety Disorder
307.47	F51.5	Nightmare Disorder
300.15	F44.9	Unspecified Dissociative Disorder
300.15	F44.89	Other Specified Dissociative Disorder
300.6	F48.1	Depersonalization/Derealization Disorder
312.8	F91.x	Conduct Disorder
313.81	F91.3	Oppositional Defiant Disorder
309.4	F43.25	Adjustment Disorder, With Mixed Disturbance of Emotions and Conduct
_____	_____	_____
_____	_____	_____

SEXUAL MISCONDUCT

BEHAVIORAL DEFINITIONS

1. Preoccupation with sexually related behavior.
2. Conviction for paraphilias (e.g., exhibitionism, exposure, voyeurism, fetishism, transvestism, sadism, masochism, etc.).
3. Conviction for sexual conduct (first, second, third, or fourth degree).
4. Recurrent intense, deviant, sexually arousing fantasies, urges, or behaviors generally involving nonhuman objects, the suffering of humiliation of oneself, another person, younger children, or any nonconsenting person.
5. Denial, rationalization, or minimization of deviant sexualized behavior.
6. Inappropriate sexual knowledge and interest for one's age.
7. Obsessive preoccupation with sex or sex-related material (e.g., pornographic magazines, Internet sites, provocative catalogs, etc.).
8. Feels driven to seek out sexual encounters.
9. Violation of the emotional, physical, or sexual rights of others.
10. Striking lack of respect for the rights of others.
11. Sexualized or seductive behavior and/or play with younger children.
12. Frequently engages in sexual encounters even at the risk of disease or arrest.

__. _____
   _____
__. _____
   _____
__. _____
   _____

LONG-TERM GOALS

1. Acknowledge and take responsibility for all inappropriate sexual behavior.
2. Eliminate all inappropriate sexual behavior.
3. Minimize anger and power/control issues that lead to perpetration of sexual crimes or other delinquent acts.
4. Improve social competency by developing nonexploitive relationships and demonstrating a respect for others that honors boundaries.
5. Enhance a positive, healthy sense of self.
6. Increase the understanding of the negative impact of sexual abuse on victims and their families.
7. Resolve issues of own sexual abuse.
8. Increase awareness of basic psychosexual development and the risk factors for reoffending.

—. _____
   _____

—. _____
   _____

—. _____
   _____

SHORT-TERM OBJECTIVES	THERAPEUTIC INTERVENTIONS
1. Provide information for the completion of a biopsychosocial assessment, including a thorough psychosexual history. (1, 2)	1. Gather a thorough biopsychosocial and sexual history of the client from both the client and his/her caregivers.
	2. Using multiple sources of information, assess the level of risk that the client represents for engaging in sexual and nonsexual criminal behavior to determine his/her required level of care.

2. The caregivers and the client provide information regarding the needs and strengths of the client and the family system. (1, 3)

1. Gather a thorough biopsychosocial and sexual history of the client from both the client and his/her caregivers.

3. Conduct a needs-and-strengths assessment and refer the client and his/her family to appropriate services (e.g., social services, vocational training center, community recreational center, legal services, etc.).

3. Complete psychological testing and receive the results. (4)

4. Conduct a psychological assessment to determine current emotional, social, academic, and intellectual functioning. Give feedback to the client and his/her family or guardian.

4. Comply with any investigation by child protective services or criminal justice officials and cooperate with recommendations. (5)

5. Report any sexual abuse that is revealed by the client to child protective services or appropriate criminal justice officials.

5. Meet with a probation officer as ordered by the court and comply with rules of probation. (6, 7)

6. Monitor how the client and his/her family are complying with recommendations of relevant professionals. Make additional recommendations, including a more restrictive setting, if necessary.

7. Encourage the client to collaborate and comply with probation officer.

6. Attend group therapy sessions focused on sexual abuse perpetration. (8)

8. Refer the client to an inpatient or outpatient group for juveniles who have perpetrated sexual offenses.

7. Attend a sexually oriented values clarification group. (9)

9. Refer the client to a therapeutic psychoeducational group that focuses on sexual values clarification (e.g., gender-role values, sexual decision making, anatomy, etc.).

8. Caregivers follow through on referrals for family therapy and a support group. (10, 11)

10. Refer the client's caregiver to a support group for parents with children who exhibit sexual impulse problems and/or parenting classes.

11. Refer the client and his/her family to family therapy, promoting healthy familial patterns.

9. Cooperate with a medical evaluation for psychotropic medication. (12)

12. Arrange for evaluation by a physician to assess the appropriateness of psychotropic medication for the client.

10. Take prescribed medications and report on their effectiveness and side effects. (13)

13. Monitor the client's psychotropic medication for effectiveness and side effects.

11. Demonstrate a trusting relationship with the therapist as evidenced by sharing thoughts and feelings openly. (14, 15)

14. Build rapport with the client by encouraging him/her to talk openly about his/her concerns, fears, and desires for improvement in his/her life.

15. Build trust by expressing unconditional positive regard and acknowledging to the client that you expect that his/her story will become more complete as he/she begins to open up.

12. Increase verbal acknowledgment of perpetrating the abuse while demonstrating appropriate affect at least 75 percent of the time. (16, 17)

16. Assign the client to write about the details of his/her offense.

17. Provide repeated opportunities for the client to report on the details of his/her offense, facilitating increased self-disclosure and responsibility for his/her actions.

13. List at least three decisions made or actions taken that confirm own responsibility for the abuse. (18)

18. Ask the client to list at least three decisions he/she has made or actions he/she has taken that have led to someone being sexually abused; confront avoidance of responsibility.

14. Complete an autobiography that focuses on factors contributing to perpetration of sex abuse. (19)

19. Instruct the client on how to write an autobiography by detailing internal factors (e.g., thoughts, feelings, behaviors, etc.) and external factors (e.g., people, places, things, situations, etc.) that have contributed to his/her offending behavior.

15. Identify thinking errors and/or cognitive distortions that increase the incidence of impulsive sexual behavior. (20)

20. Teach the concept of cognitive distortions and assist the client in identifying his/her errors in thinking that contribute to the perpetration of sexual abuse.

16. Challenge rationalizations or cognitive distortions by substituting healthy alternative statements. (21)

21. Assist the client in identifying realistic, healthy cognitions to replace the distorted thoughts that contribute to sexual abuse perpetration.

17. Identify and acknowledge the risks and/or consequences involved with sexual misconduct. (22, 23)

22. Facilitate the client's understanding of the consequences and negative outcomes relating to his/her sexual acting out.

18. Verbalize familiarity with laws that govern inappropriate sexual behavior. (24)

19. Write about the details of the planning and grooming behaviors associated with sexual abuse perpetration. (16, 25)

20. Create a relapse prevention plan that includes a list of thoughts, actions, feelings, and environments that increase risk for sexual acting out. (26, 27, 28)

21. Verbalize the details of the circumstances that led to the most recent relapse and why coping strategies were unsuccessful. (16, 25, 29)

23. Help the client to examine whether his/her life is better or worse as a result of acting on inappropriate sexual impulses.

24. Educate the client regarding the laws governing inappropriate sexual behavior and the consequences of unlawful behavior.

16. Assign the client to write about the details of his/her offense.

25. Help the client to understand the precursors to his/her offending behavior, including planning and grooming behavior.

26. Use everyday examples to explain the concepts of cycles and behavior chains.

27. Reinforce the client's use of self-monitoring to heighten his/her awareness of the thoughts, feelings, and events that trigger sexual acting out.

28. Assist the client in completing and updating a relapse prevention plan.

16. Assign the client to write about the details of his/her offense.

25. Help the client to understand the precursors to his/her offending behavior, including planning and grooming behavior.

29. Explore what coping strategies were used or not

used in the most recent incident of sexual abuse perpetration.

22. Identify and verbalize fantasies and paraphilias that contribute to sexual misconduct or interfere with the development of healthy relationships. (30)

23. Develop a list of at least five alternative behaviors or coping strategies to use when confronted by triggers. (31)

24. Decrease the frequency of sexual references in daily speech and actions by 85 percent. (32, 33)

25. Identify cognitive distortions related to gender roles, anger, power, and control issues and verbalize at least three healthy alternative statements. (34, 35, 36)

30. Assist the client in identifying his/her sexual fantasies and deviant sexual arousal patterns that may trigger sexual abuse.

31. Reduce the client's deviant sexual arousal by assisting him/her in developing coping strategies (e.g., verbal satiation, covert sensitization, aversive conditioning, thought-stopping technique, progressive muscle relaxation, imagery, self-talk and distraction, etc.)

32. Point out to the client sexual references and content in his/her speech and behavior; help him/her to recognize when his/her behavior is inappropriate.

33. Instruct the client to gather feedback from teacher and caregivers regarding sexual references in his/her speech and behavior so that he/she is able to rate his/her progress in this area daily. Process the feedback with the client and look at alternatives.

34. Administer surveys and questionnaires (see *Assessing Sexual Abuse: A Resource Guide for Practitioners* by Prentky and Edmunds; see also

www.sinclairseminars.com/
shop/browse.php) that help the
client understand his/her
beliefs related to gender roles,
hostility, power, and control
issues.

35. Instruct the client to
complete a collage that
reflects his/her beliefs related
to how the two genders
should function in society.
Process the collages in therapy session.

36. Assist the client in developing
a list of cognitive distortions
related to gender roles, hostility, power, and control issues.
Proceed by helping the client
develop healthy alternative
self-statements to challenge
his/her distortions.

26. Acknowledge instances when
sex was used to express anger,
control, or revenge. (37)

37. Process with the client how
attitudes related to hostility,
power, and control have contributed to the choices that
he/she has made, especially
those related to sexual
misconduct.

27. Identify internal and external
anger cues and external anger
triggers; verbalize strategies to
manage anger. (38)

38. Teach the client how to
recognize internal (e.g.,
thoughts, physiological
changes, emotions, etc.)
and external (e.g., people,
places, things, situations, etc.)
anger cues and the techniques
to manage his/her anger (e.g.,
thought-stopping techniques,
distraction, relaxation techniques, healthy physical activity, reframing, etc.)

28. Recognize and express feelings related to past abuse (physical, sexual, and/or emotional) and how these feelings impact current functioning. (39, 40, 41)

39. Gently inquire about the client's past sexual abuse by asking him/her to discuss experiences when he/she felt that others violated his/her boundaries, especially physical boundaries.

40. Encourage the client to talk about similarities and differences related to the feelings he/she experiences when remembering his/her own sexual abuse victimization as opposed to his/her sexual abuse perpetration.

41. Educate the client about posttraumatic stress disorder and other phenomena that can occur when someone has been abused.

29. Attend a sexual abuse survivors group. (42)

42. Refer the client to a group for survivors of sexual abuse.

30. Acknowledge what emotional rewards are received as a result of offending behavior. (43)

43. Help the client to formulate what positive emotional reinforcement he/she is seeking when offending, and help him/her to find appropriate means of achieving these feelings.

31. Identify and challenge distorted beliefs and self-statements that interfere with the ability to form healthy relationships and get social and/or emotional needs met. (44)

44. Support the client in developing a list of distorted beliefs and self-statements that interfere with his/her ability to form healthy relationships. Assist him/her in developing alternative healthy and positive self-statements.

32. Increase understanding of the victim's perspective by writing

45. Assist the client in writing letters of responsibility and

a letter of responsibility and apology for perpetrating sexual abuse and by participating in other empathy exercises. (45, 46)

apology to the victim of his/her abuse to develop empathy without seeking excuse or escape from responsibility for the sexual abuse.

46. Expose the client to the feelings of victims by incorporating letters and audio- or videotapes of real victims into the session.

33. Verbalize accurate facts about sexual development and list at least three healthy values related to sexual identity to be incorporated into a new belief system. (47, 48)

47. Invite speakers (e.g., Planned Parenthood) to discuss sexual development (e.g., basic reproduction, sexual diseases, contraception, etc.)

48. Promote the development of nonexploitive relationships by assisting the client in identifying his/her values that contradict healthy, heterosexual relationships; teach those values that promote healthy relationships.

34. Sign a no-sexual-contact agreement. (49, 50)

49. Develop and monitor a behaviorally specific no-sexual-contact agreement, giving both positive and negative feedback as warranted.

50. Monitor the no-sexual-contact agreement and the relapse prevention plan while the client is in aftercare.

35. Caregivers implement effective boundary-setting and parenting techniques. (51, 52)

51. Teach the caregivers effective parenting and boundary-setting techniques and/or refer them to a structured parenting class.

52. Assign caregivers to read books on effective parenting (e.g., *Assertive Discipline for Parents* by Canter and Canter; *Setting Limits* by MacKenzie; *Toughlove* by York, York, and Wachtel; *Parents and Adolescents: Living Together,* Vol. 1: *The Basics* and Vol. 2: *Family Problem Solving* by Patterson and Forgatch); process the material read.

__. _____   __. _____
   _____   _____
__. _____   __. _____
   _____   _____
__. _____   __. _____
   _____   _____

DIAGNOSTIC SUGGESTIONS:

ICD-9-CM	*ICD-10-CM*	*DSM-5* Disorder, Condition, or Problem
312.9	F91.9	Unspecified Disruptive, Impulse Control, and Conduct Disorder
312.89	F91.8	Other Specified Disruptive, Impulse Control, and Conduct Disorder
312.81	F91.1	Conduct Disorder, Childhood-Onset Type
312.82	F91.2	Conduct Disorder, Adolescent-Onset Type
302.2	F65.4	Pedophilic Disorder
302.4	F65.2	Exhibitionistic Disorder
302.82	F65.3	Voyeuristic Disorder
302.9	F65.9	Unspecified Paraphilic Disorder
302.9	F65.89	Other Specified Paraphilic Disorder
995.53	T74.22XA	Child Sexual Abuse, Confirmed, Initial Encounter
995.53	T74.22XD	Child Sexual Abuse, Confirmed, Subsequent Encounter
_____	_____	_____
_____	_____	_____

SEXUAL PROMISCUITY

BEHAVIORAL DEFINITIONS

1. Engages in sexual relations with multiple partners while feeling little or no emotional attachment to them.
2. Engagement in sexual intercourse without taking precautions against unplanned pregnancy or being in position to assume responsibility for a baby.
3. Sexual involvement with one partner, but with little or no desire to make long-term commitment.
4. Failure to use safe-sex practices.
5. Routinely dressing in sexually provocative or seductive manner.
6. Numerous conversations that center around sexual themes or topics.
7. Excessive bragging or boasting about sexual encounters or activity.
8. Lack of empathy or sensitivity to how sexually promiscuous behavior negatively affects the partner's emotional, physical, sexual, or social well-being.
9. Strong preoccupation or fascination with viewing pornographic materials (e.g., magazines, videos, Internet sites, and provocative catalogs).
10. Low self-esteem as evidenced by self-disparaging remarks and predictions of future failure.
11. Depression as evidenced by irritability, social isolation, low energy, and sad affect.
12. Abuse of alcohol and/or drugs that alters mood and impairs judgment prior to and during sexual activity.
13. Advanced knowledge of sexuality for one's age.
14. History of being sexually abused as a child.
15. Family history of sexual promiscuity, infidelity, or sexualization of relationships.

—. _____

_____

—. _____

_____

—. _____

_____

LONG-TERM GOALS

1. Eliminate all sexual promiscuity and other inappropriate sexual behavior.
2. Terminate sexual behavior that does not reflect commitment, emotional intimacy, or a caring, mature relationship.
3. Implement effective birth control measures and use safe-sex practices.
4. Significantly reduce the frequency of sexual comments or innuendos during everyday conversations.
5. Demonstrate lasting commitment and genuine concern, empathy, and caring for one partner.
6. Establish and maintain close, meaningful interpersonal relationships that meet deeper needs for intimacy, closeness, and affection.
7. Resolve underlying emotional conflicts that contribute to the emergence of sexually promiscuous or inappropriate behavior.
8. Resolve conflicts within the family system and establish appropriate parent-child boundaries that reflect healthy attitudes about sexuality and minimize sexualization of relationships.

—. _____

_____

—. _____

_____

—. _____

_____

SHORT-TERM OBJECTIVES

1. Provide a detailed history of past and present sexual activity. (1, 2)

2. Identify the factors contributing to the emergence of sexually promiscuous behavior. (3, 4, 5, 6)

THERAPEUTIC INTERVENTIONS

1. Establish a rapport and actively build the level of trust with the client in individual sessions through consistent eye contact, active listening, unconditional positive regard, and warm acceptance so that he/she is able to talk openly about his/her past and present sexual activity.

2. Gather a detailed psychosexual history from the client and his/her caregivers that includes number of partners, frequency of activity, initial sexual experiences, degree of emotional attachment to partner(s), use of birth control and/or safe-sex practices, past sex education, and family attitudes about sexuality.

3. Probe the client's internal thoughts (e.g., "Sexual activity will bring me acceptance," or "Having sex will prove my masculinity or femininity") or precipitating external events (e.g., rejection from peers, family trauma, sexual abuse, academic failure, etc.) that contribute to sexually promiscuous behavior.

4. Explore the client's sexual fantasies that may provide insight into the factors contributing to his/her sexual promiscuity.

5. Have the client list the reasons why he/she has chosen to engage in premature or excessive sexual activity. Process this list with the client in session.

6. Instruct the client to use a journal as a self-monitoring device to record dates and times when he/she experienced strong sexual urges and identify external factors (e.g., people, places, events, etc.) that provoked strong desires. Process these journal entries to heighten his/her awareness of situations that produce strong sexual urges.

3. Disclose a history of sexual victimization that occurred in childhood or early adolescent years. (7)

7. Explore the client's background for a history of sexual abuse that may contribute to the emergence of sexually promiscuous behavior. (See the chapter entitled "Sexual Abuse Victim" in this Planner).

4. Verbalize insight into how past sexual victimization contributes to current sexual promiscuity. (8)

8. Assist the client in making a connection between his/her painful emotions about being victimized or treated as a sexual object in childhood by a perpetrator and currently treating others as impersonal sexual objects.

5. Express the emotions that are associated with past sexual victimization. (9, 10)

9. Encourage and support the client in expressing thoughts and feelings about the past sexual victimization. (See the chapter entitled "Sexual Abuse Victim" in this Planner.)

10. Refer the client to a group for survivors of sexual abuse.

6. Recognize and verbalize the connection between sexually promiscuous behavior and underlying feelings of low self-esteem or painful emotions. (11)

11. Explore sources of the client's feelings of depression, anxiety, or low self-esteem (e.g., parental criticism or rejection; physical, sexual, or emotional abuse; academic or social failures, etc.) and how they contribute to the emergence of sexually promiscuous behavior.

7. Identify constructive steps to take to build healthy self-image and reduce feelings of depression or anxiety. (12, 13)

12. Point out to the client the self-defeating nature of trying to build self-esteem or reduce feelings of depression and anxiety through sexual promiscuity. Assist him/her in developing an action plan to build a healthy self-image and reduce feelings of depression or anxiety. (See the chapter entitled "Low Self-Esteem" in this Planner.)

13. Assign the client the home-work exercise entitled "Three Ways to Change Yourself" from *The Brief Adolescent Therapy Homework Planner* (Jongsma, Peterson, and McInnis) in which the client is asked to draw pictures of the desired changes in himself/herself.

8. Verbalize a value for sexual activity beyond physical pleasure and/or trying to get someone to like you. (14, 15, 16)

14. Teach the value of reserving sexual intimacy for a relationship that has commitment, longevity, and maturity.

15. Teach the client that sexual intimacy is most rewarding when it is performed as a mutual expression of love and

respect versus being sexual to try to get someone to love you or only to meet your own needs for pleasure or conquest.

16. Assign the client to view videos that teach the value of making responsible decisions and respecting the thoughts, feelings, and needs of others about issues related to sexuality or sexual activity (e.g., *The Dating Bill of Rights; Sexual Harassment: Stop It Now; Let's Talk about Sex,* available through the Guidance Channel).

9. Verbalize an understanding of the serious risks that are involved in not using birth control or safe-sex practices, and commit to a firm implementation of the same. (17, 18, 19, 20)

17. Explore any underlying wishes (e.g., wanting a pregnancy to feel loved by a child, allowing a pregnancy to occur to secure a long-term commitment, death wishes, etc.) that have influenced the client's maladaptive behavior and not using birth control or safe-sex practices.

18. Counsel the client about the risks that are involved in sexually promiscuous behavior or unsafe-sex practices (e.g., sexually transmitted diseases, HIV/AIDS, unplanned or unwanted pregnancy, etc.).

19. Assign the client readings that educate him/her about the risks that are involved in unsafe sex (e.g., *Everything You Need to Know about Teen Pregnancy* by Hughes, *Everything You Need to Know about Teen Fatherhood* by Ayer,

Everything You Need to Know about Teen Motherhood by Hammerslough, and *Everything You Need to Know about Being HIV-Positive* by Shire). Process these readings in session.

20. Have the client view videos in session that increase his/her awareness of the dangerous consequences of engaging in sexually promiscuous or unsafe-sex practices (e.g., *STDs, AIDS, and the Clean Love Solution* and *Teen Pregnancy,* both available through the Guidance Channel). Process his/her feelings after viewing the video(s).

10. Read accurate literature about human sexual development. (21)

21. Assign readings to the preadolescent or early adolescent client that educate him/her about sexual development or physical changes, and answer any questions he/she may have about emerging sexuality (e.g., *What's Happening to My Body? Book for Boys or What's Happening to My Body? Book for Girls* by Madaras).

11. Identify and list effective birth control methods. (22, 23)

22. Teach the client the value of using birth control.

23. Educate the client about effective birth control methods (e.g., birth control pills, IUDs, condoms, etc.). Discuss the pros and cons of each method.

12. Attend a sexually oriented values clarification group. (24)

24. Refer the client to a therapeutic psychoeducational group that focuses on sexual values

clarification (e.g., gender-role values, sexual decision making, anatomy, etc.).

13. Decrease the frequency of rationalizations or excuses for inappropriate sexual behavior or talk. (25, 26)

25. Firmly confront the client's sexually promiscuous behavior, bragging about sexual behavior, or provocative talk. Point out the consequences for himself/herself and others.

26. Confront statements in which the client rationalizes or makes excuses for his/her inappropriate sexual behavior or talk and fails to accept responsibility for his/her misbehavior.

14. Identify and acknowledge the laws or legal consequences that are involved with sexual harassment or misconduct. (27, 28)

27. Educate the client about the possible legal consequences of sexual harassment or inappropriate sexual behavior.

28. Consult with the caregivers, school officials, probation officer, or juvenile justice officials about appropriate consequences for the client's inappropriate sexual behavior or sexual harassment (e.g., suspension from school, after-school detention, extension of probation, offer a formal apology, etc.).

15. List the negative impact that inappropriate sexual talk or behavior has on others. (29, 30, 31)

29. Instruct the client to offer a verbal or written apology to individuals whom he/she has offended with sexualized talk or inappropriate sexual behavior.

30. Use guided imagery and fantasy techniques to help the client to visualize possible consequences that he/she may experience as a result of sexual

promiscuity or unsafe-sex practices (e.g., unwanted pregnancy, sexually transmitted diseases, added responsibilities, etc.).

31. Ask the client to list between 5 and 10 negative consequences that his/her inappropriate sexual talk or behavior has had on other individuals to increase his/her empathy and sensitivity to the thoughts, feelings, and needs of others. Process this list with the client in a therapy session.

16. Identify irrational or distorted cognitive messages that increase the incidents of sexually promiscuous or inappropriate behavior. (3, 32, 33)

3. Probe the client's internal thoughts (e.g., "Sexual activity will bring me acceptance," or "Having sex will prove my masculinity or femininity") or precipitating external events (e.g., rejection from peers, family trauma, sexual abuse, academic failure, etc.) that contribute to sexually promiscuous behavior.

32. Assist the client in developing an awareness of the irrational or distorted cognitive messages that contribute to the emergence of sexually promiscuous or inappropriate behavior (e.g., "Pregnancy won't happen to me"; "I know he'll love me if we have sex together"; "Having multiple partners will make me popular"; etc.).

33. Explore the client's private logic or irrational thoughts (e.g., sense of entitlement, focus on his/her needs, desire

to elevate status in peer group, etc.) that influence him/her to engage in sexually promiscuous behavior.

17. Replace irrational or distorted cognitive messages with rational, reality-based thoughts. (34)

34. Teach the client to replace irrational or distorted thoughts about sexual behavior or activity with rational, reality-based cognitive messages (e.g., "I don't want to ruin my future plans by risking an unwanted pregnancy"; "A sexual relationship will not ensure that I will feel loved"; etc.).

18. Identify effective coping strategies to control sexual desires or impulses. (35)

35. Teach the client effective coping strategies (e.g., verbal satiation, covert sensitization, aversive imagery, thought-stopping techniques, progressive muscle relaxation, positive self-talk, and behavior substitution) to control strong sexual urges or impulses.

19. Sign a no-sexual-contact agreement. (36, 37)

36. Design and implement a behaviorally specific no-sexual-contact agreement whereby the client signs a contract and agrees not to engage in sexually promiscuous or deviant sexual talk.

37. Monitor the effectiveness of the no-sexual-contact agreement. Praise and reinforce the client for successfully adhering to the terms of the contract or explore factors contributing to his/her failure to follow the conditions.

20. Decrease the frequency of sexual references in daily speech by 85 percent. (25, 38, 39)

25. Firmly confront the client's sexually promiscuous behavior, bragging about sexual

behavior, or provocative talk. Point out the consequences for himself/herself and others.

38. Challenge and confront the client about the numerous sexual references that he/she verbalizes in everyday conversation. Assist the client in recognizing how his/her numerous sexual references may cause others to feel uncomfortable or view him/her in a negative light.

39. Help the client to realize how his/her bragging or boasting about sexual exploits or conquests harms social reputation for both himself/herself and others.

21. Increase the frequency of participation in meaningful conversations at home, school, or in the community without making any references to sexual topics or behavior. (40)

40. Encourage the caregivers and teachers to provide frequent praise and encouragement for the client when he/she is able to hold meaningful conversations or make positive contributions to family or classroom discussions without making any references to sexual topics of behavior.

22. Verbally identify prosocial behaviors to achieve status, recognition, and acceptance from peers. (41, 42, 43)

41. Assist the client in identifying more meaningful or healthy ways to achieve status, acceptance, or recognition from peers other than through engaging in sexually promiscuous behavior or boasting about his/her sexual conquests.

42. Direct the client to develop a list of positive social, responsible, recreational, or leisure activities (e.g., complete

school or homework assignments, go rollerblading, play video games at an arcade with friends, etc.). Encourage the client to engage in these activities, instead of acting on strong sexual desires or impulses.

43. Teach the client positive social skills (e.g., demonstrate active listening, compliment others, show interest or respond to other peers' problems, converse about nonsexual topics, etc.) to help him/her begin to establish close, meaningful peer relationships.

23. Verbalize the connection between sexual promiscuity and feelings of rejection or alienation by peers. (44, 45, 46)

44. Explore past experiences of rejection or alienation by peers that contributed to the emergence of the client's sexually promiscuous behavior. (See the chapter entitled "Peer Conflict" in this Planner.)

45. Encourage and support the client in the expression of painful emotions surrounding past rejection or alienation experiences by peers.

46. Have the client identify and discuss three situations where he/she felt rejected, alienated, or ostracized by peers shortly before engaging in sexually promiscuous behavior. Assist him/her in identifying more adaptive ways to deal with painful emotions other than through sexual acting out.

24. Describe involvement with pornography. (47)

47. Assess the client's interests and/or involvement with

pornographic materials (e.g., pornographic magazines, videos, provocative catalogs, Internet sites, etc.). Review the list of pornographic materials that lead to sexual arousal to assess specific sexual fantasies.

25. The caregivers enforce rules against the client viewing pornography. (48)

48. Assist the caregivers in establishing clearly defined rules, boundaries, and consequences for the client viewing or bringing pornographic materials into the home. Have the client repeat the rules to demonstrate that he/she understands the expectations.

26. The caregivers establish effective family rules and boundaries surrounding sexuality and sexual behavior. (49, 50, 51)

49. Conduct family therapy sessions to assess family values or beliefs about sexuality and boundaries for sexual behavior.

50. Explore the client's family background for a history of sexual promiscuity, infidelity, or inappropriate sexual behavior that provides modeling or reinforcement for his/her promiscuous behavior.

51. Teach the family members how to establish appropriate boundaries or rules surrounding sexuality or sexual behavior.

27. Family members verbalize healthy attitudes and values about sexuality and sexual behavior. (52, 53)

52. Confront or challenge the caregivers to cease making inappropriate sexual remarks, jokes, or innuendos in the presence of the client. Point out how such remarks reinforce his/her desire to engage in sexually promiscuous behavior.

53. Assess whether the parents' overly rigid discipline or strict beliefs and values about sexuality contribute to the client's desire to rebel and engage in sexually promiscuous behaviors as a maladaptive way to gain autonomy or greater independence.

28. Identify and list healthy and adaptive ways to gain autonomy. (54)

54. Conduct individual therapy sessions with the client to identify healthy or adaptive ways to achieve greater autonomy or independence other than through sexual acting out.

29. Describe the role of substance abuse in sexual acting out. (55)

55. Conduct or arrange for a substance abuse evaluation to determine whether substance abuse issues are contributing to the client's poor use of judgment and impulsivity prior to and during sexual activity. Refer the client for chemical dependence treatment, if indicated. (See the chapter entitled "Substance Abuse" in this Planner.)

30. Complete psychological testing and accept the feedback of the results. (56)

56. Arrange for psychological testing to assess whether emotional factors, attention-deficit/hyperactivity disorder (ADHD), or mania may be contributing to the client's impulsivity and poor use of judgment prior to and during engagement in sexual activity. Provide feedback on the evaluation findings to the client and his/her caregivers.

31. Cooperate with a physician's evaluation. (57)

57. Refer the client to a physician to evaluate his/her general medical condition, check for the presence of sexually transmitted diseases, and assess the need for medication for an affective disorder or ADHD.

__. _____
    _____

__. _____
    _____

__. _____
    _____

__. _____
    _____

__. _____
    _____

__. _____
    _____

DIAGNOSTIC SUGGESTIONS:

ICD-9-CM	_ICD-10-CM_	_DSM-5_ Disorder, Condition, or Problem
296.xx	F32.x	Major Depressive Disorder, Single Episode
296.xx	F33.x	Major Depressive Disorder, Recurrent Episode
300.4	F34.1	Persistent Depressive Disorder
296.89	F31.81	Bipolar II Disorder
296.xx	F31.xx	Bipolar I Disorder
303.90	F10.20	Alcohol Use Disorder, Moderate or Severe
305.00	F10.10	Alcohol Use Disorder, Mild
304.30	F12.20	Cannabis Use Disorder, Moderate or Severe
305.20	F12.10	Cannabis Use Disorder, Mild
312.8	F91.x	Conduct Disorder
314.01	F90.1	Attention-Deficit/Hyperactivity Disorder, Predominately Hyperactive /Impulsive Presentation
995.53	T74.22XA	Child Sexual Abuse, Confirmed, Initial Encounter
995.53	T74.22XD	Child Sexual Abuse, Confirmed, Subsequent Encounter
_____	_____	_____
_____	_____	_____

STEALING/BREAKING AND ENTERING

BEHAVIORAL DEFINITIONS

1. Recurrent pattern of stealing items of trivial value at home, school, or in the community.
2. History of stealing items of high value or worth without confronting a victim.
3. History of stealing items while confronting a victim (e.g., mugging, purse snatching, extortion, armed robbery, etc.).
4. Illegal breaking and entering into a home, car, building, or place of business.
5. Acts of vandalism or destruction of property after breaking and entering into a home, car, building, or business.
6. Affiliation with negative peer groups that contributes to acts of stealing or illegal breaking and entering.
7. Impulsivity as manifested by repeatedly seeking instant gratification of needs, exercising poor judgment, taking inappropriate risks, and failing to stop and think about the consequences of stealing and/or breaking-and-entering behaviors.
8. Lack of guilt, remorse, or empathy for how stealing negatively impacts others.
9. Consistent failure to accept responsibility for illegal activities accompanied by a pattern of rationalizing or making excuses for stealing and/or breaking and entering.
10. Intense feelings of anger or rage that are channeled into stealing and/or breaking and entering.
11. Sense of entitlement and/or preoccupation with a desire for material goods, status, or power.
12. Underlying feelings of depression, anxiety, or insecurity that lead to stealing as a cry for help.
13. Deep-seated feelings of deprivation arising out of past losses, abandonment, or rejection experiences.

14. Overt or tacit approval of stealing by parents or other family members.

__. _____

_____

__. _____

_____

__. _____

_____

LONG-TERM GOALS

1. Cease all incidents of stealing or illegal breaking and entering.
2. Demonstrate respect for the rights and property of others on a consistent basis.
3. Obtain material goods through purchases after being paid for honest effort, performing chores, or maintaining steady employment.
4. Resolve the core conflicts that contribute to the emergence and maintenance of stealing or breaking-and-entering behaviors.
5. Express anger through appropriate verbalizations and healthy physical outlets instead of channeling anger into acts of stealing or breaking and entering.
6. Establish and maintain close friendships and meaningful interpersonal relationships to fulfill the need for acceptance and overcome feelings of deprivation or rejection.
7. Comply with all the conditions of probation or mandates of the criminal justice system.
8. Parents establish and maintain appropriate parent-child boundaries, setting firm consistent limits with the client's stealing, allowing him/her to experience legal consequences of illegal actions.

__. _____

_____

__. _____

_____

__. _____

_____

SHORT-TERM OBJECTIVES

THERAPEUTIC INTERVENTIONS

1. Complete psychological testing. (1, 4)

2. Complete a psychoeducational evaluation. (2, 4)

3. Complete a substance abuse evaluation and comply with the recommendations offered by the evaluation findings. (3, 4)

1. Arrange for psychological testing to assess whether emotional factors, psychotic process, or attention-deficit/hyperactivity disorder (ADHD) are contributing to the client's pattern of stealing or breaking and entering.

4. Provide feedback to the client, his/her caregivers, school officials, or criminal justice officials regarding psychological, substance abuse, and/or psychoeducational assessments.

2. Arrange for a psychoeducational evaluation of the client to rule out the presence of a learning disability or possible intellectual limitations that may be contributing to his/her poor use of judgment and acts of stealing or breaking and entering.

4. Provide feedback to the client, his/her caregivers, school officials, or criminal justice officials regarding psychological, substance abuse, and/or psychoeducational assessments.

3. Conduct or arrange for a substance abuse evaluation to determine whether substance abuse issues are contributing to the client's stealing or

breaking and entering. Refer the client for treatment if indicated. (See the chapter entitled "Substance Abuse" in this Planner).

4. Provide feedback to the client, his/her caregivers, school officials, or criminal justice officials regarding psychological, substance abuse, and/or psychoeducational assessments.

4. Provide a detailed history of past incidents of stealing or breaking and entering. (5, 6)

5. Gather a detailed history of the client's stealing behavior, including age of onset, frequency, value of stolen goods, and sequence of events leading up to stealing, to help provide insight into the factors contributing to illegal behavior.

6. Obtain copies of the client's pertinent police investigation reports or court records to gain insight into the factors contributing to stealing or breaking and entering.

5. Increase compliance with the rules or conditions of probation. (7)

7. Consult with criminal justice officials about the appropriate consequences for the client's stealing and/or breaking and entering (e.g., probation, pay restitution, perform community service, offer an apology letter, etc.).

6. Move to an appropriate alternative setting to manage impulsivity and deter stealing/illegal breaking and entering. (8, 9)

8. Consult with the caregivers and criminal justice officials about the need to place the client in a detention facility or alternative setting (e.g., foster home, group home, or

residential program) because of his/her recurrent stealing or breaking-and-entering behaviors.

9. Confer with the caregivers, attorneys, or criminal justice officials about whether the adolescent client should be referred to the adult court system for trial and/or sentencing because of his/her repeated offenses or the seriousness of the charges (e.g., theft involving violence or harm inflicted upon others, felony charges, etc.).

7. Return all stolen goods to rightful owners. (10)

10. Recommend that the caregivers require the client to return stolen goods to rightful owners or places of business.

8. Make restitution or pay for stolen items or damaged property. (11, 12)

11. Insist that the client make restitution (e.g., pay for stolen items or damaged property, perform chores or community service, etc.).

12. Assign the client household tasks or chores to make restitution for stolen goods and/or damages incurred during breaking and entering.

9. Offer sincere apology to victims of stealing/illegal breaking and entering. (13)

13. Assign the client to offer a verbal or written apology to victim(s).

10. The caregivers report incidents of stealing or illegal breaking and entering to police or appropriate criminal justice officials. (14)

14. Challenge the caregivers not to protect the client from the legal consequences of his/her stealing and/or illegal breaking

and entering and to report his/her illegal behavior to the police or criminal justice officials.

11. The caregivers develop clear rules and follow through with consequences for stealing and/or illegal breaking and entering. (12, 15, 16)

12. Assign the client household tasks or chores to make restitution for stolen goods and/or damages incurred during breaking and entering.

15. Assist the client's caregivers in establishing clearly defined (and written) rules and consequences for stealing or breaking and entering. Inform the client and have him/her repeat rules or consequences to demonstrate an understanding of the expectations.

16. Refer the caregivers to parenting classes to help them establish appropriate parent-child boundaries and to learn effective disciplinary techniques.

12. Reduce the frequency and severity of stealing or breaking-and-entering behavior. (17, 18)

17. Establish a contingency contract with the client and his/her caregivers that clearly outlines consequences if he/she is caught stealing. Have the client sign the contract, and post it in a visible place in the home.

18. Teach mediational and self-control strategies (e.g., guided imagery; relaxation; "stop, look, listen, and think"; etc.) to help the client resist the urge to steal or engage in breaking and entering behaviors.

13. Identify and list potential consequences for self and others if problems with stealing or breaking and entering persist. (15, 19, 20, 21)

15. Assist the client's caregivers in establishing clearly defined (and written) rules and consequences for stealing or breaking and entering. Inform the client and have him/her repeat rules or consequences to demonstrate an understanding of the expectations.

19. Firmly confront the client's stealing or breaking and entering, pointing out the consequences for himself/herself and others.

20. Use role-playing and role-reversal techniques to help the client develop an awareness of how his/her stealing and/or breaking and entering negatively affect the victims, and ask the client to list 10 negative effects on others.

21. Explore the client's private logic or irrational thoughts (e.g., sense of entitlement, preoccupation with wealth or status, etc.) that influence him/her to steal. Assist the client in discovering for himself/herself how stealing produces negative consequences.

14. Increase the number of statements that reflect the acceptance of responsibility for stealing and/or illegal breaking and entering, and decrease the frequency of excuses or

22. Teach the client the value of respect for others and their property as the basis for building trust and mutual respect in all relationships.

verbalizations that project the blame for stealing and/or illegal breaking and entering onto other people. (22, 23)

15. Identify family problems that may be contributing to stealing behavior. (24)

16. The caregivers increase the frequency of praise and positive reinforcement for the client's positive social or responsible behaviors. (25, 26)

17. Increase time spent with the uninvolved or detached caregiver(s) in leisure, school, or household activities. (27)

23. Confront statements in which the client rationalizes or makes excuses for his/her stealing and fails to accept responsibility for misbehavior.

24. Conduct family therapy sessions to explore the family dynamics that may contribute to the emergence of the client's stealing or breaking and entering (e.g., poverty, lack of parental supervision, neglect, abuse, antisocial role modeling by the caregivers, etc.).

25. Encourage the caregivers to provide frequent praise and positive reinforcement for the client's positive social behaviors or responsible actions (sharing personal items with peers and siblings, performing chores, postponing leisure activities until homework is complete, etc.). Instruct the caregivers to look for opportunities to catch the client being responsible or good.

26. Instruct the caregivers to spend between 10 and 15 minutes each day in one-on-one time with the client so that he/she can talk about his/her concerns, problems, or daily activities.

27. Give a directive to the uninvolved or disengaged caregivers to spend more time with the client in leisure, school, or household activities.

18. The caregivers cease the pattern of giving the client whatever he/she wants. (28, 29)

28. Probe factors that contribute to the client's sense of entitlement or overemphasis on acquiring material goods or status (e.g., overindulgence by the caregivers, underlying feelings of deprivation, rejection experiences, etc.).

29. Assess whether the caregivers' pattern of giving the client whatever he/she demands contributes to his/her sense of entitlement and stealing behavior. Challenge the caregivers to cease their pattern of overindulgence and to set limits with the client's demanding or manipulative behaviors.

19. The caregivers cease providing tacit approval and/or reinforcing stealing and/or breaking-and-entering behavior. (30, 31)

30. Confront and challenge the caregivers to cease behaviors that model disrespect for the law (e.g., lying about children's age to get them into a movie for half price, boasting about cheating on income tax, etc.). Point out to the caregivers that such behavior sends a message to the client that stealing is acceptable in some situations.

31. Confront the caregivers or other family members to stop giving overt or tacit approval for the client's stealing behavior (e.g., the client witnesses his/her caregivers or family members shoplifting; the caregivers involve children in shoplifting; the caregivers

ignore and allow stealing because the family benefits from material goods; etc.).

20. Verbalize an understanding of how current stealing and/or illegal breaking-and-entering behaviors are associated with past neglect, abuse, loss, or abandonment. (24, 32, 33)

24. Conduct family therapy sessions to explore the family dynamics that may contribute to the emergence of the client's stealing or breaking and entering (e.g., poverty, lack of parental supervision, neglect, abuse, antisocial role modeling by the caregivers, etc.).

32. Explore the client's family background for a history of neglect, abuse, abandonment, imprisonment, or drug and/or alcohol usage that may contribute to his/her stealing or breaking and entering.

33. Encourage and support the client in expressing feelings that are associated with past neglect, abuse, abandonment, or a family member's chemical dependency. Assist him/her in making the connection to stealing or breaking-and-entering behaviors.

21. Identify and verbally express feelings associated with past neglect, abuse, loss, or abandonment. (33, 34, 35)

33. Encourage and support the client in expressing feelings that are associated with past neglect, abuse, abandonment, or a family member's chemical dependency. Assist him/her in making the connection to stealing or breaking-and-entering behaviors.

34. Assign the client to the task of writing a letter to the absent caregiver. Process the content of this letter in a follow-up session to help him/her express feelings about separation or abandonment issues.

35. Use the empty chair technique to provide the client with the opportunity to express feelings of anger, hurt, or sadness in a constructive manner toward the abusive or uninvolved caregiver.

22. Recognize and verbalize how unmet needs and painful emotions are connected to stealing and/or illegal breaking and entering. (36)

36. Assist the client in making a connection between unmet needs or underlying painful emotions (e.g., fearfulness, anxiety, depression, deprivation, etc.) and stealing or breaking and entering.

23. Identify supportive people who can assist in meeting emotional nurturance needs. (37)

37. Assist the client in identifying supportive people to whom the client can turn for emotional support and acceptance instead of continuing to steal as a cry for help.

24. Identify and implement actions that will lead to constructive satisfaction of unmet needs. (38, 39, 40, 41)

38. Help the client to identify more constructive ways to meet his/her unfulfilled needs (e.g., friendship, intimacy, material goods, etc.) other than through stealing.

39. Praise and reinforce the client for taking constructive steps to meet deeper, more meaningful needs and resisting the urge or impulse to steal.

40. Give the client a homework assignment of identifying between three and five role models and listing the reasons why he/she admires each role model. Explore the factors that contributed to the role model's success. Encourage the client to take similar positive steps to achieve his/her goals other than through illegal behaviors.

41. Employ the Three Wishes Game from *The Brief Adolescent Therapy Homework Planner* (Jongsma, Peterson, and McInnis) to identify the client's needs or wishes. Process the content of the client's drawing and help him/her to identify constructive ways to meet needs.

25. Express anger through appropriate verbalizations and healthy physical outlets. (42, 43, 44)

42. Teach the client effective anger management techniques (e.g., "stop, look, listen, and think"; count to 10; relaxation techniques; etc.) to help him/her express feelings of anger through appropriate verbalizations and healthy physical outlets instead of channeling anger or aggressive impulses into stealing.

43. Explore whether the client's stealing or breaking and entering are related to a need for revenge or retaliation. Help the client to identify more effective ways to express anger or cope with past or perceived hurt or disappointments by

others (e.g., use "I" messages to express anger; identify and verbalize positive changes that he/she desires from the other person; directly express hurt and sadness; etc.).

44. Teach the client effective conflict resolution skills (e.g., identify the problem, brainstorm alternate solutions, select an option, implement a course of action, and evaluate the outcome) to help him/her resolve conflict more effectively instead of enacting revenge through acts of stealing or vandalism.

26. Identify and list coping strategies to help control the impulse to steal. (45, 46)

45. Explore periods of time when the client demonstrated good impulse control and did not engage in any acts of stealing and/or illegal breaking and entering. Reinforce any positive coping mechanisms that the client used in the past to control the impulse to steal or break and enter.

46. Introduce the idea that the client can cease his/her pattern of stealing by asking, "What will you be doing in the future when you stop getting into trouble?" Process the client's responses and assist him/her in developing an action plan to achieve his/her goals or desired changes in behavior.

27. Verbalize how affiliation with negative peer groups contributes to stealing and/or illegal breaking and entering. (47)

47. Teach the power of peer group influence over decision making. Review instances in which the client was negatively influenced by peers.

28. Report instances of assertively resisting peer pressure to steal or break and enter. (48, 49, 50)

48. Refer the client for group therapy to improve his/her judgment, impulse control, peer influence management, and interpersonal skills.

49. Teach the client effective communication and assertiveness skills to successfully resist negative peer influences or pressures to steal.

50. Assign the client to view the video entitled *Refusal Skills* (available from Childswork/Childsplay, LLC) to teach effective assertiveness skills and help him/her resist negative peer influences to steal.

29. Increase the frequency of socially appropriate behaviors with peers. (48, 51)

48. Refer the client for group therapy to improve his/her judgment, impulse control, peer influence management, and interpersonal skills.

51. Assist the client in identifying more constructive ways to earn peer approval and acceptance other than through affiliating with negative peers who steal (e.g., compliment others, attend school social activities, try out for a school play or a sports team, etc.).

30. Increase verbalizations of empathy and sensitivity to how stealing and/or breaking-and-entering behaviors negatively impact other people. (20, 52, 59)

20. Use role-playing and role-reversal techniques to help the client develop an awareness of how his/her stealing and/or breaking and entering negatively affect the victims, and ask the client to list 10 negative effects on others.

52. Use the exercise entitled "Headed in the Right Direction" from *The Brief Adolescent Therapy Treatment Planner* (Jongsma, Peterson, and McInnis) to increase the client's empathy and sensitivity to how his/her stealing or breaking-and-entering behaviors negatively impact others.

59. Instruct the client to draw pictures reflecting how his/her stealing behavior affects himself/herself and others.

31. Secure and maintain steady employment to deter the impulse to steal and earn income to buy desired material goods. (53, 54, 55)

53. Refer the client to vocational training to develop basic job skills and find employment.

54. Encourage and reinforce the client's acceptance of the responsibility of a job, the authority of a supervisor, and the employer's rules.

55. Teach the client budgeting or money management skills to delay the need for immediate gratification and resist impulse buying so that he/she can save money to purchase more meaningful or valuable material goods.

32. Earn money or income through household chores or neighborhood jobs. (55, 56, 57)

55. Teach the client budgeting or money management skills to delay the need for immediate gratification and resist impulse buying so that he/she can save money to purchase more meaningful or valuable material goods.

56. Assist the caregivers in developing an allowance plan to reward the client for performing chores and provide him/her with the opportunity to earn income to buy desired material goods.

57. Encourage the younger client to earn income by performing jobs in the neighborhood or for his/her caregivers (e.g., mowing lawns, delivering papers, babysitting, shoveling snow, etc.).

33. Express feelings and identify needs through artwork and mutual storytelling. (58, 59)

58. Use puppets, dolls, or stuffed animals with the younger client to create a story that models effective ways to resist the urge to steal and meet needs through constructive actions. Then ask the client to create a story with similar characters or themes.

59. Instruct the client to draw pictures reflecting how his/her stealing behavior affects himself/herself and others.

34. Take medication as prescribed by the physician. (60, 61)

60. Arrange for a physician to perform a medication evaluation of the client to improve his/her impulse control and stabilize his/her mood.

61. Monitor the client for medication compliance, effectiveness, and side effects.

__. _____   __. _____
    _____   _____
__. _____   __. _____
    _____   _____
__. _____   __. _____
    _____   _____

DIAGNOSTIC SUGGESTIONS:

ICD-9-CM	_ICD-10-CM_	_DSM-5_ Disorder, Condition, or Problem
312.81	F91.1	Conduct Disorder, Childhood-Onset Type
312.82	F91.2	Conduct Disorder, Adolescent-Onset Type
313.81	F91.3	Oppositional Defiant Disorder
312.9	F91.9	Unspecified Disruptive, Impulse Control, and Conduct Disorder
312.89	F91.8	Other Specified Disruptive, Impulse Control, and Conduct Disorder
314.01	F90.2	Attention-Deficit/Hyperactivity Disorder, Combined Presentation
314.01	F90.1	Attention-Deficit/Hyperactivity Disorder, Predominately Hyperactive /Impulsive Presentation
296.xx	F32.x	Major Depressive Disorder, Single Episode
296.xx	F33.x	Major Depressive Disorder, Recurrent Episode
300.4	F34.1	Persistent Depressive Disorder
V71.02	Z72.810	Adolescent Antisocial Behavior
V61.20	Z62.820	Parent-Child Relational Problem
317	F70	Intellectual Disability, Mild
V62.89	R41.83	Borderline Intellectual Functioning
_____	_____	_____
_____	_____	_____

SUBSTANCE ABUSE

BEHAVIORAL DEFINITIONS

1. Caught or observed intoxicated and/or high on two or more occasions.
2. Self-report of using alcohol or illicit drugs almost daily or using them until intoxicated on a regular basis.
3. Drug paraphernalia and/or alcohol found in the client's possession or in his/her personal area (e.g., bedroom, car, school locker, backpack, etc.).
4. Exhibiting warning signs of substance abuse (e.g., change in friends to those oriented toward alcohol and/or drug use, red and glazed eyes, truancy, etc.).
5. Reduction of or elimination of social, academic, or recreational activities to pursue substance use or related activities.
6. Poor school performance, irregular attendance, suspensions, or expulsions that are related to substance use.
7. Substance-related arrests (e.g., minor in possession, driving under the influence, disorderly conduct, possession of a controlled substance, physical assault, stealing alcohol, etc.).
8. Violating a condition of probation or a court order by continuing the use of substances.
9. Continuing substance use despite the knowledge of negative physical, legal, social, and/or psychological consequences that have resulted from drug use.
10. Experiences withdrawal symptoms when not using a substance (e.g., hand tremor, sweating, stomach cramps, etc.) and/or continues to use drugs to eliminate withdrawal symptoms.
11. Using increased amounts of a substance to experience intoxication and/or experiencing a diminished effect when using the same amount of a substance.
12. Spending a great deal of time trying to obtain, use, or recover from the effects of a substance.

13. Positive family history of chemical dependence.

___. _____

_____

___. _____

_____

___. _____

_____

LONG-TERM GOALS

1. Confirm or rule out the existence of chemical dependence.
2. Eliminate the use and/or abuse of mood-altering substances.
3. Discontinue all delinquent acts, especially those associated with substance abuse.
4. Reestablish connections with relationships and groups that will support and enhance ongoing recovery from chemical dependence.
5. Improve coping skills to deal effectively with problems.
6. Caregivers support the client's chemical dependence recovery and monitor his/her behavior.
7. Increase participation in structured activities that will increase healthy functioning in the community.

___. _____

_____

___. _____

_____

___. _____

_____

SHORT-TERM OBJECTIVES	THERAPEUTIC INTERVENTIONS
1. The client, caregivers, and/or probation officer provide information about the client's substance use and other areas of functioning. (1, 2)	1. Complete a comprehensive assessment that outlines the severity and nature of the substances used by the client. Determine additional problems that require

intervention (e.g., family concerns, scholastic difficulties, legal problems, etc.).

2. Obtain a history of formal drug screens (e.g., urinalysis, Breathalyzer™, saliva test, etc.) from relevant people (e.g., previous treatment facility, probation officer, case manager, etc.).

2. Comply with a referral to a physician for evaluation and treatment of any physiological damage resulting from or exacerbated by substance use. (3, 4)

3. Require the client to have a physical examination to determine any physiological problems that have resulted from or are exacerbated by drug use.

4. Monitor the client's adherence to medical orders and/or process his/her decisions not to comply with the physician's recommendations.

3. Participate in an orientation to the therapy program, and accept feedback regarding treatment recommendations. (5, 6)

5. Outline the information about the client to be shared with agencies and/or the court and the consequences for failure to comply with treatment expectations. Obtain consents when warranted from the client and/or his/her caregivers.

6. Provide feedback to the client, his/her caregivers, and juvenile justice officials regarding the assessment results and recommendations, including the appropriate level of care (e.g., substance abuse education, outpatient services, inpatient or residential care, etc.).

4. List the benefits of participating in substance abuse treatment and consequences for not complying with treatment. (7)

7. Process with the client the benefits of participating in and completing substance abuse treatment (e.g., legal charge may be dismissed, increased freedom, improved functioning, etc.) as well as the consequences for not completing treatment (e.g., formal processing of legal charge, deteriorating health, decreased freedom, etc.).

5. The probation officer and/or case manager assist the treatment team by enforcing the client's compliance with treatment recommendations. (8, 9)

8. Collaborate with other professionals (e.g., case manager, probation officer, school officials, etc.) to keep the client engaged in treatment and to ensure that other problems are being addressed (e.g., mental health issues, school difficulties, physiological problems, employment concerns, etc.).

9. Monitor the client's substance use directly or by obtaining reports of urine screens or other drug tests from the probation officer or the case manager.

6. Disclose the connection between substance abuse and participation in illegal activities. (10, 11)

10. Explore with the client the connection between his/her substance use and his/her legal charges (e.g., stealing, assaultive behavior, prostituting, driving under the influence, etc.).

11. Review with the client each charge and determine if alcohol and/or other substances influenced his/her behavior.

7. Identify at least three cognitive distortions that support substance use and criminal activity. (12)

8. Challenge faulty thinking by identifying and implementing adaptive thoughts that support sobriety and a crime-free lifestyle. (13, 14)

9. The client and the family verbalize an understanding of the negative effects of drugs and the addiction cycle. (15, 16, 17, 18)

12. Use examples to illustrate for the client the connection between how thoughts lead to feelings that prompt us to act in specific ways. Help the client to identify his/her thoughts and beliefs that support substance use and/or criminal activity (e.g., I'm not hurting anyone; I am only going to have one drink; I got away with stealing once, I won't get caught; etc.).

13. Assist the client with creating alternative and realistic thoughts to challenge distorted, faulty thinking.

14. Assign the client to implement realistic cognitions in daily life and record his/her experiences. Process the results.

15. Use a variety of media (e.g., film, bibliotherapy, group discussion, etc.) to provide basic facts to the client and his/her family about the negative physical, psychological, and social impact that substances have on the user, family members, and society.

16. Explain the addiction cycle as it relates to the direct (effects of intoxication) and indirect (effects of withdrawal) effects of substance use (e.g., clients use substances for the direct effects and continue to use them to combat indirect effects). Underscore the need to experience discomfort (withdrawal) to break psychological or physical addiction.

17. Outline the connection between HIV and drug use (e.g., the lack of judgment that results in high-risk sex and/or intravenous drug use).

18. Assist the client in listing the negative impact that substance use has had on his/her life (e.g., poor scholastic performance, health concerns, poor family relationships, legal difficulties, etc.).

10. Reduce to one time per week or less the frequency of lying or minimizing regarding substance use. (19)

19. Confront the client when he/she has been dishonest about drug use, and encourage him/her to accept responsibility for drug use.

11. List what has motivated and encouraged substance use. (20, 21, 22)

20. Assist the client in exploring the reasons he/she engages in drug use (e.g., escape, pleasure, self-medication, peer pressure, etc.).

21. Determine with the client those factors that place him/her at risk for substance dependence (e.g., lack of positive social network, positive family history for drug use, low self-esteem, etc.).

22. Instruct the client to write an autobiography that underscores information about growing up in his/her family, including any family history of substance abuse. The history of his/her first use of substances and criminal involvement should also be detailed.

12. Identify unresolved, emotionally charged issues that may contribute to substance use. (23)

23. Explore for any unresolved, emotionally charged issues (e.g., abandonment and/or

neglect, abuse, grief or loss, etc.) that may contribute to substance abuse.

13. Implement positive self-talk to reduce negative mood states that contribute to substance use. (24, 25)

24. Assist the client with understanding the concept of self-talk (e.g., things we tell ourselves about ourselves). Encourage the client to reward himself/herself by using positive self-talk when he/she avoids drugs or criminal activities.

25. Prompt the client to recognize when he/she is resorting to negative self-talk that may lead to relapse. Assist him/her with learning to replace negative self-talk with positive self-descriptive statements.

14. Report on the implementation of assertive communication skills. (26, 27)

26. Teach the client the difference between assertive (e.g., use of "I" statements, nonthreatening body gestures, not denying others rights, etc.) and aggressive communication styles (e.g., using putdowns, threatening tone or body movement, imposing on the rights of others, etc.). Allow the client to practice new communication skills in sessions through role playing or while addressing issues with family members.

27. Assign the client to journal assertive communication experiences. Process the journal content in subsequent sessions.

15. Implement anger management techniques. (28)

28. Teach the client anger management techniques (e.g., taking a time-out, recognizing

anger cues, using positive coping statements, etc.) to reduce his/her reliance on substances to modulate anger.

16. List and implement the steps of problem solving. (29)

29. Introduce to the client the concept and steps of problem solving (e.g., identifying the problem, choosing a goal, identifying various solutions, listing the pros and cons of each possible solution, choosing a solution and examining the outcome, etc.).

17. Practice relaxation skills to reduce tension and stress. (30)

30. Teach relaxation techniques (e.g., progressive muscle relaxation, imagery techniques, deep breathing, etc.) to assist the client with managing stress.

18. Report on the implementation of new social interaction, problem solving, and relaxation skills. (31, 32)

31. Assist the client with formulating healthy, positive friendships by teaching him/her social interaction skills (e.g., ways to meet new people, practice starting conversations with others, targeting and/or changing negative ways of interacting, etc.).

32. Encourage the client to keep a journal to document his/her feelings and actions, including how he/she handles difficult situations and how he/she might have handled events differently using relaxation, social interaction, problem-solving, or anger management skills.

19. The caregivers support the client's treatment compliance. (33, 34)

33. Encourage and support the caregivers' involvement with professionals (e.g., probation officers; case managers; thera-

pists; school psychiatrists, officials; etc.) who are assisting the client's effort toward sobriety and related issues.

34. Assist the caregivers with establishing ways that they will become involved in their child's recovery (e.g., attend Al-Anon or other support groups for caregivers, commit to family therapy sessions, provide appropriate structure at home, etc.).

20. The caregivers increase structure and the use of monitoring techniques in the home to promote the client's sobriety and crime-free lifestyle. (35, 36)

35. Encourage the caregivers to outline expectations with the client regarding rules of the home and consequences for failure to abide by these conditions.

36. Foster an appropriate monitoring of the client's activities, peers, and movement by the caregivers.

21. Participate in family therapy to deal with issues that have contributed to use of substances. (37, 38)

37. Encourage the caregivers and family members to participate in family therapy sessions to diminish family dynamics that may contribute to drug use (e.g., sibling rivalry, marital discord, parental substance abuse, lack of supervision, etc.).

38. Process with the client and his/her family the impact that his/her drug use and criminal activity has had on family relationships and/or functioning.

22. Cooperate with employment training and seek employment. (39)

23. Consistently attend and give good effort to school responsibilities. (40)

24. Increase participation in positive social/recreational activities. (41)

25. List a minimum of three stressors or triggers that may lead to relapse. (42)

26. Identify strategies to deal with triggers and/or cravings that pose a threat to sobriety. (43, 44)

39. Refer and support the client's involvement in employment training and/or opportunities.

40. Support the client's return to the educational setting by helping him/her determine how drugs contributed to academic difficulties. Assist him/her in problem-solving how to deal with obstacles to educational goals.

41. Assist the client in listing alternative social and/or recreational activities to participate in instead of using drugs. Brainstorm with the client those obstacles and solutions that will allow participation in healthy activities.

42. Prompt the client to list triggers (e.g., people, emotions, high-risk situations, etc.) that will create cravings for substance use.

43. Provide the client an opportunity to discuss when he/she used strategies to cope with cravings successfully. Have the client list ways that he/she plans to deal with current triggers that prompt substance use (e.g., avoid certain people, places, or things; spend time with sober friends and/or family members; learn to cope with emotions; etc.).

44. Encourage the client to call a sober family member or friend when cravings become strong.

27. Implement the use of reminders as to the consequences of substance abuse and the benefits of sobriety. (45, 46, 47)

45. Prompt the client to list the negative consequences of participating in substance use Encourage him/her to keep the list in a visible spot to remind him/her why he/she wants to maintain sobriety.

46. Encourage the client to create a list detailing the benefits to staying drug free and to review this list when cravings happen.

47. Create with the client a scare-yourself image consisting of the vivid smells, sights, and sounds of his/her worst substance abuse–related memory and/or fear that can be conjured when he/she feels the need to use substances.

28. Use positive self-talk to guide behavior and avoid relapse. (24, 25, 48)

24. Assist the client with understanding the concept of self-talk (e.g., things we tell ourselves about ourselves). Encourage the client to reward himself/herself by using positive self-talk when he/she avoids drugs or criminal activities.

25. Prompt the client to recognize when he/she is resorting to negative self-talk that may lead to relapse. Assist him/her with learning to replace negative self-talk with positive self-descriptive statements.

48. Explain to the client how to ride out his/her craving by focusing on thoughts and feelings to counter urges to

engage in substance use. Help
the client to concentrate on
using self-talk to challenge
urges (e.g., telling himself/her-
self to walk in the opposite
direction to a friend's house
instead of going past a known
source of alcohol or drugs).

29. Report on the use of refusal
tactics when faced with an
offer of substance use. (49)

49. Provide opportunities for the
client to practice refusal tactics (e.g., using direct eye contact to say no, saying no in a
clear firm voice, not debating
when you say no, etc.) in
therapy sessions by identifying and role-playing high-risk
situations that may lead to
relapse.

30. Attend a 12-step recovery
group. (50)

50. Refer the client to a 12-step
self-help group for teens struggling with substance abuse
and/or dependence (e.g., Nar-
cotics Anonymous, Alcoholics
Anonymous, Cocaine Anony-
mous, etc.).

31. Verbalize a greater understanding of personal relapse
process. (51, 52, 53, 54)

51. Assist the client in learning the
difference between a lapse
(e.g., a brief period of drug
use or brief reemergence of
old thoughts or habits present
when using substance) and a
relapse (e.g., full-blown drug
use resulting in old feelings,
thoughts, and habits).

52. Encourage the client to list
obstacles to maintaining absti-
nence (e.g., attitudes about
drug use, peer group, desires
to self-medicate, etc.) and

assist him/her in developing coping strategies for each obstacle.

53. Confront the client when he/she has been dishonest about drug use, and encourage him/her to accept responsibility for drug use.

54. Outline with the client his/her most recent cycle of drug use (i.e., thoughts, feelings, and actions that led to substance use). Help the client to determine how he/she could have intervened at each point in the cycle to prevent substance abuse.

32. Create and monitor a relapse prevention plan that underscores how to cope with triggers and obstacles to maintaining sobriety. Make changes as treatment progresses. (55, 56)

55. Process with the client the circumstances related to his/her most recent substance use and how and/or why coping skills were ineffective. Assist the client in making appropriate changes in his/her coping strategies.

56. Assist the client with completing a relapse prevention plan that outlines obstacles or triggers to substance use and how he/she plans to cope with each obstacle or trigger.

33. Verbalize an understanding of the consequences of substance use and/or criminal involvement and review these strategies for relapse prevention. (57)

57. Process with the client the consequences of his/her continued substance use and/or criminal involvement (e.g., processing of charge, move to

detention facility, increased
probationary monitoring,
etc.).

—. _____   —. _____

  _____   _____

—. _____   —. _____

  _____   _____

—. _____   —. _____

  _____   _____

DIAGNOSTIC SUGGESTIONS:

ICD-9-CM	_ICD-10-CM_	_DSM-5_ Disorder, Condition, or Problem
303.90	F10.20	Alcohol Use Disorder, Moderate or Severe
305.00	F10.10	Alcohol Use Disorder, Mild
304.30	F12.20	Cannabis Use Disorder, Moderate or Severe
305.20	F12.10	Cannabis Use Disorder, Mild
304.20	F14.20	Cocaine Use Disorder, Moderate or Severe
305.60	F14.10	Cocaine Use Disorder, Mild
305.70	F15.10	Amphetamine Use Disorder, Mild
304.40	F15.20	Amphetamine Use Disorder, Moderate or Severe
305.30	F16.10	Other Hallucinogen Use Disorder, Mild
304.60	F16.20	Other Hallucinogen Use Disorder, Moderate or Severe
305.50	F11.10	Opioid Use Disorder, Mild
304.00	F11.20	Opioid Use Disorder, Moderate or Severe
305.90	F18.10	Inhalant Use Disorder, Mild
304.60	F18.20	Inhalant Use Disorder, Moderate or Severe

304.10	F13.20	Sedative, Hypnotic, or Anxiolytic Use Disorder, Moderate or Severe
305.40	F13.10	Sedative, Hypnotic, or Anxiolytic Use Disorder, Mild
312.81	F91.1	Conduct Disorder, Childhood-Onset Type
312.82	F91.2	Conduct Disorder, Adolescent-Onset Type
313.81	F91.3	Oppositional Defiant Disorder
V71.02	Z72.810	Adolescent Antisocial Behavior
300.02	F41.1	Generalized Anxiety Disorder
——	——	——————————————
——	——	——————————————

SUICIDAL IDEATION/SELF-HARM

BEHAVIORAL DEFINITIONS

1. Recurrent thoughts of or preoccupation with death and/or self-injurious behavior.
2. Vague desire to die without a specific plan.
3. Persistent suicidal ideation accompanied by a concrete plan, serious intent, and the means to complete the act.
4. Recent suicide attempt.
5. Chronic depression accompanied by excessive substance abuse.
6. Family and/or peer history that is significant for suicide attempts and/or completed suicide.
7. Feelings of extreme hopelessness, helplessness, and sadness.
8. Recent stressor (e.g., parental divorce, death of a friend or family member, relationship breakup, etc.) followed by a stated desire to die.
9. Lack of concern for personal safety as evidenced by self-destructive behavior (e.g., excessive substance abuse, risk-taking behaviors, targeted physical aggression, gun play, etc.).
10. Parasuicidal behavior to gain attention, induce guilt, or express anger toward others (e.g., seriously injuring body parts, cutting, excessive head banging, etc.).

__. _____
    _____
__. _____
    _____
__. _____
    _____

LONG-TERM GOALS

1. Terminate suicidal ideation and return to the highest level of previous daily functioning.
2. Accept placement in an appropriate level of care to stabilize the suicidal crisis.
3. Work through the underlying emotional conflicts that contribute to self-injurious or self-destructive behaviors.
4. Restore a sense of hope for the future.
5. Learn methods of affect regulation and problem solving.
6. Improve coping skills to alleviate depressive symptoms.
7. Increase social interactions with family members and peers.

—. _____
_____

—. _____
_____

—. _____
_____

SHORT-TERM OBJECTIVES

1. Verbalize current suicidal ideation and/or recent attempts to engage in self-injurious behavior. (1, 2)

2. Acknowledge when the suicidal ideation and/or acts of self-injurious behavior are uncontrollable, and comply

THERAPEUTIC INTERVENTIONS

1. Ask the client to disclose current suicidal ideation and/or recent attempts to engage in self-injurious behavior.

2. Assess the client's suicidal ideation including past attempts, past attempts among the family or peers, the presence of a specific plan, and whether the client has the means and intent to follow through with his/her plan.

3. Determine the appropriate level of care, given the client's risk level. Implement the appropriate intervention

with a more restrictive and protective placement.
(3, 4, 10, 11, 15)

(e.g., 24-hour family supervision, inpatient hospitalization, partial hospitalization, or increasing the frequency of outpatient services).

4. Facilitate the client's acceptance of the transition into a more restrictive and protective setting if the suicidal ideation and/or acts of self-injurious behavior become uncontrollable.

10. Warn caretakers, significant others, and/or relevant juvenile justice officials of the client's suicidal ideation and attempts to harm himself/herself.

11. Discuss measures that can be taken to secure the client's environment with the caretakers, significant others, and/or juvenile justice officials (e.g., removing access to lethal weapons, increasing the level of supervision, periodic check-ins, etc.).

15. Encourage the client to contact the therapist or a suicide hotline when the urge to engage in self-injurious behavior increases.

3. Report a decrease in the frequency and intensity of the suicidal thoughts or attempts to harm oneself.
(5, 6, 7)

5. Continue to monitor the client's suicidal ideation and attempts to harm himself/herself. Move the client to a more structured, protective setting as necessary.

6. Administer depression and suicidal self-rating scales to

the client to monitor suicidal ideation and the severity of depression (e.g., Beck Depression Inventory, Beck Hopelessness Scale, Risk Rescue Rating, etc.).

7. Prompt the client to identify situations in which he/she engaged in injurious behavior within the past week.

4. Comply with psychiatric recommendations. (8)

8. Refer the client for a psychiatric assessment to determine his/her need for psychotropic medication.

5. Report on perceived effectiveness of psychotropic medications and adhere to the prescribed dosage. (5, 6, 9)

5. Continue to monitor the client's suicidal ideation and attempts to harm himself/herself. Move the client to a more structured, protective setting as necessary.

6. Administer depression and suicidal self-rating scales to the client to monitor suicidal ideation and the severity of depression (e.g., Beck Depression Inventory, Beck Hopelessness Scale, Risk Rescue Rating, etc.).

9. Monitor the client's use of prescribed psychotropic medications and assess compliance, effectiveness, and side effects.

6. The caretakers, significant others, and juvenile justice officials increase the level of the client's supervision in the home setting. (10, 11, 12)

10. Warn caretakers, significant others, and/or relevant juvenile justice officials of the client's suicidal ideation and attempts to harm himself/herself.

11. Discuss measures that can be taken to secure the client's environment with the caretakers, significant others, and/or juvenile justice officials (e.g., removing access to lethal weapons, increasing the level of supervision, periodic check-ins, etc.).

12. Encourage the caretakers, significant others, and/or juvenile justice officials to monitor the client's behavior in the home setting and seek professional assistance if the client engages in self-injurious behavior.

7. Report the perception of increased support and improved communication with caretakers, mental health professionals, and juvenile justice staff. (13, 14, 15, 16)

13. Collaborate with the caretakers, significant others, and/or relevant juvenile justice officials to offer increased support to the client during the crisis.

14. Provide the client with information on how to obtain support in the community, including the phone number for a 24-hour suicide hotline and the names and locations of local psychiatric emergency rooms.

15. Encourage the client to contact the therapist or a suicide hotline when the urge to engage in self-injurious behavior increases.

16. Increase the caretakers' and therapeutic contact with the client during the crisis (e.g.,

more frequent visits, daily telephone check-ins, etc.).

8. Develop a contract for safety that stipulates a crisis intervention plan to implement when a serious urge to harm oneself arises. (17, 18)

17. Develop a contract for safety with the client that clearly stipulates a crisis intervention plan to implement when he/she is experiencing a severe urge to engage in self-injurious behavior (e.g., calling a member of the support network, calling the suicide hotline, going to the psychiatric emergency room, etc.).

18. Obtain a commitment from the client that he/she will implement the contract for safety prior to engaging in self-injurious behavior.

9. Process negative thoughts and feelings that coincide with thoughts of self-harm. (19, 20, 21, 22, 23)

19. Assist the client in developing an awareness of cognitive distortions that contribute to the emergence of suicidal ideation (e.g., black-and-white thinking, overgeneralizing, personalizing, and should-must thinking). Encourage the client to monitor his/her cognitive distortions and process this in session.

20. Encourage the client to identify and verbalize the feelings that coincide with self-injurious behavior (e.g., depression, hopelessness, sadness, anger, frustration, hurt, etc.).

21. Use a therapeutic game (The Talking, Feeling and Doing Game; The Ungame;

A Helping Hand; or Feelings
Fair) to teach the client skills
in self-expression.

22. Ask the client to complete and
process an exercise from the
SOS HELP for Emotions
(Clark) or *The Depression
Workbook: A Guide for Living
with Depression and Manic
Depression* (Copeland) to
work through the depression.

23. Conduct play therapy sessions
to explore the client's feelings
surrounding his/her self-
perception and relationship
with his/her family and peers.

10. Identify how the negative feelings resulting from recent
stressors and events might
contribute to the urge to harm
oneself. (24, 25)

24. Assist the client in identifying
recent stressors and how they
have resulted in negative feelings.

25. Process how the client's negative feelings (e.g., hopelessness,
helplessness, disappointment,
sadness, etc.) regarding family
relationships, peer relationships, or recent stressors contribute to the urge to harm
oneself.

11. The caretakers acknowledge
and discuss the client's negative feelings and suicidal
ideation and/or self-injurious
behavior.
(26, 27, 28)

26. Conduct family therapy sessions to discuss the client's
negative feelings (e.g., depression, hopelessness, sadness,
etc.) regarding his/her conflicted relationships or other
recent stressors.

27. Facilitate the development of
direct communication between
the client and his/her caretakers in family therapy sessions

(e.g., maintaining direct eye contact, speaking assertively, using "I" statements, etc.).

28. Encourage the caretakers and significant others to identify situations that place the client at risk for engaging in self-destructive behaviors, and discuss strategies to prevent harm to him/her.

12. Identify and process the underlying reasons for wanting to harm oneself. (29)

29. Assist the client in identifying the underlying reasons for wanting to harm himself/herself (e.g., unresolved feelings about past traumas or loss, feelings of rejection or inadequacy, fear of consequences for antisocial behavior, etc.).

13. Establish and discuss the relationship between depressed mood, substance abuse, and the urge to engage in self-injurious behavior. (30)

30. Discuss with the client and his/her caretakers the relationship between depressed and or impulsive mood, substance abuse, and attempts to engage in self-injurious behavior. Refer the client for a substance abuse evaluation and treatment.

14. Process the consequences for self and others of all previous attempts to harm oneself. (31, 32, 33)

31. Assist the client in identifying the short- and long-term consequences of previous self-injurious behaviors on himself/herself, family members, significant others, and peers.

32. Explore what the client hopes to accomplish through his/her self-injurious behavior (e.g., communicate anger and frustration, gain attention,

avoid dealing with difficult or painful feelings, etc.).

33. Process how the intended outcome of previous self-injurious behaviors differed from the actual outcome.

15. Brainstorm and implement safe and healthy ways to address problems rather than engaging in self-injurious behavior. (34, 35, 36)

34. Assist the client in identifying safe and appropriate ways to accomplish his/her goals rather than engaging in self-injurious behavior (e.g., communicating feelings directly, seeking contact with others, using coping skills, etc.). Process the effectiveness in session.

35. Teach and monitor the use of relaxation techniques (e.g., visualization, meditation, breathing, progressive muscle relaxation, etc.) and coping skills (e.g., thought stopping, positive affirmations, positive self-talk, etc.) to assist the client in reducing depressive symptoms.

36. Use therapeutic games to explore alternative ways for the client to meet his/her needs without resorting to self-injurious behavior (e.g., Don't Be Difficult or The Good Behavior Game available from Childswork/Childsplay).

16. Reestablish a consistent pattern of self-care and activities of daily living. (37, 38)

37. Discuss the importance of healthy eating, sleeping, and hygiene habits with the client. Identify obstacles to establishing and maintaining a

routine of healthy eating, sleeping, and hygiene habits.

38. Encourage the client to monitor daily eating, sleeping, and hygiene habits, and process this in session.

17. Discuss family and/or peer history of engaging in self-destructive behavior. Identify patterns of poor coping skills. (39)

39. Explore the client's prior exposure to suicidal and self-injurious behavior among family and/or peers. Process these behaviors in terms of ineffective coping skills.

18. Identify how it feels to survive the suicide of a peer or family member and express grief and anger. (40, 41)

40. Assist the client in establishing closure by writing a good-bye letter to express how it feels to mourn and survive a peer or family member who died from suicide.

41. Discuss typical reactions to traumatic loss, including anger, denial, bargaining, and acceptance.

19. Increase the frequency of expressions of hope and future-oriented thinking. (42, 43)

42. Praise the client for expressions of hope and future-oriented thinking shared during the therapy sessions. Facilitate elaborations of these plans for the future.

43. Encourage the caregivers to provide frequent praise and positive reinforcement for the client's expressions of hope and future-oriented thinking in the home setting.

20. Identify the positive aspects of life, including past or present achievements, satisfying relationships, and situations

44. Assist the client in identifying positive aspects of his/her life (e.g., past academic success, athletic achievement, large

involving healthy coping. (44, 45)

peer group, close relationship with an adult mentor, etc.).

45. Reinforce the client for initiating a discussion about healthy coping skills that were implemented during the last week without prompting (e.g., maintaining healthy hygiene, increasing social interactions, initiating physical exercise, etc.).

21. Increase the social support network by initiating social contact with local community groups or religious organizations and/or participating in social activities with peers. (46, 47)

46. Encourage the client to participate in one social activity per week with peers.

47. Assist the client in identifying supports in the local community or religious groups that offer structured social interaction. Monitor and process this involvement in session.

__. _____
   _____
__. _____
   _____
__. _____
   _____

__. _____
   _____
__. _____
   _____
__. _____
   _____

DIAGNOSTIC SUGGESTIONS:

ICD-9-CM	_ICD-10-CM_	_DSM-5_ Disorder, Condition, or Problem
296.xx	F31.xx	Bipolar I Disorder
296.89	F31.81	Bipolar II Disorder
300.4	F34.1	Persistent Depressive Disorder
311	F32.9	Unspecified Depressive Disorder
311	F32.8	Other Specified Depressive Disorder
296.xx	F32.x	Major Depressive Disorder, Single Episode
296.xx	F33.x	Major Depressive Disorder, Recurrent Episode
309.81	F43.10	Posttraumatic Stress Disorder
301.83	F60.3	Borderline Personality Disorder
_____	_____	_____
_____	_____	_____

TRUANCY

BEHAVIORAL DEFINITIONS

1. Chronic pattern of missing entire days at school that cannot be attributed to legitimate health problems or medical concerns.
2. Refusal to get out of bed in the morning to attend school upon prompting by the caregivers.
3. Extensive history of leaving school early and/or arriving late at school.
4. Frequent absences from isolated or specific class(es) that are due to peer conflict, clashes with the teacher, and/or anxiety about the academic subject.
5. Lowered academic performance or failing grades that result from frequent absences.
6. Boredom or disinterest with academic subjects or schoolwork.
7. Affiliation with negative peer groups who encourage or reinforce truancy.
8. Use of drugs or alcohol either alone or with peers contributes to absence from school.
9. Excessive or unrealistic pressure placed on the client by caregivers to achieve academic success to a degree that it contributes to his/her desire to miss or leave school.
10. Family history of members having academic problems, failures, or disinterest.
11. Underlying feelings of depression, anxiety, or insecurity about learning that contribute to school avoidance.
12. Frequent tendency to procrastinate or postpone doing school or homework assignments in favor of engaging in recreational and leisure activities.
13. Strong desire to skip school because of the fear of possible physical or emotional harm and/or wanting to avoid peer conflict or rejection.

14. Significant decrease in school attendance that occurs in response to family-related stress (e.g., parents' divorce, death of a loved one, family relocation, etc.).

—. _____

_____

—. _____

_____

—. _____

_____

LONG-TERM GOALS

1. Attend school on a consistent, full-time basis and arrive on time for all classes on a regular basis.
2. Terminate all unexcused absences from school.
3. Demonstrate consistent interest, initiative, and motivation in academics, and bring performance up to the expected level of academic functioning.
4. Complete school and homework assignments on a regular and consistent basis.
5. Achieve and maintain a healthy balance between accomplishing academic goals and meeting social, emotional, and self-esteem needs.
6. Resolve peer conflicts that lead to school avoidance.
7. Resolve emotional conflicts that are related to family stressors.
8. The caregivers establish realistic expectations of the client's academic performance and implement effective interventions that deter truancy and motivate the client to attend school regularly.

—. _____

_____

—. _____

_____

—. _____

_____

SHORT-TERM OBJECTIVES

1. Complete a psychoeducational evaluation. (1)

2. Complete psychological testing. (2)

3. Complete a substance abuse evaluation and comply with the recommendations offered by the evaluation findings. (3)

4. Verbalize acceptance of the results of the evaluations. (4)

THERAPEUTIC INTERVENTIONS

1. Arrange for psychoeducational testing to evaluate the presence of a learning disability that may be contributing to the client's truancy. Integrate findings with other sources of information (e.g., parent-teacher reports, school grades, achievement tests, etc.) to determine whether the client is eligible to receive special education services.

2. Arrange for psychological testing to assess whether possible emotional factors or attention-deficit/hyperactivity disorder (ADHD) are interfering with the client's academic performance and willingness to leave or miss school.

3. Conduct or arrange for a substance abuse evaluation to determine whether substance abuse issues are contributing to his/her truancy or frequent absences from school. Refer the client for treatment if indicated (see Substance Abuse chapter in this Planner).

4. Provide feedback to the client, his/her caregivers, school officials, or criminal justice officials regarding psychoeducational, psychological, and/or substance abuse evaluations.

5. Provide a detailed history of the truancy. (5)

5. Gather a detailed history of the client's truant behavior including age of onset, frequency, periods of regular school attendance, and the sequence of events leading up to his/her truant behavior, to help provide insight into the factors contributing to his/her truancy or unexcused absences.

6. Cooperate with the hearing, vision, and/or medical examination. (6)

6. Refer the client for hearing, vision, and/or medical examination to rule out possible hearing, visual, and/or health problems that may be interfering with school performance and poor attendance.

7. Comply with the mandates and requirements of the criminal justice system. (7)

7. Consult with the caregivers, probation officer, or court officials about the appropriate consequences for the client's truant behavior. Recommend that the client's regular attendance at school be a mandatory condition of probation.

8. Move to an appropriate alternative setting to deter truancy and ensure regular school attendance. (8)

8. Consult with the caregivers, probation or truant officer, and criminal justice officials about the need to place the client in a juvenile detention facility or alternative setting (e.g., foster home, day treatment program, highly structured special education school program, etc.) as a consequence of chronic truancy and unexcused absences.

9. Comply with the recommendations made by the multidisciplinary evaluation team at school regarding educational interventions. (9, 10)

9. Attend an Individualized Educational Planning Committee (IEPC) meeting with the caregivers, teachers, and school officials to determine the client's eligibility for special education services, establish educational goals, and design intervention strategies that motivate him/her to remain in school.

10. Consult with the client, caregivers, and school officials about designing effective intervention strategies that build on the client's strengths, compensate for his/her weaknesses, and motivate him/her to attend school.

10. Participate in outside tutoring to improve skills in the area of academic weakness and increase motivation to remain in school. (11)

11. Recommend that the client receive peer tutoring at school, or the caregivers seek outside tutoring after school to boost the client's skills in the areas of his/her academic weakness (e.g., reading, mathematics, or written expression) and increase his/her interest or motivation to remain in school.

11. Identify the consequences of continued truancy. (12, 13, 14, 15, 16, 17)

12. Monitor the client's school attendance and reinforce consistent compliance. Confront noncompliance and point out or implement the consequences.

13. Establish a contingency contract with the client, caregivers, school officials, and

probation officer that clearly outlines the consequences if the client is truant in the future. Have him/her sign the contract and post it in a visible place in the home.

14. Consult with school officials about the appropriate consequences for truancy (after-school detentions, Saturday school, lowered grades, etc.). Discourage school officials from suspending the client from school for truant behavior.

15. Assist the client's caregivers in establishing clearly defined and written rules and consequences for truancy. Inform the client and have him/her repeat these rules or consequences to demonstrate that he/she understands the expectations.

16. Instruct the caregivers to contact the probation or truant officer if the client is truant from school or receives any unexcused absences.

17. Assign the client added household chores or responsibilities on the days that he/she is caught skipping school.

12. The caregivers maintain regular communication with school officials, probation or truant officer. (18, 19)

18. Encourage the caregivers to maintain regular (daily or weekly) communication with school officials, probation or truant officer to monitor the client's school attendance and

ensure that he/she is not leaving or missing school.

19. Instruct the caregivers to require that the client make up or complete any school and/or homework assignments that he/she missed because of truancy.

13. The caregivers consistently monitor the client's school attendance. (20, 21)

20. Insist that the caregivers transport the client to school and accompany him/her into the school building to ensure school attendance.

21. Challenge and confront the caregivers about failing to monitor the client's school attendance and/or imposing consequences for truant behavior.

14. Caregivers and teachers identify and use a variety of reinforcers to reward the client's regular school attendance and completion of school and/or homework assignments. (22, 23, 24)

22. Refer the caregivers to parenting classes to help them learn to establish appropriate parent-child boundaries, effective disciplinary techniques to deter truant behavior, and to praise behavioral improvement.

23. Encourage the caregivers to give frequent praise to the client for regularly attending school, putting forth good effort, and achieving academic goals.

24. Identify a variety of positive reinforcers or rewards to maintain the client's interest and motivation to attend school regularly. Encourage

the caregivers to use these reinforcers regularly.

15. The caregivers become more involved in the client's school-related activities. (25)

25. Encourage the caregivers to demonstrate and/or maintain regular interest and involve-ment in the client's schoolwork and activities (e.g., reading school-to-home note or checking a planner for home-work assignments, joining a parent-teacher association, attending school sporting events or plays, helping with homework, etc.).

16. Incr ease to 90% the comple-tion of school and/or home-work assignments (26, 27)

26. Assist the client and his/her caregivers in developing a routine schedule that allows the client to achieve a healthy balance of completing school and/or homework assign-ments and engaging in recre-ational, leisure, or social activities.

27. Use the program entitled "Getting It Done" from *The Brief Adolescent Therapy Homework Planner* (Jongsma, Peterson, and McInnis) to help the client complete school and homework assignments on a regular, consistent basis.

17. Identify and list the negative consequences for not attend-ing school regularly. (28, 29)

28. Firmly confront the client's truant behavior, pointing out the long-term consequences for himself/herself.

29. Have the client write an essay as part of a school assignment or condition of probation that

identifies his/her reasons for truancy, its self-defeating consequences, and solutions to increase school attendance.

18. Verbalize positive educational goals for self. (30)

30. Assist the client in establishing clearly defined educational and career goals for himself/herself. Point out how regular school attendance will enable him/her to achieve his/her goals and how truancy will lead to failure.

19. Decrease the frequency of excuses or verbalizations that project the blame for truant behavior onto other people. (31, 32)

31. Confront statements in which the client rationalizes or makes excuses for his/her truancy (e.g., blaming peers, teachers, or school officials for unexcused absences and truant behavior).

32. Explore the client's "private logic" or irrational thoughts that influence him/her to leave or miss school. Assist the client in discovering the distortions in his/her thinking.

20. Resolve anger without leaving school. (33, 34)

33. Teach the client positive coping mechanisms (e.g., relaxation techniques, positive self-talk, effective problem-solving approaches, etc.) to help him/her resist the urge to skip school and for him/her to use when encountering anger, frustration, or anxiety with schoolwork, peer interactions, and authority conflicts.

34. Teach and model effective anger management techniques and problem-solving strategies to help the client effectively resolve conflicts with peers or teachers without leaving school.

21. Express feelings that are associated with past neglect, abuse, loss, or abandonment. (35, 36)

35. Explore the client's family background for a history of neglect, abuse, loss, or abandonment that may contribute to truancy and irresponsible behaviors at school.

36. Encourage and support the client in expressing feelings associated with past neglect, abuse, loss, or abandonment. Assist him/her in making the connection to truancy and lack of motivation to perform well at school.

22. Caregivers terminate excessive anger or power struggles over school attendance. (37, 38)

37. Instruct the caregivers to avoid unhealthy power struggles (e.g., lengthy arguments, shouting matches, hostile remarks, etc.) over school attendance or performance. Encourage the caregivers to calmly follow through with consequences for truancy or irresponsible school behaviors.

38. Give the caregivers a homework assignment to observe and record between three and five responsible or positive behaviors between therapy sessions that the client demonstrates in regard to school attendance and/or

performance (e.g., client wakes himself/herself up in the morning, completes homework at scheduled times, calls a peer or teacher to solve a learning problem, etc.). Have the caregivers bring in this list to the next therapy session and process with the therapist.

23. Participate regularly in extracurricular or positive peer group activities at school to increase interest or motivation to attend school. (39)

39. Encourage the client to participate in extracurricular or positive peer group activities at school to increase his/her interest or motivation to attend school; assist him/her in identifying activities that are of interest.

24. Identify resource people in school to whom the client can turn for support, assistance, or instruction for learning or interpersonal problems. (40)

40. Identify a list of individuals within the school to whom the client can turn for support, assistance, or instruction when he/she experiences a desire to skip school or encounters problems with learning or interpersonal relationships.

25. Implement assertiveness and other constructive strategies to counteract negative peer group influence. (41, 42, 43)

41. Teach the client effective communication and assertiveness skills to successfully resist negative peer influences or pressures to skip school.

42. Assist the client in identifying more constructive ways to earn peer approval and acceptance other than through affiliating with negative peers who regularly skip or leave school (e.g., verbalizing one positive comment daily about another

student, attending a school dance, agreeing to write articles for the school newspaper, etc.).

43. Assign the client to view the video entitled *The Refusal Skills* (available from Childswork/Childsplay, LLC) to teach effective assertiveness skills and help him/her resist negative peer influences to skip school.

26. Increase the frequency of positive statements about school experiences. (44, 45, 46)

44. Assign the client the task of making one positive self-statement daily to himself/herself about school and recording it in a journal.

45. Reinforce the client's successful school experiences and positive statements about school.

46. Confront the client about verbalizing excessive, negative, or disparaging remarks about school. Reframe into a positive perspective.

27. Identify and verbalize at least three steps to take to achieve career aspirations or goals. (47, 48)

47. Give the client a homework assignment of identifying between three and five role models and listing reasons why he/she admires each role model. Identify in the next session how these role models achieved success by attending school and achieving educational goals. Encourage the client to take similar positive steps to achieve his/her goals.

48. Refer the client to vocational training to increase his/her motivation to attend school, develop basic job skills, and find employment.

28. Disclose peer conflict experiences. (49)

49. Explore the client's experience of rejection by peers and the possible causes for this alienation (e.g., hostility toward them, hypersensitivity to teasing, target of scapegoat rejection, poor social skills, etc.).

29. Identify coping strategies for peer conflict. (50)

50. Teach the client means of coping with and improving conflicted peer relationships (e.g., social skills training, outside intervention with bullies, conflict resolution training, reaching out to build new friendships, identifying empathic resource peers or adults in school to turn to when hurt, lonely, or angry, etc.).

__. _____
_____

__. _____
_____

__. _____
_____

__. _____
_____

__. _____
_____

__. _____
_____

DIAGNOSTIC SUGGESTIONS:

ICD-9-CM	*ICD-10-CM*	*DSM-5* Disorder, Condition, or Problem
314.01	F90.2	Attention-Deficit/Hyperactivity Disorder, Combined Presentation
296.xx	F32.x	Major Depressive Disorder, Single Episode
296.xx	F33.x	Major Depressive Disorder, Recurrent Episode
300.4	F34.1	Persistent Depressive Disorder
300.02	F41.1	Generalized Anxiety Disorder
315.00	F81.0	Specific Learning Disorder With Impairment in Reading
315.10	F81.2	Specific Learning Disorder with Impairment in Mathematics
315.2	F81.2	Specific Learning Disorder With Impairment in Written Expression
V62.3	Z55.9	Academic or Educational Problem
317	F70	Intellectual Disability, Mild
_____	_____	_____
_____	_____	_____

VANDALISM/TRESPASSING

BEHAVIORAL DEFINITIONS

1. Willful or malicious destruction, injury, disfigurement, or defacement of any public or private property without the consent of the owners or persons having custody or control.
2. Smashing mailboxes, trashing someone's property, drawing graffiti in public places, breaking windows, or destroying abandoned buildings.
3. Occupying an abandoned commercial building or house without the consent of the owner.
4. Intruding on another person's property without permission.
5. Forcibly entering into another's property.
6. Unlawful or unwarranted intrusion upon the rights of another.
7. Thrusting oneself into the company of another without being asked or wanted.
8. Encroaching on the property of others to harass them because of their race, religion, or sexual orientation.

—. _____
_____

—. _____
_____

—. _____
_____

LONG-TERM GOALS

1. Eliminate all illegal behaviors.
2. Cease the malicious destruction of public or private property.

3. Repair the willful destruction or defacement of property.
4. Make restitution for acts of vandalism.
5. Demonstrate a significant improvement in impulse control.
6. Demonstrate a sense of respect for others by honoring personal and property boundaries.

__. _____
   _____
   _____

__. _____
   _____
   _____

__. _____
   _____

SHORT-TERM OBJECTIVES

1. Admit and take responsibility for own acts of vandalism and/or trespassing. (1, 2, 3)

2. Acknowledge and accept legal consequences of trespassing and/or vandalism. (4, 5)

THERAPEUTIC INTERVENTIONS

1. Explore the client's history of acts of vandalism and/or trespassing.

2. Confront the client's denial of responsibility for his/her behavior and projection of responsibility on to others.

3. Praise the client for acknowledging and accepting responsibility for acts of trespassing and/or vandalism, particularly situations when he/she did not suffer legal consequences.

4. Consult with juvenile justice officials to determine the appropriate sanctions for the client's trespassing and/or vandalism (e.g., restitution, community service, fines, probation, boot camp, etc.), and discuss these with the client and his/her caretakers.

5. Assist the client in developing an understanding of the legal consequences for vandalism and/or trespassing.

3. Identify obstacles to complying with the recommendations and/or requirements of the juvenile justice system. (6, 7)

6. Assist the client in identifying obstacles (e.g., lack of creative outlets, excessive pride and difficulty accepting responsibility, heightened vulnerability to peer pressure, lack of financial resources to pay restitution, etc.) that interfere with his/her ability to comply with the recommendations and/or requirements of the juvenile justice system.

7. Help the client to problem-find ways to work through obstacles that interfere with his/her ability to comply with the recommendations and/or requirements of the juvenile justice system.

4. Acknowledge and comply with the need to move to an appropriate alternative setting or juvenile detention facility. (8, 9)

8. Consult with the caretakers and juvenile justice officials about the need to place the client in a more restrictive or alternative setting (e.g., juvenile detention facility, partial hospitalization, group home, or residential program).

9. Facilitate the client's acceptance of placement in a more restrictive or alternative setting.

5. Discuss how trespassing and/or vandalism perpetuates involvement with the juvenile justice system. (10)

10. Prompt the client to identify the negative consequences that arise from trespassing and/or vandalism (e.g., more

restrictive settings, tether, increased supervision, etc.) and the positive consequences that arise from compliant behavior (e.g., less restrictive setting, terminating probation, increased independence, etc.).

6. Verbalize an awareness of how trespassing and/or vandalism affects family members and family relation- ships. (11, 12)

11. Process the short- and long- term consequences of trespassing and/or vandalism on family members (e.g., financial burden to pay restitution; social isolation from community members; feelings of resentment, anger and mistrust toward the client; etc.).

12. Prompt the client and family members to identify the family dynamics, stress factors, and/or precipitating events that elicited acts of vandalism and/or trespassing in a family therapy session.

7. Verbalize the painful emotions and monetary loss experienced by victims of own vandalism. (13, 14, 15)

13. Encourage the client to participate in victim-offender mediation in order to recon- cile and mutually agree upon reparation for the client's harm.

14. Have the client write a letter to himself/herself in which he/she has to assume the perspective of the victim of the vandalism and/or trespassing.

15. Assist the client in writing a letter of apology to the victims of the trespassing and/or

vandalism to foster a sense of responsibility, remorse, and empathy.

8. Make restitution for acts of trespassing or vandalism. (16, 17)

16. Encourage the client to make restitution for acts of vandalism by restoring the damaged or defaced property to the original condition or providing compensation for the loss or damages.

17. Arrange for the client to participate in programs within the community that seek to repair the willful destruction of property (e.g., repairing damage caused by vandalism, participating in a graffiti paint-out, working on the beautification of a plot of land piled high with trash, etc.).

9. The client and caretakers identify behavioral choices that have contributed to the vandalism and/or trespassing. (18, 19)

18. Assist the client in identifying seemingly unimportant decisions that resulted in trespassing and/or vandalism (e.g., spending time in vacant lots or stores, substance abuse, school truancy, etc.).

19. Encourage the caretakers to identify behaviors or situations that place the client at risk for trespassing and/or vandalism (e.g., lack of supervision, lack of clearly defined rules and expectations regarding appropriate behavior, lack of consequences for acting-out behaviors, etc.).

10. Identify patterns in social interactions that frequently trigger or coincide with trespassing and/or vandalism. (20)

20. Assist the client in recognizing patterns of social interaction that place him/her at risk for trespassing and/or vandalism (e.g., associating with gangs, substance abusers, or peers who have been involved in illegal activities). Encourage avoidance of these social interactions.

11. Discuss the destructive nature of prejudice. (21, 22)

21. In a group therapy session, use the video entitled *The Teen Files: The Truth about Hate* (available from the American Correctional Association) to engage the client in a discussion about his/her attitudes including racism, ethnic bigotry, religious hatred, and sexual discrimination.

22. Explore in a family therapy session the family dynamics that contribute to hate crimes.

12. Identify and verbalize the importance of respecting personal and property boundaries. (23, 24, 25)

23. Discuss the importance of limits and boundaries with the client and his/her caretakers in a family therapy session.

24. Prompt the client to identify boundary violations that have occurred within the last week in session.

25. Help the client to identify how his/her boundaries have been violated in the past. Encourage him/her to recognize patterns between his/her past victimization and how he/she currently attempts to violate the boundaries of others.

13. Make a commitment to avoid potential obstacles to successfully refrain from trespassing and/or vandalism. (26, 27, 28)

26. Identify and process the obstacles to successfully refrain from trespassing and/or vandalism (e.g., not maintaining sobriety, not complying with curfew, not consistently attending school, etc.), and develop coping strategies to deal with each obstacle (e.g., scare-yourself imagery, self-talk, support groups, etc.).

27. Encourage the client to sign a no-vandalism-and/or-trespassing contract. Ensure that he/she makes a commitment to avoid potential obstacles to successfully refraining from trespassing and/or vandalism as part of the contract.

28. Identify situations when the client violates the rights of others or major age-appropriate societal norms. Assist the parents and/or caretakers and/or juvenile justice officials in creating a plan to redirect the client's disrespect for others and/or property.

14. Identify and replace distorted thoughts that trigger the desire to engage in trespassing and/or vandalism. (29, 30)

29. Assist the client in developing an awareness of thinking errors that contribute to the emergence and maintenance of vandalism and/or trespassing (e.g., I'm just playing; Nobody will care if I paint this wall; Nobody owns this building so I can do whatever I want; etc.). Encourage the client to monitor his/her thinking errors and process in session.

30. Teach the client prosocial realistic self-talk to replace his/her thinking errors (e.g., others' property and boundaries deserve respect; someone will be angry and disappointed if I deface their property; since I do not own this property, I do not have the right to change it in any way; etc.).

15. Verbalize the underlying causes for the trespassing and/or vandalism. (31, 32)

31. Encourage the client to identify and verbalize the feelings that elicit illegal behaviors such as trespassing and/or vandalism (e.g., anger, jealousy, frustration, etc.).

32. Explore the underlying causes for the trespassing and/or vandalism with the client (e.g., to communicate anger and frustration, to gain access to money and/or goods, to express individuality and creativity, etc.).

16. Identify and implement safe and appropriate ways to cope with problems rather than engaging in trespassing and/or vandalism. (33, 34, 35)

33. Assist the client in identifying prosocial ways to address his/her problems rather than engaging in trespassing and/or vandalism (e.g., using coping skills, communicating feelings directly, obtaining a job, enrolling in a class and/or club that provides increased opportunity for artistic expression, etc.).

34. Use therapeutic workbooks to explore alternative ways to have needs met without resorting to trespassing and/or

vandalism (e.g., *The Problem Solving Workbook* by Zimmerman or *I Can Problem Solve* by Shure).

35. Encourage the client to implement problem-solving strategies during the week, and process the effectiveness in session.

17. Use relaxation and self-control techniques three times daily to decrease impulsive behavior. (36, 37)

36. Teach the client and monitor his/her implementation of relaxation techniques using *The Relaxation and Stress Reduction Workbook* (Davis and McKay) to assist him/her in dealing with stress more effectively.

37. Use therapeutic games (e.g., In Control: A Book of Games to Teach Self-Control Skills or The Self-Control Patrol Game available from Childswork/Childsplay) to teach the client self-control techniques.

18. The caregivers, school personnel, and juvenile justice officials clearly communicate expectations for the client's behavior, as well as consequences for his/her trespassing and/or vandalism. (38, 39)

38. Educate the caregivers and the school personnel on the importance of establishing firm expectations for the client and implementing consistent consequences for his/her behavior in the home setting.

39. Encourage the caregivers, school personnel, and juvenile justice officials to communicate and implement consequences for any act that violates the rights of others.

19. The caregivers, school officials, and juvenile justice officials increase the frequency of praise and positive reinforcement when the client complies with expectations. (40, 41)

40. Encourage the caregivers, school personnel, and juvenile justice officials to provide frequent praise and positive reinforcement for the client's prosocial behaviors.

41. Teach the caregivers to use contingency management techniques to shape the client's behavior (e.g., identify target behavior and make rewards contingent on enactment of this behavior).

20. The caregivers encourage the client to accept responsibility for his/her trespassing and/or vandalism. (42, 43)

42. Encourage the caregivers to help the client accept responsibility for his/her trespassing and/or vandalism, and deter the caregivers from protecting the client from the legal consequences of his/her illegal behavior.

43. Confront the caregivers' efforts to sabotage limit-setting, negative consequences, and redirection provided by the therapist, school officials, or juvenile justice officials based on the client's misbehavior.

21. Establish and maintain employment to structure free time and deter impulsive and acting-out behaviors. (44, 45)

44. Refer the client to vocational training programs to develop job skills and find employment opportunities.

45. Prompt the client to acknowledge the importance of keeping his/her time structured by productive activities in an

effort to avoid boredom and involvement in illegal activities.

22. Enroll in organized extracurricular activities or increase participation with positive peer group activities. (46, 47)

46. Encourage the client to participate in organized extracurricular activities to provide positive peer interactions in a structured setting.

47. Refer the client to the Police Athletic League, Big Brothers/Big Sisters, or local community groups to provide an opportunity for interaction with peer and adult role models.

___. _____
    _____

___. _____
    _____

___. _____
    _____

___. _____
    _____

___. _____
    _____

___. _____
    _____

DIAGNOSTIC SUGGESTIONS:

ICD-9-CM	_ICD-10-CM_	_DSM-5_ Disorder, Condition, or Problem
312.81	F91.1	Conduct Disorder, Childhood-Onset Type
312.82	F91.2	Conduct Disorder, Adolescent-Onset Type
313.81	F91.3	Oppositional Defiant Disorder
312.9	F91.9	Unspecified Disruptive, Impulse Control, and Conduct Disorder
312.89	F91.8	Other Specified Disruptive, Impulse Control, and Conduct Disorder
314.01	F90.2	Attention-Deficit/Hyperactivity Disorder, Combined Presentation
V71.02	Z72.810	Adolescent Antisocial Behavior
_____	_____	_____
_____	_____	_____

Appendix A

BIBLIOTHERAPY SUGGESTIONS

ACADEMIC UNDERACHIEVEMENT

Bloom, J. (1990). *Help Me to Help My Child.* Boston: Little, Brown and Company.

Levine, M. (1991). *Keeping Ahead in School: A Student's Book About Learning Disabilities and Learning Disorders.* Cambridge, MA: Editor's Publishing Service, Inc.

Martin, M., and C. Greenwood-Waltman, eds. (1995). *Solve Your Child's School-Related Problems.* New York: HarperCollins.

Pennington, B. (1991). *Diagnosing Learning Disorders.* New York: Guilford.

Silverman, S. (1998). *13 Steps to Better Grades.* Plainview, NY: Childswork/Childsplay, LLC.

Stern, J. (1996). *Many Ways to Learn: Young People's Guide to Learning Disabilities.* Washington, D.C.: Magination Press.

ASSAULTIVE/AGGRESSIVE BEHAVIORS

Bertolino, B. (1999). *Therapy with Troubled Teenagers.* New York: John Wiley & Sons.

Canter, L., and P. Canter (1988). *Assertive Discipline for Parents.* New York: Harper-Collins.

Clark, L. (1998). *S.O.S. Help for Emotions.* Bowling Green, KY: Parents Press.

Greene, R. (1998). *The Explosive Child.* New York: HarperCollins.

Kaye, D. (1991). *Family Rules: Raising Responsible Children.* New York: St. Martins.

Licata, R. (1999). *Everything You Need to Know about Anger.* New York: Rosen Publishing Group.

Potter-Efron, R. (1994). *Angry All the Time.* Oakland, CA: New Harbinger.

Redl, F., and D. Wineman (1951). *Children Who Hate.* New York: Free Press.

Shapiro, L. E. (1995). *How I Learned to Control My Temper.* Plainview, NY: Childswork/Childsplay, LLC.

Shore, H. (1994). *The Angry Monster Workbook.* Plainview, NY: Childswork/Childsplay, LLC.

York, P., D. York, and T. Wachtel (1997). *Toughlove.* New York: Bantam Books.

ATTENTION-DEFICIT/HYPERACTIVITY DISORDER (ADHD)

Barkley, R. (1995). *Taking Charge of ADHD: The Complete, Authoritative Guide for Parents.* New York: Guilford Press.

Crist, J. (1997). *ADHD—A Teenager's Guide.* Plainview, NY: Childswork/Childsplay, LLC.

Hallowell, E., and J. Rafey (1994). *Driven to Distraction.* New York: Pantheon.

Ingersoll, B. (1988). *Your Hyperactive Child.* New York: Doubleday.

Nadeau, K. (1998). *Help4ADD High School.* Niagara Falls, NY: Advantage Books.

Parker, H. (1992). *The ADD Hyperactivity Handbook for Schools.* Plantation, FL: Impact Publications.

Quinn, P. (1995). *Adolescents and ADD: Gaining the Advantage.* Washington, D.C.: Magination Press.

Silver, L. (1999). *Dr. Larry Silver's Advice to Parents on Attention Deficit Hyperactivity Disorder.* New York: Times Books.

Zeigler Dendy C. (1995). *Teenagers with ADD: A Parents' Guide.* Bethesda, MD: Woodbine House.

CRUELTY TO ANIMALS

Bean, B., and S. Bennett (1993). *The Me Nobody Knows: A Guide for Teen Survivors.* San Francisco: Jossey Bass Publishing.

Rosenbloom, D., and M. Williams (1999). *Life after Trauma: A Workbook for Healing.* New York: Guilford Publishing.

Rubinstein, F. D. (1999). *Furious Fred.* Westport, CT: Franklin Learning Systems.

Rubinstein, F. D. (1997). *Breaking the Chains of Anger.* Westport, CT: Franklin Learning Systems.

Rubinstein, F. D. (2000). *From Rage to Reason.* Westport, CT: Franklin Learning Systems.

The Talking, Feeling and Doing Game. Cresskill, NJ: Creative Therapeutics. 1998.

DECEITFUL AND MANIPULATIVE BEHAVIOR

Kincher, J., and P. Espeland (1992). *The First Honest Book about Lies.* Minneapolis, MN: Free Sprit Publishing.

Moser, A., and D. Melton (1998). *Don't Tell a Whopper on Fridays, The Children's Truth Control Book.* Kansas City, MO: Landmark Editions.

Lite, L., and H. Botelho (1998). *The Affirmation Web: A Believe In Your Self Adventure.* Athens, OH: Speciality Press.

Lewis, B. (1997). *What Do You Stand For: A Children's Guide to Build Character.* Minneapolis, MN: Free Sprit Publishing.

Daniels, T. (1985). *Honesty and Positive Thinking.* Basalt, CO: Trenna Productions.

DEPRESSION

Cobain, B., and E. Verdick (1998). *When Nothing Matters Anymore: A Survival Guide for Depressed Teens.* Minneapolis, MN: Free Spirit Publishing.

Ingersoll, B., and S. Goldstein (1995). *Lonely, Sad and Angry: A Parent's Guide to Depression in Children and Adolescents.* New York: Doubleday.

Kerns, L. (1993). *Helping Your Depressed Child.* Rocklin, CA: Prima.

Moser, A. (1994). *Don't Rant and Rave on Wednesdays!* Kansas City, MO: Landmark Editions.

Sanford, D. (1993). *It Won't Last Forever.* Sister, OR: Questar.

DRUG SELLING

Bachel, B. K. (2000). *What Do You Really Want?: How to Set a Goal and Go For It! A Guide for Teens.* Minneapolis, MN: Free Spirit Publishing.

Becker, J. (1994). *Mentoring High-Risk Kids.* Center City, MN: Hazelden Booklet.

Bernstein, N. (1996). *Treating the Unmanageable Adolescent: A Guide to Oppositional and Conduct Disorders.* Northvale, NJ: Jason Aronson.

Czudner, G. (1999). *Small Criminals Among Us: How to Recognize and Change Children's Antisocial Behavior—Before They Explode.* Far Hills, NJ: New Horizon Press.

Glodosla, R., A. Fahden, with J. Grant (1998). *How to Be a Successful Criminal. The Real Deal on Crime, Drugs And Easy Money.* Colorado Springs, CO: Turn Around Publishing.

Hipp, E. (1994). *Feed Yourself Some Real Excellent Stuff on Being Yourself.* Center City, MN: Hazelden Information and Educational Services.

Jacobs, T. A. (1997). *What Are My Rights? 95 Questions About Teens and The Law.* Minneapolis, MN: Free Spirit Publishing Co.

Kipnis, A. R. (1999). *Angry Young Men: How Parents, Teachers and Counselors Can Help Bad Boys Become Good Men.* San Francisco: Jossey-Bass.

Samenow, S. E. (1998). *Before It's Too Late: Why Some Kids Get Into Trouble—and What Parents Can Do About It.* New York: Times Book

Williams, T. (2001). *Stay Strong. Simple Life Lessons for Teens.* New York: Scholastic.

ENURESIS

Arnold, S. (1997). *No More Bedwetting: How to Help Your Child Stay Dry.* New York: John Wiley & Sons.

Houts, A. C., and M. W. Mellon (1989). "Home-Based Treatment for Primary Enuresis," in C. E. Schaefer and J. M. Briesmeister (eds.), *Handbook of Parents Training: Parents as Co-Therapists for Children's Behavior Problems,* pp. 60–80. New York: John Wiley & Sons.

Ilg, F., L. Ames, and S. Baker (1981). *Child Behavior: Specific Advice on Problems of Child Behavior.* New York: Harper and Row.

Mack, A., and D. Wilensky (1990). *Dry All Night: The Picture Book Technique that Stops Bedwetting.* Boston: Little, Brown and Company Children's Book Division.

FAMILY INSTABILITY/VIOLENCE

Crary, E. (1994). *I'm Furious.* Seattle, WA: Parenting Press.

Crary, E. (1984). *Kids Can Cooperate.* Seattle, WA: Parenting Press.

Dobson, J. (1996). *The New Dare to Discipline.* Wheaton, IL: Tyndale House Publishers.

Faber, A., and E. Mazlish. (1987). *Siblings without Rivalry.* New York: W. W. Norton.

Patterson, G. R., and M. Forgatch (1987). *Parents and Adolescents: Living Together.* Vol. 1: *The Basics.* Eugene, OR: Castalia.

Haley, J. (1976). *Problem-Solving Therapy.* San Francisco: Jossey-Bass.

Trottier, M. (1997). *A Safe Place.* Morton Grove, IL: Albert Whitman and Co.

FAMILY/SOCIETAL REINTEGRATION

Applestein, C. D. (1994). *The Gus Chronicles: Reflections from an Abused Kid.* Needham, MA: Albert E. Trieschman Center.

Boulden, J., and J. Boulden (1996). *A New Beginning.* Weaver, CA: Boulden Publishing.

Boulden, J., and J. Boulden (1997). *My New Family.* Weaver, CA: Boulden Publishing.

Otto, L. B. (1996). *Helping Your Child Choose a Career: A Book for Parents, Teachers, Counselors, and Students.* Indianapolis, IN: Jist Works.

Montague, M. (1991). *Job-Related Social Skills Book.* Reston, VA: Exception Publications.

Robertus, P. (1998). *The Dog Who Had Kittens.* New York: Holiday House.

FIRE SETTING

Greene, R. (1998). *The Explosive Child.* New York: HarperCollins.

Licata, R. (1999). *Everything You Need to Know About Anger.* New York: Rosen Publishing Group.

Millman, H., and C. Schaefer (1977). *Therapies for Children: A Handbook of Effective Treatments for Problem Behaviors.* San Francisco: Jossey-Bass.

Shore, H. (1994). *The Angry Monster Workbook.* Plainview, NY: Childswork/Childsplay, LLC.

Whittenhouse, E., and W. Pudney (1996). *A Volcano in My Tummy.* Denver, CO: New Social Publishers.

GANG INVOLVEMENT

Atkin, B. (1996). *Voices from the Streets: Young Former Gang Members Tell Their Stories.* New York: Little, Brown and Company.

Devore, C. (1994). *Kids and Gangs.* Edina, MN: Abdo Publication Company.

Goldentyer, D. (1994). *Gangs (Teen Hot Line).* Austin, TX: Raintree/Steck Vaughn.

Greenburg, K. (1992). *Out of the Gang.* Minneapolis, MN: Lerner Publication Company.

Palmer, P., and M. Froehner (1989). *Teen Esteem: Self Direction Manual for Young Adults.* Manassas Park, Va: Impact Publication.

Williams, S., and B. Becnel (1997). *Gangs and Wanting to Belong.* Center City, MD: Hazelden.

Williams, S., and B. Becnel (1997). *Gangs in Your Neighborhood (Tookie Speaks out against Gang Violence).* Center City, MD: Hazelden.

GRIEF AND ABANDONMENT ISSUES

Fitzgerald, H. (2000). *The Grieving Teen: A Guide for Teenagers and Their Friends.* New York: Simon and Schuster.

Hipp, E. (1995). *Helping through Hard Times: Getting through Loss.* Center City, MD: Hazelden.

Moser, A., and D. Melton (1998). *Don't Despair on Thursdays! The Children's Grief Management Book.* Kansas City, MO: Landmark Editions.

Moser, A., and D. Melton (2000). *Don't Fall Apart on Saturdays! The Children's Divorce Survival Book.* Kansas City, MO: Landmark Editions.

Mundy, M., and A. Alley (1989). *Sad Isn't Bad: A Good Grief Guide Book for Kids Dealing with Loss.* Meinrad, IN: Abbey Press.

Traisman, E. (1992). *Fire in My Heart, Ice in My Veins: A Journal for Teenagers Experiencing A Loss.* Omaha, NE: Centering Corporation.

Winsch, J., and P. Keating (1995). *After the Funeral.* Mahwah, NJ: Paulist Press.

ISOLATED/DISTRUSTFUL/ANGRY

Bertolino, B. (1999). *Therapy with Troubled Teenagers.* New York: John Wiley & Sons.

Canter, L., and P. Canter (1988). *Assertive Discipline for Parents.* New York: Harper-Collins.

Greene, R. (1998). *The Explosive Child.* New York: HarperCollins.

Kaye, D. (1991). *Family Rules: Raising Responsible Children.* New York: St. Martins.

York, P., D. York, and T. Wachtel (1997). *Toughlove.* New York: Bantam Books.

LOW SELF-ESTEEM

Briggs, D. (1970). *Your Child's Self-Esteem.* Garden City, NY: Doubleday.

Burns, D. (1993). *Ten Days to Self-Esteem.* New York: William Morrow.

Dobson, J. (1974). *Hide or Seek: How to Build Self-Esteem in Your Child.* Old Tappan, NJ: F. Revell.

Glenn, H., and J. Nelsen (1989). *Raising Self-Reliant Children in a Self-Indulgent World.* Rocklin, CA: Prima.

Hanson, L. (1996). *Feed Your Head: Some Excellent Stuff on Being Yourself.* Center Court, MN: Hazelden.

Harris, C., R. Bean, and A. Clark (1978). *How to Raise Teenager's Self-Esteem.* Los Angeles: Price Stern Sloan.

Loomans, D., and J. Loomans (1994). *Full Esteem Ahead! 100 Ways to Build Self-Esteem.* Tiburon, CA: H. J. Kramer.

Moser, A. (1991). *Don't Feed the Monster on Tuesdays!* Kansas City, MO: Landmark Editions.

Pipher, M. (1994). *Reviving Ophelia.* Newburgh, NY: Courage to Change.

Powell, J. (1969). *Why I'm Afraid to Tell You Who I Am.* Allen, TX: Argus Communications.

Sanford, D. (1986). *Don't Look at Me.* Portland, OR: Multnomah Press.

Scott, S. (1997). *How to Say No and Keep Your Friends.* Highland Ranch, CO: HRC Press.

Shapiro, L. (1993). *The Building Blocks of Self-Esteem.* King of Prussia, PA: Center for Applied Psychology.

PEER CONFLICT

Baruch, D. (1949). *New Ways in Discipline.* New York: Macmillan.

Bieniek, D. (1996). *How to End the Sibling Wars.* King of Prussia, PA: Childswork/Childsplay, LLC.

Faber, A., and E. Mazlish (1999). *How to Talk So Kids Will Listen and Listen So Kids Will Talk.* New York: Avon Books.

Faber, A., and E. Mazlish (1987). *Siblings without Rivalry.* New York: Norton.

Ginott, H. (1965). *Between Parent and Child.* New York: Macmillan.

Ginott, H. (1969). *Between Parent and Teenager.* New York: Macmillan.

Nevick, R. (1996). *Helping Your Child Make Friends.* King of Prussia, PA: Childswork/Childsplay, LLC.

PHYSICAL ABUSE VICTIM

Burke, R., and R. Herron (1996). *Common Sense Parenting: A Proven Step-By-Step Guide for Raising Responsible Kids and Creating Happy Families.* Boys Town, NE: Boys Town Press.

Divinyi, J., and E. Fallon (1997). *Good Kids, Difficult Behavior: A Guide to What Works and What Doesn't.* Wellness Connection.

Fay, J., and F. Cline (1993). *Parenting Teens with Love and Logic: Preparing Adolescents for Responsible Adulthood.* Colorado Springs, CO: Pinon Press.

Miller, A. (1984). *For Your Own Good.* New York: Farrar Straus Giroux.

Monahon, C. (1983). *Children and Trauma: A Parent's Guide to Helping Children Heal.* New York: Lexington Press.

PROBATION NONCOMPLIANCE

Barkley, R. A., and C. Benton (1998). *Your Defiant Child: Eight Steps to Better Behavior.* New York: Guilford Press.

Bluestein, J. (1993). *Parents, Teens, and Boundaries: How to Draw the Line.* Deerfield Beach, FL: Health Communications.

Dobson, J. C. (1992). *The New Dare to Discipline.* Wheaton, IL: Tyndale House Publishers.

Gardner, R. A. (1990). *The Girls and Boys Book about Good and Bad Behavior.* Cresskill, NJ: Creative Therapeutics.

Gordon, T. (1976). *P.E.T. in Action: Parent Effectiveness Training.* New York: Putnam Publishing Group.

Patterson, G. R., and M. Forgatch (1987). *Parents and Adolescents: Living Together.* Vol. 1: *The Basics.* Eugene, OR: Castalia Publishing.

Shapiro, L. E. (1995). *How I Learned to Think Things Through: A Storybook and Workbook of Activities to Help Children Think before They Act.* Plainview, NY: Childswork/Childsplay, LLC.

Shapiro, L. E. and H. Shore (1997). *Don't Be Difficult: A Workbook to Help Children Consider the Consequences of Both Positive and Negative Choices.* King of Prussia, PA: Center for Applied Psychology.

Wachtel, T., D. York, and P. York (1985). *Toughlove.* New York: Bantam Books.

RUNAWAY/STREET LIVING

Artenstein, J. (1993). *Runaways in Their Own Words: Kids Talking about Living on the Streets.* New York: Tor Books.

Fenwick, E., and T. Smith (1996). *Adolescence: The Survival Guide for Parents and Teenagers.* New York: DK Publishing.

SEXUAL ABUSE VICTIM

Carnes, P. (1983). *Out of the Shadows: Understanding Sexual Addictions.* Minneapolis, MN: Comp Care Publications.

Davis, L. (1991). *Allies in Healing.* New York: HarperCollins.

Hindman, J. (1983). *A Very Touching Book . . . For Little People and for Big People.* Durkee, OR: McClure-Hindman Associates.

Katherine, A. (1991). *Boundaries: Where You End and I Begin.* New York: Simon and Schuster.

SEXUAL MISCONDUCT

Allred, T., and G. Burns (1997). *STOP! Just for Kids: For Kids with Sexual Touching Problems, by Kids with Sexual Touching Problems.* Brandon, VT: The Safer Society Program & Press.

Canter, L., and P. Canter (1988). *Assertive Discipline for Parents.* New York: Harper-Collins.

Gil, E. (1987). *Children Who Molest: A Guide for Parents of Young Sex Offenders.* Rockville, MD: Launch Press.

Patterson, G. R., and M. Forgatch (1987). *Parents and Adolescents: Living Together.* Vol. 1: The Basics. Vol. 2: *Family Problem Solving.* Eugene, OR: Castalia.

Pithers, W. D., A. S. Gray, C. Cunningham, and S. Lane (1997). *A Guide for Parents with Children with Sexual Behavior Problems.* Brandon, VT: The Safer Society Program & Press.

Tallmadge, A., and G. Forster (1998). *Tell It Like It Is: A Resource Guide for Youth in Treatment.* Brandon, VT: The Safer Society Program & Press.

York, P., D. York, and T. Wachtel (1997). *Toughlove.* New York: Bantam Books.

SEXUAL PROMISCUITY

Ayer, E. (1998). *Everything You Need to Know about Teen Fatherhood.* New York: The Rosen Publishing Group.

Hammerslough, J. (1997). *Everything You Need to Know about Teen Motherhood.* New York: The Rosen Publishing Group.

Hughes, T. (1999). *Everything You Need to Know about Teen Pregnancy.* New York: The Rosen Publishing Group.

Kuriansky, J. (1999). *The Complete Idiot's Guide to Dating.* New York: Alpha Books.

Madara, L. (1988). *What's Happening to My Body? Book for Boys: A Growing up Guide for Parents and Sons.* Minneapolis, MN: Econo-Clad Books.

Madara, L. (1988). *What's Happening to My Body? Book for Girls: A Growing up Guide for Parents and Daughters.* Minneapolis, MN: Econo-Clad Books.

Pipher, M. (1994). *Reviving Ophelia.* Newburgh, NY: Courage to Change.

Scott, S. (1997). *How to Say No and Keep Your Friends.* Highland Ranch, CO: HRC Press.

Shire, A. (1997). *Everything You Need to Know about Being HIV-Positive.* New York: The Rosen Publishing Group.

STEALING/BREAKING AND ENTERING

Bertolino, B. (1999). *Therapy with Troubled Teenagers.* New York: John Wiley & Sons.

Canter, L., and P. Canter (1988). *Assertive Discipline for Parents.* New York: HarperCollins.

Covey, S. (1997). *The 7 Habits of Highly Effective Families: Building a Beautiful Family Culture in a Turbulent World.* New York: Golden Books.

Glenn, S., and J. Nelsen (1989). *Raising Self-Reliant Children in a Self-Indulgent World.* Rocklin, CA: Prima.

Katherine, A. (1991). *Boundaries: Where You End and I Begin.* New York: Simon and Schuster.

Shapiro, L. E. (1996). *Teens' Solution Workbook.* Plainview, NY: Childswork/ Childsplay, LLC.

York, P., D. York, and T. Wachtel (1997). *Toughlove.* New York: Bantam Books.

SUBSTANCE ABUSE

Anonymous, Sparks, B. M. (ed.) (1998). *Go Ask Alice.* New York: Avon Books.

Cohen, P. R. (1991). *Helping Your Chemically Dependent Teenager Recover: A Guide for Parents and Other Concerned Adults.* Minneapolis, MN: Johnson Institute.

Falkowski, C. (2000). *Dangerous Drugs: An Easy-to-Use Reference for Parents and Professionals.* Center City, MN: Hazelden Foundation.

Fleming, M. (1992). *How to Stay Clean and Sober: A Relapse Prevention Guide for Teenagers.* Center City, MN: Hazelden Information and Educational Services.

Folker, G., and J. Engelmann (1997). *Taking Charge of My Mind and Body: A Girl's Guide to Outsmarting Alcohol, Drug, Smoking, and Eating Problems.* Minneapolis: Free Spirit Publishing.

Hodgson, H. W. (1986). *A Parent's Survival Guide: How to Cope When Your Kid Is Using Drugs.* Cambridge, NY: Harper/Hazelden.

Packer, A. J. (2000). *Highs! Over 150 Ways to Feel Really, Really Good . . . Without Alcohol or Other Drugs.* Minneapolis, MN: Free Spirit Publishing.

Johnson, V. (1999). *Everything You Need to Know about Chemical Dependence: Vernon Johnson's Complete Guide for Families.* Center City, MN: Hazelden Information and Educational Services.

LaFountain, W. L. (1981). *Setting Limits: Parents, Kids and Drugs.* Center City, MN: Hazelden Pamphlet.

Langsen, R. C. (1996). *When Someone in the Family Drinks Too Much.* New York: Dial Books for Young Readers

Leite, E., and P. Espeland (1989). *Different Like Me: A Book for Teens Who Worry about Their Parent's Use of Alcohol/Drugs.* Center City, MN: Hazelden Information and Educational Services.

Ryglewicz, H., B. Pepper, and J. Massaro (1994). *Alcohol, Street Drugs, and Emotional Problems.* Center City, MN: Hazelden Pamphlet.

Sassatelli, J. (1992). *Breaking Away: Saying Good-Bye to Alcohol/Drugs: A Guide to Help Teenagers Stop Using Chemicals.* Center City, MN: Hazelden Information and Educational Services.

Roos, S. (1993). *A Young Person's Guide to the Twelve Steps.* Center City, MN: Hazelden Information and Educational Services.

Super, G. (1990). *What are Drugs?* Frederick, MD: Twenty-First Century Books.

Zarek, D., and J. W. Sipe (1987). *Can I Handle Alcohol/Drugs? A Self-Assessment Guide for Youth.* Center City, MN: Hazelden Information and Educational Services.

SUICIDAL IDEATION/SELF-HARM

Clark, L. C. (1998). *SOS Help for Emotions: Managing Anxiety, Anger and Depression.* Bowling Green, KY: Parents Press.
Copeland, M. E., and S. Copans (1998). *Adolescent Depression Workbook.* Brattleboro, VT: Peach Press.
Copeland, M. E. (1992). *The Depression Workbook: A Guide for Living with Depression and Manic Depression.* Oakland, CA: New Harbinger Publications.
Copeland, M. E. (2000). *The Loneliness Workbook: A Guide to Developing and Maintaining Lasting Connections.* Oakland, CA: New Harbinger Publications.
Davis, M., E. R. Eshelman, and M. McKay (2000). *The Relaxation and Stress Reduction Workbook,* 5th ed. Oakland, CA: New Harbinger Publications.
Eggert, L. (1994). *Anger Management for Youth: Stemming Aggression and Violence.* Bloomington, IN: National Educational Service.
Hipp, E. (1995). *Fighting Invisible Tigers: A Stress Management Guide for Teens.* Minneapolis, MN: Free Spirit Publishing.
Lester, D., and B. Danot (1993). *Suicide behind Bars: Prediction and Prevention.* Philadelphia: Charles Press.
Rowan, J. R. (1998). *Suicide Prevention in Custody.* Lanham, MD: American Correctional Association.

TRUANCY

Canter, L., and P. Canter (1988). *Assertive Discipline for Parents.* New York: Harper-Collins.
Covey, S. (1997). *The 7 Habits of Highly Effective Families: Building a Beautiful Family Culture in a Turbulent World.* New York: Golden Books.
Kaye, D. (1991). *Family Rules: Raising Responsible Children.* New York: St. Martins.

VANDALISM/TRESPASSING

Bluestein, J. (1993). *Parents, Teens and Boundaries: How to Draw the Line.* Deerfield Beach, FL: Health Communications.
Davis, M., E. R. Eshelman, and M. McKay (2000). *The Relaxation and Stress Reduction Workbook,* 5th ed. Oakland, CA: New Harbinger Publications.
In Control: A Book of Games to Teach Self-Control Skills. Plainview, NY: Childswork/Childsplay, LLC.

The Self-Control Patrol Game. Plainview, NY: Childswork/Childsplay, LLC.

Shure, M. B. (1992). *I Can Problem Solve: An Interpersonal Cognitive Problem Solving Program.* Champaign, IL: Research Press.

The Teen Files: The Truth about Hate Video. (1999). Lanham, MD: American Correctional Association.

Zimmerman, T. (1995). *The Problem Solving Workbook.* Plainview, New York: Childswork/Childsplay, LLC.

Appendix B

RECOVERY MODEL OBJECTIVES AND INTERVENTIONS

The Objectives and Interventions that follow are created around the 10 core principles developed by a multidisciplinary panel at the 2004 National Consensus Conference on Mental Health Recovery and Mental Health Systems Transformation, convened by the Substance Abuse and Mental Health Services Administration (SAMHSA, 2004):

1. **Self-direction:** Consumers lead, control, exercise choice over, and determine their own path of recovery by optimizing autonomy, independence, and control of resources to achieve a self-determined life. By definition, the recovery process must be self-directed by the individual, who defines his or her own life goals and designs a unique path toward those goals.
2. **Individualized and person-centered:** There are multiple pathways to recovery based on an individual's unique strengths and resiliencies as well as his or her needs, preferences, experiences (including past trauma), and cultural background in all of its diverse representations. Individuals also identify recovery as being an ongoing journey and an end result as well as an overall paradigm for achieving wellness and optimal mental health.
3. **Empowerment:** Consumers have the authority to choose from a range of options and to participate in all decisions—including the allocation of resources—that will affect their lives, and are educated and supported in so doing. They have the ability to join with other consumers to collectively and effectively speak for themselves about their needs, wants, desires, and aspirations. Through empowerment, an individual gains control of his or her own destiny and influences the organizational and societal structures in his or her life.
4. **Holistic:** Recovery encompasses an individual's whole life, including mind, body, spirit, and community. Recovery embraces all aspects of life, including housing, employment, education, mental health and healthcare treatment and services, complementary and naturalistic services, addictions treatment, spirituality, creativity, social networks, community participation, and family supports as determined by the person. Families,

providers, organizations, systems, communities, and society play crucial roles in creating and maintaining meaningful opportunities for consumer access to these supports.

5. **Nonlinear:** Recovery is not a step-by-step process but one based on continual growth, occasional setbacks, and learning from experience. Recovery begins with an initial stage of awareness in which a person recognizes that positive change is possible. This awareness enables the consumer to move on to fully engage in the work of recovery.

6. **Strengths-based:** Recovery focuses on valuing and building on the multiple capacities, resiliencies, talents, coping abilities, and inherent worth of individuals. By building on these strengths, consumers leave stymied life roles behind and engage in new life roles (e.g., partner, caregiver, friend, student, employee). The process of recovery moves forward through interaction with others in supportive, trust-based relationships.

7. **Peer support:** Mutual support—including the sharing of experiential knowledge and skills and social learning—plays an invaluable role in recovery. Consumers encourage and engage other consumers in recovery and provide each other with a sense of belonging, supportive relationships, valued roles, and community.

8. **Respect:** Community, systems, and societal acceptance and appreciation of consumers—including protecting their rights and eliminating discrimination and stigma—are crucial in achieving recovery. Self-acceptance and regaining belief in one's self are particularly vital. Respect ensures the inclusion and full participation of consumers in all aspects of their lives.

9. **Responsibility:** Consumers have a personal responsibility for their own self-care and journeys of recovery. Taking steps toward their goals may require great courage. Consumers must strive to understand and give meaning to their experiences and identify coping strategies and healing processes to promote their own wellness.

10. **Hope:** Recovery provides the essential and motivating message of a better future—that people can overcome the barriers and obstacles that confront them. Hope is internalized, but can be fostered by peers, families, friends, providers, and others. Hope is the catalyst of the recovery process. Mental health recovery not only benefits individuals with mental health disabilities by focusing on their abilities to live, work, learn, and fully participate in our society, but also enriches the texture of American community life. America reaps the benefits of the contributions individuals with mental disabilities can make, ultimately becoming a stronger and healthier Nation.[1]

---

[1]From: Substance Abuse and Mental Health Services Administration's (SAMHSA) National Mental Health Information Center: Center for Mental Health Services (2004). *National consensus statement on mental health recovery.* Washington, DC: Author. Available from http://mentalhealth.samhsa.gov/publications/allpubs/sma05-4129/

The numbers used for Objectives in the treatment plan that follows correspond to the numbers for the 10 core principles. Each of the 10 Objectives was written to capture the essential theme of the like-numbered core principle. The numbers in parentheses after the Objectives denote the Interventions designed to assist the client in attaining each respective Objective. The clinician may select any or all of the Objectives and Intervention statements to include in the client's treatment plan.

One generic Long-Term Goal statement is offered should the clinician desire to emphasize a recovery model orientation in the client's treatment plan.

LONG-TERM GOAL

1. To live a meaningful life in a self-selected community while striving to achieve full potential during the journey of healing and transformation.

SHORT-TERM OBJECTIVES

1. Make it clear to therapist, family, and friends what path to recovery is preferred. (1, 2, 3, 4)

THERAPEUTIC INTERVENTIONS

1. Explore the client's thoughts, needs, and preferences regarding his/her desired pathway to recovery (from depression, bipolar disorder, posttraumatic stress disorder [PTSD], etc.).

2. Discuss with the client the alternative treatment interventions and community support resources that might facilitate his/her recovery.

3. Solicit from the client his/her preferences regarding the direction treatment will take; allow for these preferences to be communicated to family and significant others.

4. Discuss and process with the client the possible outcomes that may result from his/her decisions.

2. Specify any unique needs and cultural preferences that must be taken under consideration during the treatment process. (5, 6)

3. Verbalize an understanding that decision making throughout the treatment process is self-controlled. (7, 8)

4. Express mental, physical, spiritual, and community needs and desires that should be integrated into the treatment process. (9, 10)

5. Verbalize an understanding that during the treatment process there will be successes and failures, progress and setbacks. (11, 12)

5. Explore with the client any cultural considerations, experiences, or other needs that must be considered in formulating a mutually agreed-upon treatment plan.

6. Modify treatment planning to accommodate the client's cultural and experiential background and preferences.

7. Clarify with the client that he/she has the right to choose and select among options and participate in all decisions that affect him/her during treatment.

8. Continuously offer and explain options to the client as treatment progresses in support of his/her sense of empowerment, encouraging and reinforcing the client's participation in treatment decision making.

9. Assess the client's personal, interpersonal, medical, spiritual, and community strengths and weaknesses.

10. Maintain a holistic approach to treatment planning by integrating the client's unique mental, physical, spiritual, and community needs and assets into the plan; arrive at an agreement with the client as to how these integrations will be made.

11. Facilitate realistic expectations and hope in the client that positive change is possible, but

does not occur in a linear process of straight-line successes; emphasize a recovery process involving growth, learning from advances as well as setbacks, and staying this course toward recovery.

12. Convey to the client that you will stay the course with him/her through the difficult times of lapses and setbacks.

6. Cooperate with an assessment of personal strengths and assets brought to the treatment process. (13, 14, 15)

13. Administer to the client the *Behavioral and Emotional Rating Scale (BERS): A Strength-Based Approach to Assessment* (Epstein).

14. Identify the client's strengths through a thorough assessment involving social, cognitive, relational, and spiritual aspects of the client's life; assist the client in identifying what coping skills have worked well in the past to overcome problems and what talents and abilities characterize his/her daily life.

15. Provide feedback to the client of his/her identified strengths and how these strengths can be integrated into short-term and long-term recovery planning.

7. Verbalize an understanding of the benefits of peer support during the recovery process. (16, 17, 18)

16. Discuss with the client the benefits of peer support (e.g., sharing common problems, receiving advice regarding successful coping skills, getting encouragement, learning of helpful community

resources, etc.) toward the client's agreement to engage in peer activity.

17. Refer the client to peer support groups of his/her choice in the community and process his/her experience with follow-through.

18. Build and reinforce the client's sense of belonging, supportive relationship building, social value, and community integration by processing the gains and problem-solving the obstacles encountered through the client's social activities.

8. Agree to reveal when any occasion arises that respect is not felt from the treatment staff, family, self, or the community. (19, 20, 21)

19. Discuss with the client the crucial role that respect plays in recovery, reviewing subtle and obvious ways in which disrespect may be shown to or experienced by the client.

20. Review ways in which the client has felt disrespected in the past, identifying sources of that disrespect.

21. Encourage and reinforce the client's self-concept as a person deserving of respect; advocate for the client to increase incidents of respectful treatment within the community and/or family system.

9. Verbalize acceptance of responsibility for self-care and participation in decisions during the treatment process. (22)

22. Develop, encourage, support, and reinforce the client's role as the person in control of his/her treatment and responsible for its application to his/her daily life; adopt a supportive role as a resource

10. Express hope that better functioning in the future can be attained. (23, 24)

person to assist in the recovery process.

23. Discuss with the client potential role models who have achieved a more satisfying life by using their personal strengths, skills, and social support to live, work, learn, and fully participate in society toward building hope and incentive motivation.

24. Discuss and enhance internalization of the client's self-concept as a person capable of overcoming obstacles and achieving satisfaction in living; continuously build and reinforce this self-concept using past and present examples supporting it.

Appendix C

BIBLIOGRAPHY

Armstrong, T. L., (ed). (1991). *Intensive Interventions with High-Risk Youths: Promising Approaches.* Monsey, NY: Criminal Justice Press.

Barnum, R., and Keilitz, I. (1992). "Issues in Systems Interactions Affecting Mentally Disordered Juvenile Offenders." In J. J. Cocozza (ed.), *Responding to the Mental Health Needs of Youth in the Juvenile Justice System.* Seattle, WA: The National Coalition for the Mentally Ill in the Criminal Justice System, pp. 49–91.

Braithwaite, K., J. Duff, and I. Westworth (1999). *Conduct Disorder in Children and Adolescents.* www.adhd.com.au/conduct.html.

Branch, C. W. (1997). *Clinical Interviews with Gang Adolescents and Their Families.* Boulder, CO: HarperCollins Publishers and Westview Press.

Burchard, J. D. (1987). "Social and Political Challenges to Behavioral Programs with Delinquents and Criminals." In E. K. Morris and C. J. Braukmann (eds.) *Behavioral Approaches to Crime and Delinquency: A Handbook of Application, Research, and Concepts.* New York: Plenum Press, pp. 577–96.

Cellini, H. R. (1995). "Assessment and Treatment of the Adolescent Sexual Offender. In B. K. Schwartz and H. R. Cellini (eds.), *The Sex Offender: Vol. 1. Corrections, Treatment and Legal Practice,* Kingston, NJ: Civic Research Institute, pp. 6.1–6.12.

Center for Substance Abuse Treatment. (1999). *Strategies for Integrating Substance Abuse Treatment and the Juvenile Justice System: A Practical Approach.* Washington, DC: U.S. Department of Health and Human Services.

Cohen, J. A. (2000). *Treating Trauma in Children and Adolescents.* Thousand Oaks, CA: Sage.

Corsica, J. Y. (1993). Employment Training Interventions. In A. Goldstein and C. R. Huff (eds.), *The Gang Intervention Handbook.* Champaign, IL: Research Press.

Cunningham, C., and K. Macfarland (1998). *When Children Abuse Group Treatment Strategies for Children with Impulse Control Problems.* Brandon, VT: Safer Society Press.

Curtis, P. A., J. C. Kendall, and G. Dale, Jr. (eds) (1999). *The Foster Care Crisis: Translating Research into Policy and Practice.* Lincoln, NB: University of Nebraska Press.

Dattilio, F. M., and A. Freeman (1994). *Cognitive Behavioral Strategies in Crisis Intervention.* New York: Guilford Press.

Eggert, L. (1994). *Anger Management for Youth: Stemming Aggression and Violence.* Bloomington, IN: National Educational Service.

Elliot, D. S., S. S. Ageton, and D. Huizinga (1985). *Multiple Problem Youth: Delinquency, Substance Abuse and Mental Health Problems.* New York: Springer-Verlag.

ERIC Clearinghouse on Urban Education. (In press). *School Violence: What Practitioners Should Know.* New York: Teachers College, ERIC Clearinghouse on Urban Education.

Eth, S. (ed.) (2001). *PTSD in Children and Adolescents.* Washington, DC: American Psychiatric Press Incorporated.

Forman, S. G. (1993). *Coping Skills Interventions for Children and Adolescents.* San Francisco: Jossey-Bass.

Friedman, A. S., and A. Utada (1989). "A Method for Diagnosing and Planning the Treatment of Adolescent Drug Abusers (The Adolescent Drug Abuse Diagnosis [Adad] Instrument)." *Journal of Drug Education,* 19: 285–312.

Goldstein, A. P., and C. R. Huff (eds). (1993). *The Gang Intervention Handbook.* Champaign, IL: Capital City Press.

Gullotta, T. P. (1994). "The What, Who, Why, Where, When and How of Primary Prevention." *Journal of Primary Prevention,* 15: 3–28.

Hegar, R. L. L., and M. Scannapieco (1998). *Kinship Foster Care: Policy, Practice and Research.* New York: Oxford University Press.

Henggeler, S. W., G. B. Melton, and L. A. Smith (1992). "Family Preservation Using Multi-Systemic Therapy: An Effective Alternative to Incarcerating Serious Juvenile Offenders." *Journal of Consulting and Clinical Psychology,* 60: 953–961.

Hollin, C. R. (1989). *Cognitive-Behavioral Interventions with Offender.* New York: Praeger.

James, B. (1989). *Treating Traumatized Children.* New York: Lexington Books.

Johnson, K. (1998). *Trauma in the Lives of Children: Crisis and Stress Management Techniques for Counselors, Teachers and Other Professionals.* Alameda, CA: Hunter House Publisher.

Jongsma, A., L. Peterson, and W. McInnis (1999). *Brief Adolescent Therapy Homework Planner.* John Wiley & Sons.

Jongsma, A., L. Peterson, and W. McInnis (1999). *Brief Child Therapy Homework Planner.* John Wiley & Sons.

Kaduson, H., and C. Schaefer (eds.) (1990). *101 Favorite Play Therapy Techniques.* Northvale, NJ: Jason Aronson.

Kahn, T. J. (1997). *Pathways: A Guided Workbook for Youth Beginning Treatment.* Brandon, VT: Safer Society Press.

Kanfer, F. H., S. Englund, C. Lennhoff, and J. Rhodes (1995). *A Mentor Manual: For Adults Who Work with Pregnant and Parenting Teens.* Washington, DC: Child Welfare League of America.

Kipke, M. D., S. B. Montgomery, R. R. Simon, and E. F. Iverson (1997). "Substance Abuse Disorders among Runaway and Homeless Youth." *Substance Use and Misuse,* 32: 965–982.

Lal, S. R., D. Lal and C. R. Achilles (1993). *Handbook on Gangs in Schools: Strategies to Reduce Gang-Related Activities.* Newbury Park, CA: Corwin Press.

Land, K. C., P. L. McCall, and J. R. Williams (1992). "Intensive Supervision of Status Offenders: Evidence on Continuity of Treatment Effects for Juveniles and a 'Hawthorne Effect' for Counselors." In: J. McCord and R. Tremblay (eds.), *Preventing Antisocial Behavior: Interventions from Birth through Adolescence.* New York: Guilford Press.

Lundman, R. J. (1993). *Prevention and Control of Juvenile Delinquency.* New York: Oxford University Press.

Malekoff, A. (1997). *Group Work with Adolescents: Principles and Practice.* New York: Guilford Press.

Mash, E. J. and R. A. Barkley (1989). *Treatment of Childhood Disorders.* New York: Guilford Press.

Millman, H., and C. Schaefer (1977). *Therapies for Children: A Handbook of Effective Treatments for Behaviors.* San Francisco: Jossey-Bass.

Millman, H., C. Schaefer, and J. Cohen (1980). *Therapies for School Behavioral Problems.* San Francisco: Jossey-Bass.

O'Connor, K. J. (1983). "The Color Your Life Technique." In: C. E. Schaeffer and K. J. O'Connor (eds.), *Handbook of Play Therapy,* pp. 251–258. New York: John Wiley & Sons.

O'Connor, K. J. (1991). *The Play Therapy Primer: An Integration of Theories and Techniques.* New York: John Wiley & Sons.

O'Hanlon, B., and S. Beadle (1997). *A Guide to Possibility Land.* New York: W. W. Norton.

Otto, R. K., J. J. Greenstein, M. K. Johnson, and R. M. Friedman (1992). "Prevalence of Mental Disorders among Youth in the Juvenile Justice System." In J. J. Cocozza (ed.), *Responding to the Mental Health Needs of Youth in Juvenile Justice System.* Seattle, WA: The National Coalition for the Mentally Ill in the Criminal Justice System.

Pardeck, J. T., and J. A. Pardeck (1998). *Children in Foster Care and Adoption: A Guide to Bibliotherapy.* Westport, CT: Greenwood Publishing Group.

Pennington, B. (1991). *Diagnosing Learning Disorders.* New York: Guilford Press.

Prentky, R., and S. Edmunds (1997). *Assessing Sexual Abuse: A Resource Guide for Professionals.* Brandon, VT: Safer Society Press.

Rasmussen, L. A. (1999). "Factors Related to Recidivism among Juvenile Sexual Offenders." *Sexual Abuse: A Journal of Research and Treatment,* 11(1): 69–85.

Ray, J., V. Smith, T. Peterson, J. Gray, J. Schaffner, and M. Houff (1995). "A Treatment Program for Children with Sexual Behavior Problems." *Child and Adolescent Social Work Journal,* 12(5): 331–343.

Robertson, J. F. (1989). "A Tool for Assessing Alcohol Misuse in Adolescence." *Social Work,* 34: 39–44.

Robin, A. L., and S. L. Foster (1989). *Negotiating Parent/Adolescent Conflict.* New York: Guilford Press.

Ryan, G. D. (1997). *Juvenile Sexual Offending: Causes, Consequences and Correction.* San Francisco: Jossey-Bass.

Salter, A. C. (1998). *Treating Child Sex Offenders and Their Victims: A Practical Guide.* Beverly Hills, CA: Trade Paperback.

Saxe, S. (1997). "The Angry Tower." In: H. Kaduson and C. Schaefer (eds.), *101 Favorite Play Therapy Techniques,* pp. 246–249. Northvale, NJ: Jason Aronson.

Schiff, M. F. (1998). "Restorative Justice Interventions for Juvenile Offenders: A Research Agenda for the Next Decade." *Western Criminology Review* 1(1). [Online]. Available: http://wcr.sonoma.edu/v1n1/schiff.html.

Selekman, M. D. (1991). *Family Therapy Approaches with Adolescent Substance Abusers.* Boston: Allyn and Bacon.

Selekman, M. D. (1993). *Pathways to Change: Brief Therapy Solutions with Difficult Adolescents.* New York: Guilford Press.

Selekman, M. D. (1997). *Solution-Focused Therapy with Children.* New York: Guilford Press.

Sholver, G. P. (ed.) (1995). *Conduct Disorders in Children and Adolescents.* Washington, DC: American Psychiatric Press.

Shure, M. B. (1992). *I Can Problem Solve: An Interpersonal Cognitive Problem Solving Program.* Champaign, IL: Research Press.

Silver, J. A., B. J. Amster, and T. Haecker (eds.) (1999). *Young Children and Foster Care: A Guide for Professionals.* Baltimore, MD: Paul H. Brookes Publishing.

Stahl, A. L. (2000). "Juvenile Vandalism." *Office of Juvenile Justice and Delinquency Prevention.* www.ojjdp.ncjrs.org.

Straus, M. A. (1979). "Measuring Interfamily Conflict and Violence: The Conflict Tactics (CT) Scale." *Journal of Marriage and the Family,* 41: 75–88.

Strayhorn, J. M. (1988). *The Competent Child.* New York: Guilford Press.

Stumphauzer, J. S. (1986). *Helping Delinquents Change: A Treatment Manual of Social Learning Approaches.* Springfield, IL: Haworth Press.

Wadeson, H. (1980). *Art Psychotherapy.* New York: John Wiley & Sons.

Wadeson, H. (1995). *The Dynamics of Art Psychotherapy.* New York: John Wiley & Sons.

Wagner, E., and H. Wagner (eds.) (2001). *Innovations in Adolescent Substance Abuse Interventions.* New York: Pergamon.

Watzlawick, P., J. Weakland, and R. Fisch (1974). *Change.* New York: W. W. Norton.

Wilkes, T. C. R., G. Belsher, J. A. Rush, and E. Frank (1994). *Cognitive Therapy for Depressed Adolescents.* New York: Guilford Press.

Ziegler, R. G. (1992). *Homemade Books to Help Kids Cope.* New York: Magination Press.

Appendix D

RESOURCES FOR THERAPEUTIC GAMES, WORKBOOKS, TOOLKITS, VIDEOTAPES, AND AUDIOTAPES

A.D.D. Warehouse
300 Northwest 70th Avenue,
   Suite 102
Plantation, FL 33317
Phone: 1-800-233-9273
www.addwarehouse.com

Boys Town Press
14100 Crawford Street
Boys Town, NE 68010
www.girlsandboystown.org

Childswork/Childsplay, LLC
P.O. Box 1604
Secaucus, NJ 07096-1604
Phone: 1-800-962-1141

Courage to Change
P.O. Box 1268
Newburgh, NY 12551
Phone: 1-800-440-4003

Creative Therapeutics
P.O. Box 522
Cresskill, NJ 67626-0522
Phone: 1-800-544-6162
www.rgardner.com

The Guidance Channel
135 Dupont Street
P.O. Box 760
Plainview, NY 11803-0760
Phone: 1-800-99YOUTH
www.guidancechannel.com

Sinclair Seminars
www.sinclairseminars.com/shop/bro
   wse.php

Western Psychological Services
Division of Manson Western
   Corporation
12031 Wilshire Boulevard
Los Angeles, CA 90025-1251
Phone: 1-800-648-8857
www.wpspublish.com